AN XRX BOOK

PUBLISHER
Alexis Yiorgos Xenakis

EDITOR
Elaine Rowley

TECHNICAL EDITOR
Traci Bunkers

ASSISTANT EDITORS
Holly Brunner
Joni Coniglio
Rick Mondragon

FASHION DIRECTOR
Nancy J. Thomas

PHOTO STYLIST
Rick Mondragon

PHOTOGRAPHER
Alexis Yiorgos Xenakis

PUBLISHING DIRECTOR
David Xenakis

GRAPHIC DESIGNER
Bob Natz

PRODUCTION DIRECTOR
Denny Pearson

PRODUCTION COORDINATOR
Natalie Sorenson

DIGITAL COLOR SPECIALIST
Jason Bittner

DIGITAL PRODUCTION
Everett Baker
Jay Reeve

TECHNICAL ILLUSTRATIONS
Carol Skallerud

MARKETING DIRECTOR
Karen Bright

FIRST PUBLISHED IN USA IN 2002 BY XRX, INC.
PO BOX 1525, SIOUX FALLS, SD 57101-1525

COPYRIGHT ©2002 XRX, INC.

ISBN 1-893762-03-3

Produced in Sioux Falls, South Dakota, by XRX, Inc., 605.338.2450

Printed in the USA

Front cover: Beaded Ruana designed by Cheryl Oberle in yarns from
Weaving Southwest.
Endpapers: Splatters of dye on the wall of a hand-dye studio.

Other publications from **XRX** BOOKS:

A Gathering of Lace

Jean Moss Sculptured Knits

Sally Melville Styles

Magnificent Mittens

Ethnic Socks and Stockings

The Great American Afghan

The Great American Kids Afghan

The Great North American Afghan

Socks • Socks • Socks!

Kids • Kids • Kids!

The Best of Knitter's Shawls and Scarves

The Best of Weaver's Huck Lace

The Best of Weaver's Thick n' Thin

Knitter's Magazine

HandpaintCountry

a knitter's journey with...

Cheryl Potter - narration
Alexis Xenakis - photography

 BOOKS

DEDICATION

To Alexis, without his pictures, there could have been no words.

I wish to thank the hand-dyers who generously shared their time, thoughts, work spaces, and often their homes with us; the designers who helped make the beautiful yarns even less resistible; and all the people at XRX, Inc. who took care of the myriad details that make a complex project like this possible. I especially appreciate the work of Traci Bunkers, who took on the gargantuan job of pattern editing; Bob Natz, whose expertise with layout and design brought this book to life; and Elaine Rowley, who logged endless hours on the computer, over the light table, at the airport, and in the van. Thank you all.

Cheryl Potter

INTRODUCTION

Sit back and relax—you're about to go on a knitter's journey, criss-crossing the country to visit the studios and shops of our most talented hand-dyers. Along the way, we'll tell you their stories and show you their yarns. Throughout your travels, you'll meet the designers who transformed these unique yarns into wearable art. We invite you to consider their advice, try their patterns, revel in their inspiration—and read on.

Like any good travel book, this one is a resource guide. Feel free to take a side trip and delve into the handpaint hints, design tips, knitting techniques, and yarn source pages. We hope this is a book you'll refer to again and again for information as well as inspiration.

We also hope our words and photographs have captured the strength and beauty of the landscape and the creative diversity of the hand-dyers we visited.

For us, this journey demystified the world of hand-dyed yarns. Share this discovery—and your yarn world will never be the same.

Bonkers Handmade Originals 619 East 8th Street, Studio 3D
  Lawrence, KS 66044   785-843-5875

Brown Sheep Company 100662 County Road
  Mitchell, NE 69357   308-635-2198

Chasing Rainbows Dyeworks 1700 Hilltop Drive
  Willits, CA 95490   707-459-8558

Cherry Tree Hill Yarn PO Box 659
  Barton, VT 05822   802-525-3311

Cheryl Oberle Designs 3315 Newton Street
  Denver, CO 80211   303-433-9205

The Drop Spindle 417 East Central
  Santa Maria, CA 93454   805-922-1295

Ellen's 1/2 Pint Farm 85 Tucker Hill Road
  Norwich, VT 05055   802-649-5420

Exquisitely Angora 1222 Mackay Place
  St. Louis, MO 63104   314-771-6302

Fiesta Yarns 206 Frontage Road
  Rio Rancho, NM 87124   505-892-5008

The Great Adirondack Yarn Co. RD #7 Hagaman Road
  Amsterdam, NY 12010   518-843-3381

Interlacements PO Box 3082
  Colorado Springs, CO 80934   719-578-8009

Joslyn's Fiber Farm 5738 East Klug Road
  Milton, WI 53563   608-868-3224

Koigu Wool Designs RR1 Williamsford, Ontario
  H0H 2V0 Canada   519-794-3066

La Lana Wools 136 Paseo Norte
  Taos, NM 87571   505-758-9631

Liisu Yarns PO Box 143
  Meadows of Dan, VA 24120   276-952-2558

Mountain Colors PO Box 156
  Stevensville, MT 00598   406-777-3377

Oak Grove Yarns PO Box 531
  Putney, VT 05346   802-387-5934

Prism Yarns 2595 30th Avenue North
  St. Petersburg, FL 33713   727-327-3100

Tess' Designer Yarns 33 Strawberry Point
  Steuben, ME 04680   207-546-2483

Valentina Devine 1222 Big Rock Loop
  Los Alamos, NM 87544   505-662-1440

Weaving Southwest 216B Pueblo Norte
  Taos, NM 87571   505-758-0433

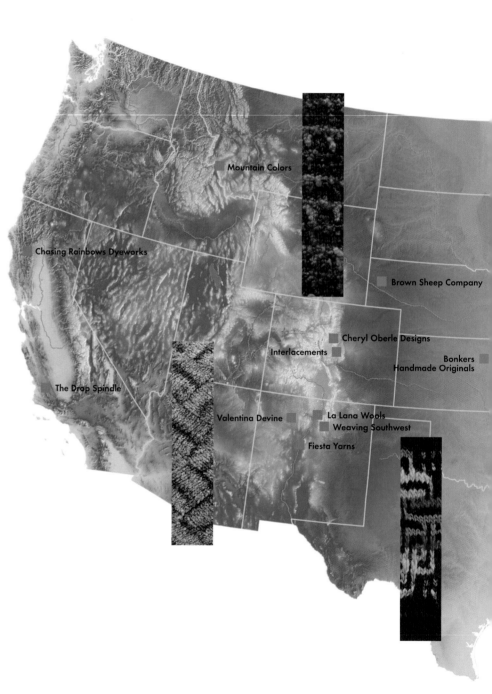

Tess' Designer Yarns

Cherry Tree Hill Yarn

Ellen's 1/2 Pint Farm

Koigu Wool Designs   Oak Grove Yarns
                            Great Adirondack Yarn Co.

Joslyn's Fiber Farm

Contents

HandpaintCountry

Exquisitely Angora

Liisu Yarns

a knitter's journey with...

Cheryl Potter - narration
Alexis Xenakis - photography

Prism Yarns

Southwest

WEAVING SOUTHWEST RACHEL BROWN

Taos, New Mexico

Our Southwest journey begins in Albuquerque, New Mexico. We drive north through bleached grass and sage punctuated by deep green piñon trees. Threading our way through dry washes and over high desert, we approach foothills rising before flat mesas and mountains dusted with their first snow.

Rachel Brown

We reach Taos after dark, squinting at adobe shapes that rush past, only able to make out the pink neon lights of our motel. Morning finds us up early and ready to take photos of the adobe wall outside our rooms, the Mission-style church down the street, fences shaped like cacti, and all things Southwestern. As we wander past the ancient buildings of the historic district, almost by accident we find Rachel Brown.

Above: Highly textured Jumbo Loop mohair shown in colorway Peacock.

Center: Cheryl Oberle's Beaded Ruana combines tweed-dyed apparel yarns in Mojave Mauve, Winter Plum, and Gunmetal with approximately 200 glass beads for mix-and-match fun. Rachel Brown achieves the complex colors through a sequential dye method which takes the yarn through four different dye processes.

Below: Interior of Weaving Southwest gallery with rugs, tapestries, and pillows by area weavers.

"What I do here is everything that I love," Rachel Brown declares, sitting in the sun before Weaving Southwest, her gallery and showroom in Taos. Although she has owned this store only 16 years, she has been a fixture in the weaving and hand-dyeing community for nearly 40 years. The popularity of her ground-breaking work, *The Weaving, Spinning, and Dyeing Book,* first published in 1978 and now in its 11th printing, has made her a matriarch and mentor to many fiber enthusiasts. She smiles and says, "Once I got started, I decided I would cover absolutely everything."

A pioneer in her field Looking at this small, tanned woman with elfin features and cropped white hair, we can hardly fathom all that she has accomplished since she moved to Taos in 1956. Although she studied fine arts at Radcliffe College and was a member of the Art Students League in New York City, she considers herself self-taught.

When she came to New Mexico, her few neighbors were Spanish-speaking women who wove blankets from wool they dyed themselves. Rachel rescued her first loom from becoming firewood, picked up some Rit dye at the grocery store, and got started. After a few years she had the hang of both loom and dye, and developed the sequential dye method she prefers to this day. In this method the exhaust water is never thrown out, an advantage in an arid region.

It was 1963, the hippie era, when Rachel began her first business, a yarn and weaving cooperative called The Craft House. There, she was able to dye as much as 150 pounds of wool a day in huge pots outside. Rachel tried her hand at production weaving and taught so many classes in spinning, weaving, and dyeing that friends suggested she write a book. Eventually she sold the Craft House and travelled to Mexico, Guatemala, and South America to learn new techniques. She may never have returned except for a postcard she received that read, "Book accepted. Return to NY ASAP to sign contract." She spent the next five years writing.

Spreading the word After Rachel's book was published, she found time to weave and show her own tapestries, but she never stopped spreading the word. Luisa Gelenter and her then-partner, Madeline Johannes, who were dyeing wool with "weeds and natural things," hooked up with Rachel, and together they founded the Wool Products Association in 1981 to provide a venue for farmers to market animal fiber. In 1983, they held the first Taos Wool Festival, a fiber arts fair that now overtakes the historic district for a week each fall. Rachel's belief in self-sufficiency and cottage industry led her to

spend the next five years developing a teaching curriculum for Tierra Wools in Los Ojos. She went on to establish several co-ops and galleries, some of which (Open Space, Taos Artisans) still exist.

In 1978, Rachel designed the Rio Grande Wheel from a spinning wheel built by her husband. She went on to manufacture and sell the wheel and specialized looms along with her spinning fiber and hand-dyed rug and apparel yarns. But it wasn't until 1988, when she opened Rio Grande Weaving Supply, that Rachel found her calling. As she began to dye more textured yarns in a broader spread of colors, the color theory classes she had taken so long ago in college suddenly made sense. She concluded that this was what she was trained to do.

Land of enchantment New Mexico's cultural and artistic melting pot stimulates Rachel's creativity, and the clear skies and light colors of the natural surroundings inspire her color choices. "When I take my walks in the morning, I see about 25 light to medium neutral colors. I want to do them all and I could, but it wouldn't be practical," Rachel explains. Some of her colorways, like Winter Plum, are based on the season; others are derived from the landscape. Her Mojave Mauve is an unusual combination of

earth tones reminiscent of the desert. Rachel finds that knitters and weavers are becoming more and more sophisticated about color, and she enjoys presenting them with new blends.

At one time, Rachel dyed all her yarns herself; she now employs two assistants. Each hand-dyes a different yarn for tapestry, rugs, or apparel. In typical cottage-industry style, these trained dyers process yarn off-site and bring it to the store for retail sale. Rachel works only with animal fibers, and the dyeing is done year-round, primarily outdoors. She uses two main dye techniques that produce totally different results: gradation dyeing to produce semi-solid tones, and resist dyeing to produce "tweeds." With her gradation-dyeing technique, she dyes tapestry yarns in 20 semi-solid colors, each in five "grades" or shades.

Conversely, the resist-dye technique consists of "four different dyeings based on primaries and secondaries that mix, followed by an overall wash." Rachel says this overdye process works best with closely related colors. With a base of about ten colors she can achieve a hand-painted look using the resist-dye method. Because Rachel doesn't offer yarns to the wholesale market, she feels no pressure to precisely reproduce colorways, which allows her freedom to explore. However, she is able to repeat colors. Over the years, she has developed 300 colorways that remain in her repertoire.

The start-to-finish gallery The synchronicity of Rachel's yarns, gallery, and equipment was born of her tenacity—she never lets a barrier stop her. When she needed equipment, she found a way to make it; when her inventory of pieces required a gallery, she started one. Her shop consists of two spaces, a salesroom and showroom, which she calls her "start-to-finish gallery." Here, one can go from yarn to finished product. Rachel's customers are visiting the source: they can buy a well-crafted weaving, try out the looms Weaving Southwest manufactures, or choose from her hand-dyed yarns.

Although now primarily a weaver, Rachel began knitting at the age of eight and calls it her first fiber art. Her weaving yarns cross over for use in knitting, and she finds that knitters are most interested in the tweed-dyed yarns. "They have a certain unevenness that is desirable," Rachel says. Her apparel yarns offer a palette of texture as well as color, because, as she explains, "Color has a life to it. It's not a dead, flat surface."

Much of Rachel's fiber is custom-spun at the Taos Valley Wool Mill. Her best-selling yarns are the baby loop tweed and a rug yarn that comes in 78 colors. Rachel loves that her knitters are into "weird colors" like "strange pink and blue neutrals." She dyes dark, rich browns, pairing them with light colors such as antique ivory for contrast. Rachel believes "it's going to be a long time—if ever—before people are going to be sick of creative color expression."

Future watch As a weaver and teacher interested in sharing her knowledge, Rachel plans to write another book, one promoting tapestry weaving in New Mexico, which is home to Navajo, Hispanic, and contemporary weavers. As Rachel puts it: "New Mexico is a hotbed of activity when it comes to textiles."

Rachel sees the endless possibilities of the Internet as her new frontier. Currently she is developing new colorways for handknitters because "the customer is looking for an art object in their finished product." As hand-painted yarn begins to achieve mass appeal, Rachel is not surprised that commercial yarn companies are copying the look. "Anytime that you come up with something good, there are always going to be copycats. That keeps you on your toes and makes you find something new. And that's the way the whole thing progresses."

As we wander through Weaving Southwest one last time (the name was changed from Rio Grande Weavers Supply in 1999), we are overwhelmed by rooms filled with gorgeous yarns, the sound of looms and spinning wheels at work, and the gallery of extraordinary rugs and tapestries. Rachel tells us, "I love creating a beautiful environment. I'm fascinated with equipment, fascinated with color, and fascinated with yarn."

Above: Patrons can see both the rug yarns and the finished rug at Rachel's start-to-finish gallery.

Bottom: Tweed-dyed apparel yarns against an adobe wall outside Weaving Southwest.

Beaded ruana designed by Cheryl Oberle

It's foolproof and fun to work with this rich blend of color and texture—changing yarns and placing beads as you wish.

"The shawl is an exercise in randomness. There is no set pattern for placing the colors and textures. Since the Weaving Southwest palette works together so well, you can't go wrong. Don't worry about making the two sections match; asymmetry makes for a more interesting garment. Try to use as much mohair yarn as possible to keep the shawl lightweight."

Cheryl Oberle

MATERIALS

Yarn Weaving Southwest Tweed-dyed yarns in the following colors: *A* Winter Plum, *B* Mojave Mauve, *C* Gunmetal - *Jumbo Loop* 1 skein each A, B, and C (each 4oz/114g, 60yds/55m, 96% Lincoln wool, 4% mohair); *Mohair Loop* 1 skein each A, B, and C (each 3½oz/100g, 215yds/197m, 78% mohair, 13% wool, 9% nylon); *Thick & Thin* 1 skein B (4oz/114g, 122yds/112m, 100% wool); *Worsted Singles* 2 skeins A, 1 skein B (each 4oz/114g, 190yds/174m, 100% wool); *Brushed Mohair* 1 skein each A and B (each 3½oz/100g, 215yds/197m, 78% mohair, 13% wool, 9% nylon).

Needles Size 10½ (6.5mm) circular needle, 29"/74cm long *or size to obtain gauge.*

Extras Approximately two hundred ½" glass beads in different styles. Craft glue.

NOTES

1 See *Techniques*, p. 228 for long-tailed cast-on. *2* Shawl is worked in two rectangular pieces that are sewn together to form a V-shape. *3* The beads are strung onto a strand of brushed mohair and knitted into desired row. *4* The fringes are made at the beginning and end of each row. *5* Change yarns and colors as desired after knitting an odd number of rows. *6* Hole in beads must be large enough to string on brushed mohair. *7* For ease in working, mark wrong-side row.

USING BEADS

Before working a row with beads, string beads onto a strand of brushed mohair. String only the beads needed for one row at a time to keep the brushed mohair free to use in other rows in the shawl. With craft glue, coat the end of the yarn for about 3". Smooth and twist the yarn end into a point and let it dry thoroughly. Use the stiffened end like a needle to thread the beads onto the yarn. If using different kinds of beads, string them randomly. First section uses approx 30 beads per beaded row. Second section uses approx 20 beads per beaded row. The beads are knitted-in on WS rows. Work beads randomly 1–6 sts apart as follows: **Beaded row** (WS) At desired stitch, slide the bead up as close to the RH needle as possible and knit the next stitch. The bead will be on the back (RS) of the work. Rep for each bead, keeping at least one st between beads. **Next row** Knit across, knitting into the back of the st on each side of the bead to anchor it. This will twist the sts on each side of the bead and help support the weight of the bead.

FIRST SECTION

Tie 2 strands of yarn tog using an overhand knot and leaving 14" tails. Starting at the knot, cast on 138 sts using long-tail cast-on. At end of cast-on, cut both strands, leaving 14" tails. Turn. **Row 1** (WS) Leaving a 14" tail, tie a new single strand of yarn onto the tails at the end of the cast-on row and knit across. At end of row, cut yarn, leaving a 14" tail. Turn. **Row 2** (RS) Leaving a 14" tail, tie a new single strand of yarn onto the tail of the last row and knit across. At end of row, cut yarn, leaving a 14" tail. Turn. Rep row 2 for pat, cutting yarn at end of every row, even when not changing to a different yarn, and, AT SAME TIME, work beaded row on WS when piece measures 3½", 9", 11½", and 19" from beg. When piece measures 20½" from beg, end with a WS row, bind off loosely in knit.

SECOND SECTION

Work as for first section, casting on 84 sts and working beaded row on WS when piece measures 3", 7½", 10" and 16½" from beg.

FINISHING

Steam or wet block both sections. Along fringed edges, knot fringes tog with an overhand knot in groups of 7 or 8 strands each. With RS facing up, sew short edge of first section (with fringes on top and slightly overlapping) to end of a long edge of second section, forming a V-shape.

Easy

Finished measurements

Finished shawl measures approx 71" at widest point and 50" deep from top to point

First Section 50" x 20½"

Second Section 30½" x 20½"

Gauge

11 sts and 23 rows to 4"/10cm over Garter st, randomly changing yarns at end of desired rows, using size 10½ (6.5mm) needle.

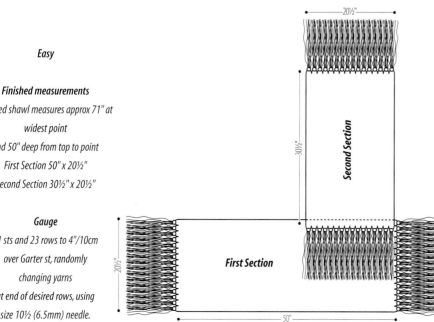

20½"

30½"

Second Section

20½"

First Section

50"

Rio designed by Cheryl Oberle

A simple shape, a simple stitch, and one multi-hued yarn—this sweater appears to be much more than the sum of its parts.

MATERIALS

Yarn Weaving Southwest *Tweed-dyed Worsted Singles* 7 (8, 9) skeins Peacock (each 4oz/114g, 190yds/174m, 100% wool).

Needles One pair each sizes 7 and 9 (4.5 and 5.5mm) needles, *or size to obtain gauge.* Size 7 (4.5mm) circular needle, 16"/40cm long.

Extras Four ½"/12.5mm buttons. Stitch holders.

NOTES

1 Slip all stitches purlwise with yarn in front (wyif).

STITCH USED

Rib pat multiple of 4 sts plus 1
Row 1 (RS) Sl 1 (selvage), k3, *sl 1 wyif, k3; rep from* to last st, k1. *Row 2* (WS) Sl 1 (selvage), k1, *sl 1 wyif, k3; rep from*, ending last rep k2. Rep rows 1–2 for pat.

BACK

With larger needles, cast on 85 (93, 101) sts. Work 12 (13½, 15)" in Rib pat, end with a WS row.

Shape armhole

Work 8 sts and place these sts on hold at beg of next 2 rows—69 (77, 85) sts. Work even in pat until piece measures 21½ (23½, 25)", end with a WS row. Place sts on hold.

FRONT

Work as for back until armhole measures 6 (6½, 6½)" from beg, end with a WS row.

Divide for neck

Next row (RS) Work 34 (38, 42) sts, k into front and back of next st (1 st inc'd), work to end. *Next row* Work 35 (39, 43) sts (right front). Place remaining 35 (39, 43) sts on

hold for left front. Turn and work in pat for 3½" for right front. Place sts on hold. With WS facing, place left front sts on needle and work in pat for 3½". Place sts on hold.

SLEEVES

With larger needles, cast on 33 (37, 37) sts. Work in Rib pat, AT SAME TIME, inc 1 st each side every 5th row 10 times, then every 6th row 15 times—83 (87, 87) sts. Work even until piece measures 22 (23, 24)" from beg. Place sts on hold.

FINISHING

Block pieces. Mark 18 (21, 25) sts each end of front and back for shoulders. Remaining sts are for lapels and back neck. With WS tog and larger needles, join shoulders using 3-needle bind-off (ridge effect). Leave remaining sts on hold.

Armholes

With RS facing and larger needles, k8 from underarm holder, pick up and k67 (71, 71) sts along armhole edge, k8 from underarm holder—83 (87, 87) sts. With WS tog, join armhole and sleeve sts from holder using 3-needle bind-off.

Neck

With circular needle and beg with left front, place front and back neck stitches from holders onto needle. Bind off in knit to the shoulder, bind off in purl across the back neck, bind off remaining sts in knit. Sew side and sleeve seams leaving 2" open at sleeve cuffs. Turn back neckline and cuffs and sew buttons to hold in place.

3-needle bind-off (ridge effect)

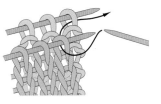

Place wrong sides together, back stitches on one needle and front stitches on another. *K2tog (1 from each needle). Repeat from * once. Pass first stitch over 2nd stitch. Continue to k2tog and bind off across.

Easy

Sizes
S (M, L)
Shown in size S.
Directions are for smallest size with larger sizes in parentheses. If there is only 1 set of numbers, it applies to all sizes.

Finished measurements
Underarm 42½ (46½, 50½)"
Length 21½ (23½, 25)"

Gauge
16 sts and 28 rows to 4"/10cm over Rib pat, using larger needles.

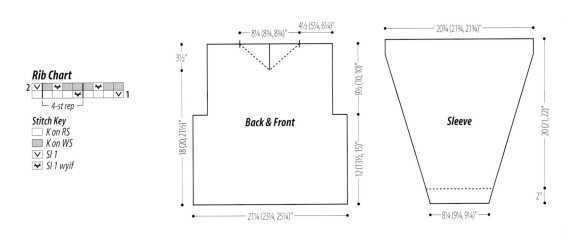

Rib Chart

2 [chart] 1
— 4-st rep —

Stitch Key
☐ K on RS
▨ K on WS
☑ Sl 1
☒ Sl 1 wyif

Back & Front
8¼ (8¾, 8¾)"
4½ (5¼, 6¼)"
3½"
18 (20, 21½)"
12 (13½, 15)"
21¼ (23¼, 25¼)"

Sleeve
20¾ (21¾, 21¾)"
9½ (10, 10)"
20 (21, 22)"
2"
8¼ (9¼, 9¼)"

LA LANA WOOLS LUISA GELENTER

Taos, New Mexico

Just down the street from Weaving Southwest, and in the heart of the historic district of Taos, is La Lana Wools, the store and gallery owned by Luisa Gelenter. For more than ten years, La Lana has been in this adobe building, the former studio of artist Bert Phillips.

Luisa Gelenter

LA LANA WOOLS LUISA GELENTER

Taos, New Mexico

Clockwise from above: Mini hanks of plant-dyed Bombyx silk; adobe oven with swatches of colorways for Judy Dercum's Kiva Night Sky; Silver Streak—a millspun yarn with a handspun look; Hand-dyed silk scarves flutter in the breeze outside Luisa's dye studio.

Although Luisa Gelenter has her hand in many pots as a store owner, hand-dyer, spinner, yarn designer, and part owner of a fiber mill, she is best known for her unique line of plant-dyed yarns. Using recipes she developed over time, Luisa dyes fiber at the studio behind her house.

Becoming a fiber fiend Looking at Luisa, with her abundantly long and curly dark hair streaked with gray, and eyes that can fix you like a mystic, we can only ask, "How did you get here?" Luisa took the first step on her path by learning to spin with a drop spindle while traveling in Bolivia in the early 1970s. There, in the marketplace, she sat with the Aymara ladies and studied their ceaseless, nimble manipulation of fiber. Soon she was back in New Mexico "fooling around with plant dyes." Her interest in producing yarn from the ground up became an obsession. "I became a fiber fiend," she admits, with a grin.

Luisa responded to the visual and tactile appeal of fiber arts even before she began her fiber adventure as a spinner who enjoyed spinning from the fleece. "A fresh, buttery, open-locked fleece—preferably in many shades of brown—was my idea of spinning Nirvana. I loved the way colors moved in random and unpredictable ways. Then I got into plant dyeing. After all, if you're going to go so far as to handspin everything, why not honor your efforts and go all the way?"

The pots have to sing to you Luisa built her studio 14 years ago on property that looks toward the Sacred Mountain, part of the Sangre de Cristo chain. Luisa leads us to her dye porch, an open-air room built onto the side of the studio, facing the peaks. Inside, it is warm and wet and fragrant with simmering herbs. Along the wall, steaming dye pots bubble slowly. We can almost feel the magic as Luisa lifts dripping

yarn from one of the pots with a long stick and then lowers it back gently. "The first law of the pots is: Love what you get."

Open spaces and the quality of light are important here, as well as the sparseness of vegetation. "You do see color in the landscape," she points out. "Subtle color. Gradual changes of light."

Luisa's color palette is derived solely from nature. Some of her dyes come from native plants, many of which she harvests at various times of the year. From kota, commonly called Navajo tea, she conjures up an array of burnt siennas, reds, rusts, and oranges. Mullein gives her green, "endless green," she is fond of saying, and goldenrod produces deep yellows.

Exotic dyes, such as indigo and cochineal, are important color sources for Luisa, as they have been for dyers since ancient times. From cochineal, she coaxes the richest reds, while indigo provides shades of blue, from pale sky to midnight. Madder yields orange tones, and logwood, pewter to deep purple.

certain green. Luisa laughs and admits, "I never met a green I didn't like."

At her store, Luisa markets both hand-spun and custom millspun yarns—cotton, hemp, wool, mohair, silk—presented in undyed shades and a wide spectrum of plant-dyed colors. "Because we have the entire palette, we're ready for everyone," Luisa says.

Designing yarns As part owner of Taos Valley Wool Mill, Luisa has the opportunity to design every aspect of a new yarn. Her custom-milled yarns are unique.

A crossover yarn and a very popular one for La Lana is Silver Streak, a millspun yarn that is both unusual and economical. Random streaks of gray and black against a natural white background give the yarn a handspun look, without the usual price tag.

Another technically interesting yarn is ¿Cómo Bouclé? which translates to "Is it like boucle?" Luisa was able to mimic boucle by spinning and then unspin-

Clockwise from above: Cochineal gives Luisa her richest reds; kota, or Navajo tea, yields burnt sienna; Como boucle, a "fake" boucle resting on a fake cactus fence; a palette of plant-dyed yarns amid the trove to be found at La Lana.

Unpredictability and serendipitous outcomes are what keep Luisa intrigued with plant dyes. "I love the fact that you are never going to get exactly the same color twice with natural dyes— each dye lot is unique," she says.

Here in her studio, Luisa has developed many unique dye techniques over the years. She does absolutely no painting of yarn or fiber, but produces the variegated look of her popular Forever Random® Blends through a series of steps. First, she hand-dyes fiber in various solids using an immersion technique complemented by overdyeing, which she calls "Immersion Plus." Then she breaks the fiber apart to be recombined as it is carded at the mill. Blending and carding produce a look of variegation that handspinning completes. This process is extremely labor-intensive, but Luisa shrugs it off as part of the experience of working with fiber. For her, color and meditation go hand in hand. "You need to be in harmony with yourself," she explains. "Otherwise, the spinning can go right out of control and the pots won't sing to you."

For most of her other hand-dyed yarns, including her wide range of solids, Luisa uses her Immersion Plus method. Sometimes she overdyes to get a particular hue she wants, for example, indigo over yellow to produce a

ning a strand of merino with a strand of silk. Como has the look of a complicated yarn but is easy to knit.

Devolution When it comes to business, Luisa does not see herself as a mass marketer. "When I started, I was a voice in the wilderness," she says. "Now, people care about things being natural; it's a great time for natural dyes and fibers."

In addition to the shop, she shows her yarns at fiber festivals across the country, services several custom-dye accounts, and has developed a large mail-order following. During the summer, she holds workshops at her studio. Until a few years ago, "I never went anywhere because my head was such a big country," she explains. "Now I get out and about."

Luisa works to spread the word that hand-dyed yarns are much more interesting to work with. "People are craving the work of the hand," Luisa confides. "I can see it when they come into my

store." She believes that as knitters, we turn to handwork for our own satisfaction, because whether we know it or not, we react to the yarn viscerally. It is an ancient, ancestral feeling. "They have to have it and they don't even know why," Luisa says of knitters who are drawn to La Lana.

For Luisa, pattern support happened by accident. She dyes for a clientele that is becoming more and more creative. She is delighted that some of her best customers, including Valentina Devine, Judy Dercum, and Linda Romens, have became her best designers.

At La Lana, Luisa encourages people to discover their roots, which often involves handwork. "It's just a matter of awakening consciousness," she explains, "Industrial devolution needs to take place." For this reason, much of what happens at her store and studio is education. "People knit less and are the poorer for it," she declares. "We have to bring them back, and it helps that people like Julia Roberts knit. She's a great poster girl."

Future watch Yarn design is Luisa's specialty and she continues to try new techniques. But, Luisa finds, with beautiful fleeces as with beautiful yarns, "The simplest way is often the best."

Luisa sees herself "continuing with the yarn adventure, wherever it takes me." She has found that hand-dyeing has given her a way to take the steps that make her path, a path that has become the thread of her life. "It doesn't matter where you begin," Luisa explains. "If you are creative, you will get there. As the *I Ching* says, 'Perseverance furthers.'"

Clockwise from above: Luisa's Finissimo Tailspun—yarn that began as a happy accident at the mill and mimics the way the fleece looks while still on the back of the mohair goat; Luisa looks out from the Sangre de Cristos range; dyed fleece drying before being spun into multicolored yarns; herbs simmer in dye pots on Luisa's open-air porch.

Facing page: Native plants that Luisa Gelenter uses in dyeing, insets from top right: Indian Paintbrush, Kota (or Navajo Tea, as it is more commonly called), Mullein, Snakeweed, Onion skins, Marigolds; in the background, sacks of dried plants gathered from the surrounding desert await the dyepots.

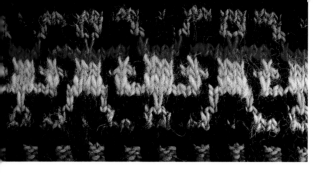

Anasazi vest designed by Linda Romens

A clever use of mosaic-stitch motifs makes this handsome vest a good way to start working with 2-color knitting. Rich hand-dyed and handspun solids add a strong ethnic appeal.

MATERIALS

Yarn La Lana plant-dyed yarns *Custom Mill Spun MC* 4 (4, 5) skeins Black, **A** 1 skein Apple Green, **B** 1 skein Purple (each 4oz/114g, 200yds/183m, 100% wool); La Lana *Hand Spun* 1 skein each **C** Misty Pebbles, **D** Yellow Brick Road, **E** Madder, **F** Tzarina (each 2oz/57g, 56yds/51m, 100% wool).

Needles One pair each sizes 7 and 9 (4.5 and 5.5mm) needles, *or size to obtain gauge*. Size 7 (4.5mm) circular needle, 29"/74cm long.

Extras Four 1"/25mm buttons. Size H/8 (5mm) crochet hook, stitch markers and holders.

NOTES

1 See *Techniques*, p. 228 for intarsia knitting, ssk, ssp, single crochet (sc), and reverse single crochet (rev sc). **2** Vest is worked in one piece to underarms, then divided for fronts and back. **3** Twist yarn at color change to avoid holes. **4** Work all shaping as full-fashioned decreases.

STITCH USED

Corrugated rib multiple of 4 sts plus 2
RS rows K2 MC, *p2 CC, k2 MC; rep from*.
WS rows P2 MC, *k2 CC, p2 MC; rep from*.

Full-fashioned decs
At beg of RS rows K1, ssk; *at end of RS rows* Work to last 3 sts, k2tog, k1.
At beg of WS rows P1, p2tog; *at end of WS rows* Work to last 3 sts, ssp, p1.

BODY

With smaller needles and MC, cast on 154 (170, 186) sts. Work 3 rows in k2, p2 rib. **Next row** (RS) Work in Corrugated rib in following color sequence for CC: 2 rows C, 2 rows A, 2 rows D, 2 rows E, 2 rows F, 2 rows B. Change to larger needles, and with MC, k 1 row, dec 7 sts evenly spaced—147 (163, 179) sts. P 1 row. Work 26 rows Chart A, then with MC, work in St st until piece measures 15 (15½, 15½)" from beg, end with a WS row.

Divide for fronts and back

Next row (RS) K33 (37, 41) sts (right front) and put those sts on hold, bind off 3 sts (underarm), work until there are 75 (83, 91) sts for back and put those sts on hold, bind off 3 sts (underarm), knit to end (left front).

LEFT FRONT

Shape armhole

Dec 1 st at armhole edge on this row, then every RS row 3 times—29 (33, 37) sts. Work 1 row even. **Begin Chart B** (RS) K2, place marker (pm), work row 1 of Chart B, pm, join 2nd ball of MC and knit to end. Work even in pat, working

sts between markers in chart pat and twisting MC with contrasting yarn at beg and end of chart to avoid holes, until armhole measures 1", end with a WS row.

Shape V-neck

Continuing in pat and dec 1 st at neck edge this row, then every 6th row 6 times—22 (26, 30) sts. Work even in St st with MC until armhole measures 8 (9, 10½)", end with a WS row.

Shape shoulder

Bind off at armhole edge 7 (9, 10) sts twice, then 8 (8, 10) sts once.

RIGHT FRONT

Shape armhole

With WS facing, join MC at armhole edge and shape as for left front. **Begin Chart B** (RS) K4 (8, 12), pm, work row 1 of Chart B, pm, join 2nd ball of MC and knit to end. Continue in pat and work as for left front, reversing neck and shoulder shaping.

BACK

Shape armhole

With WS facing, join MC at armhole edge. Shape armhole each side as for fronts. Work even in St st until armhole measures 6½ (7½, 9)", end with a WS row.

Shape neck

Row 1 (RS) K26 (30, 34), join 2nd ball of yarn and bind off 15 sts, then knit to end. Dec 1 st each neck edge on the next 2 rows, then every other row twice. When armhole measures same length as fronts to shoulder, shape shoulder each side as for fronts.

FINISHING

Sew shoulders. Place markers along left front for 4 buttonholes, with the first 1½" from the bottom, the last at beg of V-neck shaping, and others spaced evenly between.

Front bands

With RS facing, circular needle, and MC, pick up and k112 (120, 128) sts along right front to shoulder, 42 (42, 50) sts along back neck, and 112 (120,128) sts along left front to bottom—266 (282, 306) sts. Beg with p2, work 2 rows in k2, p2 rib. **Next row** (WS) Work in Corrugated rib in following color sequence for CC: 1 row C, 1 row A, 1 row D. **Next (buttonhole) row** (RS) K2 MC, *p2 E, k2 MC; rep from* across and at beg of each marker, work one-row horizontal buttonhole over 4 sts. Continuing in Corrugated rib, work 1 row F, 1 row B. Work 1 row MC only. Bind off. Sew on buttons.

Armhole bands

With RS facing and MC, work 1 rnd sc, join with a sl st in first st. Do not turn. Working left to right, chain 1, work 1 row rev sc in each sc, join with a sl st in first st.

Anasazi vest

ONE-ROW HORIZONTAL BUTTONHOLE

Step 1 At marker, bring the yarn to the front and slip the next stitch purlwise. Put the yarn to the back and leave it there. *Slip the next stitch purlwise, then pass the first slipped stitch over it. Repeat from* three times more without moving the yarn. Slip the last bound-off stitch to the left needle and turn work.

Step 2 Bring the yarn to the back and cast on 5 stitches using the cable cast-on as follows: *Insert the right needle between the first and second stitches on the left needle, wrap the yarn as if to knit, pull the loop through and place it on the left needle. Repeat from* four times more and turn work.

Step 3 Bring the yarn to the back, slip the first stitch from the left needle and pass the extra cast-on stitch over it and tighten firmly.

Step 1

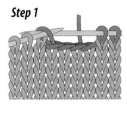

Step 2

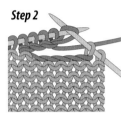

Step 3

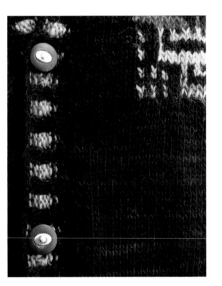

Chart A

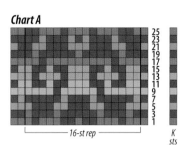

25 23 21 19 17 15 13 11 9 7 5 3 1

— 16-st rep —

K sts

Chart B

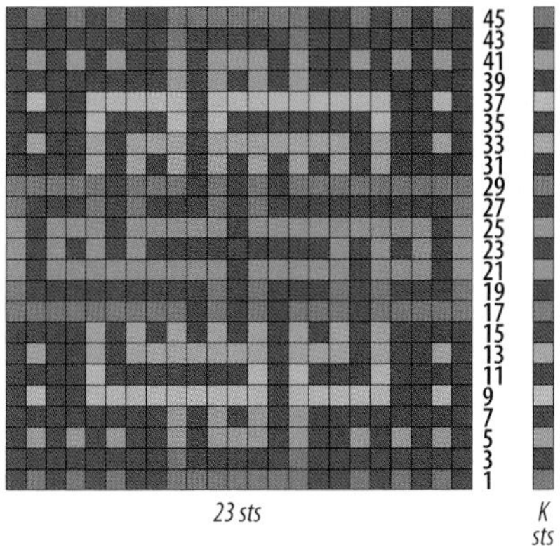

45 43 41 39 37 35 33 31 29 27 25 23 21 19 17 15 13 11 9 7 5 3 1

23 sts

K sts

Color Key
- Black (MC)
- Apple Green (A)
- Purple (B)
- Misty Pebbles (C)
- Yellow Brick Road (D)
- Madder (E)
- Tzarina (F)

Chart Notes
1. Each chart row consists of worked stitches and slipped stitches. On each row, stitches to be worked are indicated at the right of the chart. All other stitches in that row are slipped.
2. Work each chart row twice.
a. On right-side rows, reading chart from right to left, knit the indicated stitches and slip the others, slipping purlwise with yarn in back.
b. On wrong-side rows, purl the stitches that were knit on the previous row and slip the slipped stitches, slipping purlwise with yarn in front.

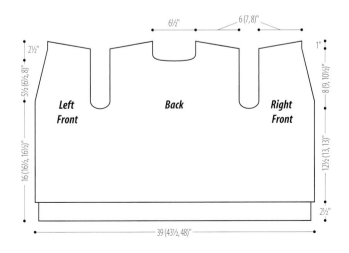

6½" 6 (7, 8)"

2½" 1"

5½ (6½, 8)" 8 (9, 10½)"

Left Front **Back** **Right Front**

16 (16½, 16½)" 12½ (13, 13)"

2½"

— 39 (43½, 48)" —

LA LANA WOOLS LUISA GELENTER
Kiva night sky designed by Judy Dercum

This one-piece, indigo-dyed cardigan features cuff-to-cuff patterning accented by multi-directional duplicate stitch in handspun silk.

Intermediate

Sizes

XS (S, M, L, XL, XXL, XXXL)

Shown in size M.

Directions are for smallest size with larger sizes in parentheses.

If there is only 1 set of numbers, it applies to all sizes.

Finished measurements

Underarm (buttoned) 39¼ (43½, 48, 52, 56¼, 60½, 64¾)"

Length 20 (20¾, 20¾, 21½, 21½, 22¼, 22¼)"

Gauge

15 sts and 22 rows to 4"/10cm over Single seed st, using larger needle.

16 sts and 22 rows to 4"/10cm over chart pat using larger needle.

MATERIALS
Yarn La Lana plant-dyed yarns: *Hand Spun MC* 8 (9, 10, 11, 12, 13, 14) skeins Deep Sea Indigo (100% wool), *A* 3 skeins Emerald City (40% Romney wool, 60% mohair) (each 2oz/57g, 56yds/51m); *Custom Mill Spun B* 1 (1, 1, 1, 2, 2, 2) skeins Purple, *C* 1 skein Medium Indigo Blue (each 4oz/114g, 200yds/183m, 100% wool); *Bombyx Silk* 1 skein each *D* Green, *E* Indigo Blue, *F* Lavender (each 1oz/28g, 59yds/54m, 100% silk).
Needles Sizes 8 and 9 (5 and 5.5mm) circular needle, 24"/60cm long *or size to obtain gauge.* One size 8 (5mm) double-pointed needle.
Extras 5 (5, 5, 5, 6, 6, 6) ¾"/20mm buttons. Crochet hook size H-8/5mm, yarn needle, stitch holders.

NOTES
1 See *Techniques,* p. 228 for M1, sl1-k1-psso, cable cast-on, invisible cast-on, chain and grafting. *2* Cardigan is worked in one piece from bottom back up to neck, increasing for sleeves, then divided for fronts and worked down to bottom front, decreasing for sleeves. *3* For ease in working, circle numbers for your size.

STITCHES USED
Single seed st multiple of 4 sts
Row 1 (RS) *K3, p1; rep from*. *Row 2 and all WS rows* Purl. *Rows 3 and 7* Knit. *Row 5* K1, *p1, k3; rep from*, end p1, k2. *Row 8* Purl. Rep rows 1–8 for pat.
Corrugated rib multiple of 2 sts plus 1
RS rows K1 MC, *p1 CC, k1 MC; rep from*.
WS rows P1 MC, *k1 CC, p1 MC; rep from*.

BACK
With smaller needle and MC, cast on 76 (84, 92, 100, 108, 116, 124) sts using invisible cast-on. Work 4 rows in St st. *Begin Single seed st* Work in Single seed st until piece measures 4¾ (5½, 5½, 6, 6, 6¾, 6¾)" from beg.
Shape sleeves
Continue in pat, working shaping as follows (working incs into pat): using cable cast-on, inc 1 st at beg of next 2 (0, 4, 8, 4, 6, 0) rows; 2 sts at beg of next 0 (6, 2, 2, 6 4, 6) rows; 3 sts at beg of next 32 (24, 22, 18, 16, 18, 28) rows; 6 sts at the beg of next 6 (8, 8, 8, 8, 6, 0) rows; 3 (3, 4, 4, 4, 4, 4) sts at the beg of the next 2 rows—216 (222, 222, 222, 228, 228, 228) sts. Work in St st until piece measures 13¼ (14, 14, 14¾, 14¾, 15½, 15½)" from beg, end with a WS row and inc 1 st in center—217 (223, 223, 223, 229, 229, 229) sts. *Begin Chart A: Next row* (RS) Using larger needle and beg where indicated for your size, work rows 1–12 of Chart A.
Divide for neck and fronts
Next row (RS) Continuing in chart pat, k102 (105, 105, 105, 106, 106, 106), join a 2nd ball of yarn and bind off

13 (13, 13, 13, 17, 17, 17) sts for back neck, k to end. Working both sides at same time, bind off 4 sts from each neck edge twice, then work 7 rows even.
Shape neck
Continue in pat, working shaping as follows (working incs into pat): *Inc row* (RS) K to 2 sts before neck edge, M1, k2, then at other neck edge, k2, M1, k to end. Rep inc row every other row 7 (7, 7, 7, 6, 6, 6) times more, then every 4th row 6 (6, 6, 6, 9, 9, 9) times. AT SAME TIME, after 36 rows of Chart A are complete, with MC and smaller needle, work in St st for 1 (1¼, 1½, 1¾, 2¼, 2¼, 2¼)".
Shape sleeves
Work in Single Seed st, working shaping as follows: bind off 3 (3, 4, 4, 4, 4, 4) sts at the beg of the next 2 rows, 6 sts at the beg of next 6 (8, 8, 8, 8, 6, 0) rows; 3 sts at beg of next 32 (24, 22, 18, 16, 18, 28) rows; 2 sts at beg of next 0 (6, 2, 2, 6 4, 6) rows; 1 st at beg of next 2 (0, 4, 8, 4, 6, 0) rows—38 (42, 46, 50, 54, 58, 62) sts each front. Work even in pat for 4 (4¾, 4¾, 5¼, 5¼, 6, 6)", then work 4 rows St st. Place sts on hold.

FINISHING
Cuffs
With RS facing, smaller needle, and MC, along wrist edge pick up and k35 (37, 37, 39, 39, 41, 41) sts. *Next row* (WS) Work in Corrugated rib in following color sequence for CC: 2 rows B, 3 rows F, 2 rows E, 1 row C, 3 rows D with A as MC, 3 rows F. With C, work 1 row in rib. Work 2–st I-cord bind-off as follows: With dpn, cable cast-on 2 sts onto LH needle, then *k1, sl 1-k1-psso, sl 2 sts back to LH needle; rep from*, ending with 2 sts on dpn. Sl 2 sts back to LH needle and bind off. Sew side and sleeve seams from bottom to cuffs, matching up rows along sleeves and body.
Bottom band
Place all bottom edge sts of cardigan onto smaller needle, removing waste yarn from invisibly cast-on sts from back—152 (168, 184, 200, 216, 232, 248) sts. With WS facing and MC, p 1 row, dec 15 (17, 17, 17, 21, 23, 23) sts evenly—137 (151, 167, 183, 195, 209, 225) sts. Work Corrugated rib in following color sequence for CC: 2 rows B, 3 rows F, 2 rows E, 1 row C, 4 rows D with A as MC, 3 rows F, 1 row B. Place all sts on hold.
Front bands
With RS facing, smaller needle, and C, beg at lower right front edge and pick up and k55 (58, 58, 61, 53, 56, 56) sts to beg of V-neck shaping, 43 (43, 43, 43, 55, 55, 55) sts along front neck shaping, 29 (29, 29, 29, 33, 33, 33) sts along back neck, 43 (43, 43, 43, 55, 55, 55) sts along front neck shaping, 55 (58, 58, 61, 53, 56, 56) sts along left front to lower edge—225 (231, 231, 237, 249, 255, 255) sts. Work Corrugated rib as follows, rep from* across on all rows: *Row 1* With C, k1, *p1, k1. *Row 2* K1 A, *p1 F, k1

Kiva night sky

Color Key
- Deep Sea Indigo (MC)
- Emerald City (A)
- Purple (B)
- Med Indigo Blue (C)
- Green (D)
- Indigo Blue (E)
- Lavender (F)

Stitch Key
- ☐ K on RS, p on WS
- ☑ Work in duplicate st after piece is complete
- ◆ Placement of Chart B center st of first or last row
- ★ Placement of Chart C center st of first or last row

Chart A

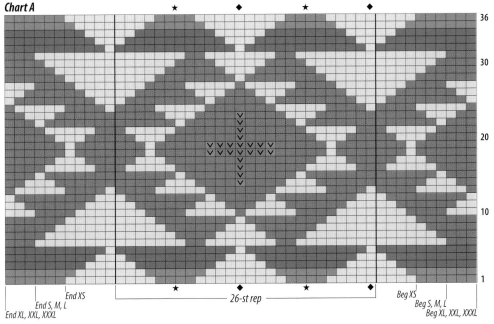

★ ◆ ★ ◆

36
30
20
10
1

End XS
End S, M, L
End XL, XXL, XXXL

★ ◆ ★ ◆
26-st rep

Beg XS
Beg S, M, L
Beg XL, XXL, XXXL

◆ **Chart B**   ★ **Chart C**

Chart D

Duplicate st
Duplicate st crosses on Chart A. Then, working above and below Chart A, duplicate st Chart B where indicated. Before working Chart C, turn work so front of sweater is at bottom and back is at top. Then duplicate st Chart C, centering it between the Chart B crosses. (**Note** Stitches in Chart B crosses appear upside down, see photo above.) Duplicate st Chart C just above bottom band, spacing it approx 2½" apart. Duplicate st Chart D between Chart C crosses.

A. **Row 3** P1 A, *k1, F, p1 A. **Row 4** K1 A, *p1 D, k1 A. **Row 5** With C, p1, *k1, p1. Place all sts on hold.

I-cord band
With RS facing, smaller needle, and short length of C, pick up and k6 sts along bottom edge of left front band. Place all bottom band sts of cardigan onto same needle. With RS facing and C, pick up on same needle and k6 sts along bottom edge of right front band, turn—149 (163, 179, 195, 207, 221, 237) sts. **Next row** (WS) With C, k1, *p1, k1; rep from* across. **Next row** With C, work 2–st I-cord bind-off to last st at right front corner, k2 and sl them back to LH needle, k1, sl 1-k1-psso, sl 2 sts back to LH needle, k2 and sl them back to LH needle, continue in I-cord bind-off around front bands to beg at left front corner. Graft end of I-cord to beg. Place markers along right front for 5 (5, 5, 5, 6, 6, 6) buttonholes, with the first at bottom, the last at beg of V-neck shaping, and others spaced evenly between. With crochet hook and WS facing, at each marker join C with a sl st to I-cord base, chain 6, skip 3 I-cord rows and join with a sl st in next I-cord row, fasten off. Sew on buttons.

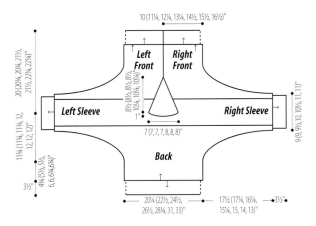

Work one repeat. Many other color cmbinations are possible. Judy Dercum experimented with other color combinations by working one repeat of Chart A.

VALENTINA DEVINE VALENTINA DEVINE

Los Alamos, New Mexico

We leave the Taos River Valley to retrace our steps south toward Santa Fe. A weak winter sun slowly warms us as we take the spur that climbs 7500 feet to Los Alamos, as yet untouched by fire. As we approach the home of Valentina Devine, we have the feeling that it's going to be a memorable day.

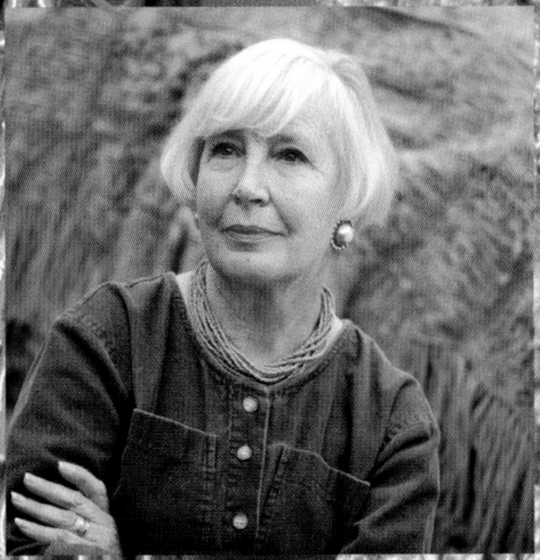

Valentina Devine

VALENTINA DEVINE VALENTINA DEVINE
Los Alamos, New Mexico

A skywalk connects Valentina Devine's kitchen to her studio, where a well-organized collection of yarns, neatly arranged by color, is stacked floor to cathedral ceiling. "I'm German," Valentina says as we view the colorful array that threatens to burst from its compartments, "and I'm very straightforward."

Born in Moscow to a German father and a Russian mother, Valentina grew up in a time when living in one country meant you were completely cut off from the other, so she has always felt a little displaced. Her mother would talk to Valentina for hours about the Russian half of her family they never saw, trying to create a sense of family history that she was unable to experience firsthand. It is perhaps for this reason that Valentina continually strives to break down barriers, especially in the fiber world.

Knitting without boundaries Everywhere we look are the shawls and wall hangings that have become Valentina's trademark, from the shaded greens and browns of "Ordinary Bamboo" in the foyer (see closeup photo on page 25) to the more abstract "New Mexico Clouds" in the living room. This piece, knit in irregularly shaped and textured naturals embellished by rows of crochet, is composed of what Valentina terms "mindless knitting, which is knit and purl whenever you feel like it." But we wonder, is it a wall hanging or an oversized shawl? Valentina makes no distinction. "It is both," she proclaims, smiling. "I like to say from wall to body, from body to wall."

Valentina found her first mentor in the early 1970s in New York, where she began working at a fiber shop owned by Irene Miller, who also taught dye workshops in the back kitchen of her Victorian house. "She had the constant, constant dye pot going on the old gas stove," Valentina remembers. It took five years for Valentina to discover the secrets of those pots, and she did this hands-on, by following Irene.

In the shop, the displays were baskets "sitting around, with hand-dyed yarn just oozing out of them," Valentina recalls. She had never before seen such color combinations applied to yarn, or yarns in such disarray. Her previous experience with yarn was choosing from the department store solids stacked in small cubicles. Valentina found that she preferred multicolored yarns exploding from baskets.

Irene then introduced Valentina to Kaffe Fassett and her color world changed forev-

er. Although he showed just a few garments and had not yet written his first book, his inspirational vision mesmerized Valentina. "I just completely went crazy. When I saw what he did," she recalls, "it changed my whole attitude towards yarn."

Since then, she has developed her own technique, Creative Knitting, which entails knitting in different directions and embellishing with surface design. In an effort to break down even more barriers, Valentina emphasizes free-form knitting without patterns and encourages combinations of knit, crochet, and embellishment all on one garment. "I love the abstract shapes," she confesses, "and using color in an abstract fashion."

She owes the inspiration for her approach to Joyce Edwards, a fellow fiber artist Valentina met at the Torpedo Factory, an art center in Alexandria, Virginia. It was there that Valentina began to exhibit her knit and crochet wall hangings. Joyce's philosophy toward fiber was, "Anything goes. If it feels good, do it," Valentina recalls. She taught Valentina to be fearless of color and fiber, to approach yarn without hesitation. It is as a tribute to Joyce that Valentina has developed knit and design workshops with titles such as "Creative Knitting,"

Top: Detail of Valentina's signature technique, Creative Knitting—multi-directional knitting, embellished with surface design. Ever seeking to break down boundaries, Valentina Devine likes to combine knit and crochet stitches within a garment. Her free-form techniques are so popular that she teaches a series of knit and design workshops based on knitting without patterns.

Right: Gypsy Moth Shawl alight on a hillside in Los Alamos.

Below: Valentina's floor-to-ceiling yarn collection is arranged by color and texture on the back wall of her lofty studio.

"Beyond Creative Knitting," and "Knitting Without Boundaries."

Creative business Valentina has been selling at shows and fiber fests for nearly twenty years. From her beginnings at the Torpedo Factory, she went on to show hand-dyed yarns at the Maryland Sheep and Wool Festival, where she has a booth to this day. Another favorite venue is the Estes Park Wool Festival, where she has sold yarn and taught classes for the past ten years.

Although Valentina resists kits, she has made an effort to record some of her free-form designs in the past few years. "These are mostly combinations to add to the Creative Knitting workshop," she explains. "As you know, that is a very free-form, individual style, and I just put a few color families together for the knitters who agonize about which color goes with which." She currently offers about ten designs as kits. "Not many," she admits, "when you think of how many years I have been selling yarn."

For Valentina, her first love is dyeing yarn and her second is knitting freely without a pattern. "I have to push myself to sit down and write a pattern," Valentina reveals. "I don't do it well, but I realize it is a necessary

evil in order to sell kits and keep the knitter interested, so ... I do it."

Blurring the lines For Valentina, color is the most important aspect of her designs. "I like my yarn to look like hand-dyed yarn, so it's always shaded," she tells us. "When I design, I consider how the lines in the color blotches will appear in the knitted piece." Designing on the diagonal is a technique she often uses to prevent colors from forming stripes. In addition, she prefers subtle shading, finding that three to five colors applied to yarn can sometimes overstate her intention. Valentina finds that supplementing her hand-dyed yarns with textured naturals helps facilitate the subtle movement from one color to the next.

For inspiration, Valentina looks to features of the Southwest, especially the subdued tones of adobe dwellings, wintry colors, and the jagged shapes of canyons. She juxtaposes these with ideas that come to her from the many prints, carpets, furniture pieces, and paintings she has gathered during her extensive travels. Having once been culturally confined, she now makes a point of travelling freely through Turkey, Spain, Italy, Indonesia, Morocco, and Germany, where she finds an unending array of textures, colors, and unusual motifs.

Valentina hand-dyes whatever yarns come her way using simple overdye and dip-dye techniques that complement her richly embellished knitting. Allowing herself no more than three colors, she dyes yarn in semi-solid tones and then overdyes in a solid color in order to mute and create new colors. In this way she achieves the many grays and metal tones that are essential to her palette.

Future watch As her knit and dye techniques become more well known, Valentina sees herself opening the world of creative knitting to a broader audience. She continues to develop new ideas and hopes to write a book that will inspire even more knitters, crocheters, weavers, and embroiderers.

Currently, Valentina is expanding her palette by exploring new techniques with hand-dyed naturals. She reaches out internationally, teaching her craft in the universal language of color. In this way, she crosses the ethnic and cultural barriers that she was unable to overcome as a child. "There are no failures or mistakes with color," Valentina declares with a knowing look. "Absolutely none. Ever."

Clockwise from above: A heady mixture of color and texture: hand-dyed wool boucle; detail of New Mexico Clouds shawl—knitted shapes joined by crochet; silks in some of the metallic tones Valentina favors.

The light in New Mexico is like no other. At daybreak, the sun slowly warms the ancient adobes. The slant of the sun cycles throughout the day, breaking into a shadowless high noon. Soon, the gathering dusk stretches across the walks, the sun slips behind the mountains, and we move indoors to rest for tomorrow's travel.

Garter blocks designed by Valentina Devine

Garter blocks are far from mundane when knit diagonally in a splendidly textured, hand-dyed wool.

MATERIALS

Yarn Valentina Devine *Wool Bouclé* 4 skeins each of 2 different colors for 2-color afghan (Flamingo and New Mexico Sunset); 8 skeins total of 5 different colors for multi-color afghan (Monet Blues, Santa Fe Turquoise, Terracotta Mix, Wild Mushrooms, and Olive Garden) (each 8oz/228g, 154yds/141m, 96% wool, 4% nylon).
Needles One pair size 11 (8mm) needles, *or size to obtain gauge.*
Extras Large crochet hook, sewing thread, and needle (optional).

NOTE

1 See *Techniques,* p. 228 for chain (ch), half double crochet (hdc), and single crochet (sc). *2* Both afghans are made up of 24 squares that are knitted diagonally, then sewn or crocheted together.

SQUARE make 24

(**Note** For 2-color afghan, make 12 each color. For multi-color afghan, make 24 total in desired colors.)
Cast on 2 sts. Work in Garter st (knit every row), inc 1 st at beg of every row until there are 30 sts. Then continuing in Garter st, dec 1 st at beg of every row to 3 sts. Cut yarn, draw through sts and pull tightly.

FINISHING

Sew (with thread or fine yarn) or sc squares tog (with RS tog), 6 squares long by 4 squares wide. For 2-color afghan, assemble alternating colors. For multicolor afghan, assemble with colors placed as desired.

2-color afghan

Edging With desired color, join with a sc in corner at beg of a long end. **Rnd 1** Work in sc evenly spaced around; join with a sl st in first sc. **Rnd 2** *Sc in each sc to next corner, sc in next sc, [ch 1, skip 1 sc, sc in next sc] across short end to corner; rep from* around; join with a sl st in first sc. Fasten off.
Fringe With same color as edging, cut 3 strands 14" long per fringe. Attach fringe (*see illustration*) in each ch-1 space on both short ends of afghan. Trim fringe even.

Multicolor afghan

Edging With desired color, join with a sc in corner at beg of a long end. **Rnd 1** Work in sc evenly spaced around, working a multiple of 8 sc plus 5 on each short end; join with a sl st in first sc. Fasten off.
Strip-fringe With same color as edging, join with a sc in corner at beg of a short end. Ch 16, hdc in 2nd ch from hook and in each remaining ch, *sc in each of next 3 sc on afghan, ch 16, hdc in 2nd ch from hook and in each remaining ch; rep from* across short end. Tie 2 strips tog in a half knot across. Rep for opposite end.

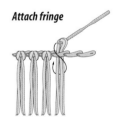

Attach fringe

Easy +

Finished measurements
approx 42" x 62" excluding fringe

Gauge
8½ sts and 16 rows to 4"/10cm
over Garter st (k every row)
using size 11 (8mm) needles.

Morning dawns crisp and bright as we wind through painted canyons, traveling from Arizona into New Mexico. Already we sense something different: the scent of sage and smudge of piñon smoke rise from old adobes, the light grows stronger by the minute. By the time we pass the outskirts of Rio Rancho, full day is upon us. We arrive at a large warehouse glistening against a desert backdrop. At the entrance, we are greeted by Cindy Brooks and Molly Cavin, partners in Fiesta Yarns.

FIESTA YARNS CINDY BROOKS & MOLLY CAVIN

Rio Rancho, New Mexico

Cindy Brooks and Molly Cavin

FIESTA YARNS CINDY BROOKS & MOLLY CAVIN
Rio Rancho, New Mexico

Clockwise from above:
The appearance of ribbon changes dramatically when knit; Gelato, a rayon ribbon, shimmers in the sun; dried red chili peppers provide local color.

From cookies to colorways "We moved down here from Santa Fe when I owned a wholesale cookie manufacturing company," explains Cindy. That was in 1991, when they needed all 15,000 square feet of their space. Cindy and Molly sold the cookie company, the Santa Fe Bite Size Bakery, in 1997. "The cookies got big and it wasn't fun anymore," she jokes. But of course, neither of them could retire, so they decided to embark on a new venture. Today, Fiesta Yarns takes up only a fraction of the warehouse.

What was I supposed to be doing? Cindy remembers asking herself. "The answer wasn't 'cleaning the house.'" Both Cindy and Molly learned to knit at a tender age, and even during their cookie days, "yarn was our thing." Before buying Fiesta from Christella San Guerrero, they explored all kinds of business ventures involving yarn, from machine knits to a retail store, until finally, "Fiesta fell into our laps," Cindy says, "as simple as that."

But it was not simple to reinvent Fiesta. Before them lay the task of turning the small dye studio into a business without losing the magic of what Christella had spent 14 years creating. Undaunted, Cindy and Molly went forward. "To us, it was wonderful," Cindy recalls. "That's what we look for when we decide to grow a business—we look for a good idea that needs a lot of fixing."

As a fiber artist, Christella was best known for a unique double-stranded yarn called La Boheme. She had an incredible color sense, Cindy notes, but she was not business-oriented, and she knew it. For example, Christella had no interest in mass production, and for that reason skein sizes tended to be random, dye lots small, and backorders the norm. These problems could be fixed by Cindy and Molly, who had a large, empty warehouse in a good location and years of manufacturing and production experience. "We saw incredible potential," Cindy says.

For Cindy, who was an art major, and Molly, whose first real job was as a potter's apprentice, the transition to the world of hand-dyeing was satisfying. "As a child, I would dream of colors I couldn't see on earth," Molly says. For Cindy, color sense came to fruition in her twenties, when she began to travel. "I still go to Mexico for a color fix," she admits, citing the bold and carefree colors she finds there.

From Christella they learned to hand-dye plant and animal fibers together, such as the rayon/mohair blend in La Boheme, which remains Fiesta's signature yarn. "When we took over, people didn't even know that Christella had any other yarns!" Cindy says with a laugh. Now that they employ two dye assistants, Molly has moved on to handling production. "Molly is the mechanical and production brains of the group," Cindy proclaims. "She can fix anything." Molly smiles, adding, "I'm very good at phone mechanics."

Fiesta's yarns are distributed wholesale, although knitting supplies and factory seconds are sold from a showroom in Rio Rancho. Since so many of Fiesta's yarn lines cross over to weaving, crocheting, machine

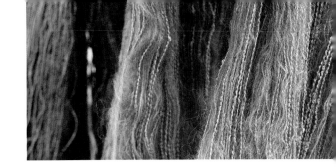

about it," Cindy notes. "We'll dye the same color two different times, and all of a sudden something magical happens. It is not something you can completely control." "It's the forces of nature," Molly adds.

Natural beauty abounds in New Mexico, the Land of Enchantment, and Cindy finds inspiration in the ever-changing light outside the studio. She believes it is the erratic weather patterns that bring out the incredible colors she sees in the desert mountains beyond. "It's a perfect environment to be dyeing in, because the colors change constantly, and we do try to capture this in the yarn," she says.

Fiesta's yarns are known for subtle color blending. The knitter will never see obvious color changes or, Cindy hopes, even distinct pools of color. Some colors become background shades that light up other colors. They may be unrecognizable, but can change the effect of other colors in the skein when knit. A wonderful example of the way color can act as a foil can be seen in La Boheme.

Clockwise from above: La Boheme, Fiesta's signature yarn, is also its oldest—the original recipe was developed 20 years ago by weavers. The unlikely duo of brushed mohair and rayon boucle combine to create a soft and shiny stranded yarn with a designer look that dresses up even the simplest design.

Fiesta has recently introduced a line of La Boheme monochromatics, shown here in Bronze and Onyx.

Lace patterning with La Boheme in the colorway Aster as shown in From the Top by Susan Meredith.

knitting, and other fiber arts, they are sold to a variety of markets.

Magical colors When Cindy and Molly purchased Fiesta, they discovered that Christella painted yarn in a "teeny tiny room." With Cindy's background in restaurant set-up, and Molly's aptitude with custom-made equipment, their first task was to design a practical, functional dye kitchen. "We didn't want to take any more steps than necessary," Cindy recalls.

Cindy and Molly do not label their dye process because they do not use techniques that produce repeatable colorways. "There are so many different colors within the skein that you really don't need to worry

Cindy and Molly inherited La Boheme from Christella, who purchased the recipe from a weaving company nearly twenty years ago. La Boheme came to them with a fixable problem. "We called it the 'oh-my-god, the mohair's growing' problem," Cindy laughs. Because it is a stranded yarn of diverse fibers, La Boheme had a tendency to misbehave. The rayon would slip and the mohair would loft, resulting in uneven plies—and phone calls from customers. "We even had compulsive customers who would unply the yarn and knit from two separate balls," Cindy recalls.

Since then, she and Molly have worked to solve this problem from a knitter's standpoint, exploring the way the yarn knits up using various colorways, stitch patterns, and winding techniques. As a result, the yarn is now machine-plied for better tension. Knitting with La Boheme has become an easier, more comfortable,

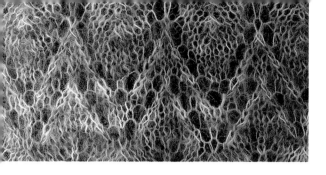

and more pleasant experience, and the phone calls have decreased.

Cindy believes that knitters want to create extraordinary garments. As knitters themselves, she and Molly strive to produce luxurious yarns that indulge the senses. Regular yarns are "scratch products—you know, flour, sugar, eggs—and then you put it together and bake a cake." Handpainted yarn *is* the cake. Cindy explains, "The garment does not need to be intricate; it does not need to take a lot of time. People want to experience the colors and texture of the yarn."

New yarns, new colors, new designs
In addition to La Boheme, which comes in 30 color blends, Fiesta offers many other yarns, available in 10 to 12 blends. They include a textured wool/mohair/rayon boucle called Clouds, a shiny rayon ribbon called Gelato, and Pebbles, a boucle cotton.

Fiesta has a line of what they call "monochromatics." Here, the range of shades stays within one color—Garnet is composed of variations of red, while Onyx is black with hints of wine, emerald, and blue. Other monochromes include Bronze, Liquid Silver, and Snow.

Pattern support is very important to Cindy and Molly. Although yarns and patterns are still available separately, Fiesta now produces a variety of kits. Some of these patterns were inherited; many more designs have been developed since the business changed hands in 1998.

Future watch
Neither Cindy nor Molly believes handpainted yarn will take over the market, despite the influx of knitters, many of them young, who are choosing high-end, designer yarns. "Of course we'd all like to dream that!" Cindy jokes, but she sees price resistance as the biggest factor.

She has plans for a line of crochet patterns. "There are a lot of crocheters out there—I don't think many of them have experimented with handpainted yarn," she notes. She would love to see them crocheting the same kind of incredible garments that are now exclusive to the knitting world.

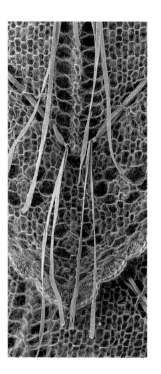

Clockwise from above: Heaven mohair in knitted lace, in the skein, and accented with ribbons.

Cindy and Molly are developing a new line of hand-dyed basics that are quite different for Fiesta. Kokopelli, their new wool/mohair blend, is now available in 28 semi-solid colors of the Southwest. This venture will offer knitters yet another choice. Why? "We purchased this company to grow it," Cindy reminds us.

Endnotes At the time of printing, Fiesta has been sold to Jeannie and Brad Duncan. They are dedicated to continuing the tradition started by Christella San Guerrero and recreated by Cindy and Molly.

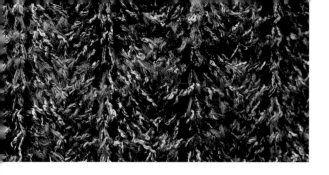

FIESTA YARNS CINDY BROOKS & MOLLY CAVIN
From the top designed by Susan Meredith

Colors undulate along the easy lace rows of this ready-to-wear-right-off-the-needles raglan.

MATERIALS
Yarn Fiesta *La Boheme* (a 2-stranded yarn) 4 (5, 6) skeins Aster (each 4oz/114g, 145yds/132m, 1 strand 100% kid mohair, 1 strand 100% rayon).
Needles Size 7 (4.5mm) circular needle, 16" and 29"/40 and 74cm long, *or size to obtain gauge.* Sizes 8 and 9 (5 and 5.5mm) circular needles, 29"/74cm long. Sizes 8, 9, and 10 (5, 5.5 and 6mm) double-pointed needles (dpn).
Extras Crochet hook size G/7 (4.5mm), stitch markers and holders.

NOTES
1 See *Techniques*, p. 228 for M1, ssk, sl 1-k2tog-psso, and single crochet (sc). *2* Pullover is worked circularly from the top down. Begin working back and forth in rows to end of neck shaping, then join and work in rounds. *3* Change needle lengths, or use double-pointed needles, as needed. *4* To maintain correct stitch count when shaping, every decrease in stitch pattern needs a corresponding yarn over.

STITCH USED
Lace pat multiple of 8 sts
(*Note* When working pat st in rnds, knit row 2.)
Row 1 (RS) *Yo, k2, sl 1-k2tog-psso, k2, yo, k1; rep from*.
Row 2 Purl.

BODY
Yoke
(*Note* Use one color for markers placed on row 9, then a different color for marker placed on Chart A, row 7, that will mark beg of rnd.)
With size 7 (4.5mm) needle, cast on 43 sts. P 1 row. *Row 1* [K1, yo] twice, k7, yo, k1, yo, [k6, k2tog, yo] twice, [k7, yo, k1, yo] twice, k1—51 sts. *Row 2 and all WS rows* Purl. *Row 3* K1, M1, [k1, yo] 3 times, k2, sl 1-k2tog-psso, k2, yo, [k1, yo] 3 times, [k2, sl 1-k2tog-psso, k2, yo, k1, yo] 3 times, [k1, yo] twice, k2, sl 1-k2tog-psso, k2, [yo, k1] 3 times, M1, k1—61 sts. *Row 5* K1, M1, k3, yo, k1, yo, k3, yo, k1, sl 1-k2tog-psso, [k1, yo, k3, yo] twice, [k1, sl 1-k2tog-psso, k1, yo, k3, yo] 3 times, k1, yo, k3, yo, k1, sl 1-k2tog-psso, k1, yo, k3, yo, k1, yo, k3, M1, k1—71 sts. *Row 7* K1, M1, [k5, yo, k1, yo, k5, yo, sl 1-k2tog-psso, yo] twice, [k5, yo, sl 1-k2tog-psso, yo], twice, k5, yo, k1, yo, k5, yo, sl 1-k2tog-psso, yo, k5, yo, k1, yo, k5, M1, k1—81 sts. *Row 9* K1, M1, k7, *yo, place marker (pm), k1, yo, pm, k3, k2tog, k2, yo, k1, yo, k2, k2tog, k3, yo, pm, k1, yo, pm*, k3, k2tog, [k2, yo, k1, yo, k2, sl 1-k2tog-psso] twice, k2, yo, k1, yo, k2, k2tog, k3; rep from* to* once, k7, M1, k1—91 sts. *Begin Chart A: Row 1* K1, M1, k1, [*yo, k2, sl 1-k2tog-psso, k2, yo, k1; rep from* to marker, sl marker, yo, k1, yo, k1, sl marker] 4 times, yo, k2, sl 1-k2tog-psso, k2, yo, k1, M1, k1. *Row 2* Purl. Work through chart row 6. *Row 7* Work

chart to last 4 sts, pm, k3, M1, k1. Cast on 5 sts at end of row for front neck and join—136 sts (32 sts between markers for front and back, 10 sts between markers for raglans, 16 sts between markers for shoulders). Begin working in rnds as follows: Knit to last marker placed (in rnd 7). Rnds now begin here. *Begin Chart B: Rnd 1* [Work rnd 1 of Lace pat to marker, work Chart B rnd 1 to marker] 4 times, work Lace pat to end. *Rnd 2* Knit. Continue as established through chart rnd 21 (29, 37)—224 (256, 288) sts.

Divide for body and sleeves
Rnd 22 (30, 38) Removing markers as you come to them (except rnd marker), [k to first raglan marker, k8 (16, 16), pm, k7 (3, 7), place next 49 (57, 65) sts on hold for sleeve, cast on 9 sts for underarm] twice, k to end—144 (160, 176) sts. *Rnd 23 (31, 39)* *Work rnd 1 of Lace pat to marker, yo, k2, sl 1-k2tog-psso (ssk, sl 1-k2tog-psso), [k2, yo] 1 (0, 1) time, k9 (7, 9), [yo, k2] 1 (0, 1) time, sl 1-k2tog-psso (k2 tog, sl 1-k2tog-psso), k2, yo, k1; rep from * once more; work rnd 1 of Lace pat to end. *Next rnd* Knit. Rep last 2 rnds once more.

Shape body
Begin Chart C [Work rnd 1 of Lace pat to marker, work dec rnd 1 of Chart C] twice, work in pat to end—4 sts dec'd. Work even in pat, working dec rnd every 6th rnd until chart complete—128 (144, 160) sts. Lace pat is now continuous at sides. Work in pat for 2 (3, 3)". Change to size 8 (5mm) needle and work for 3" more. Change to size 9 (5.5mm) needle and work 3" more. Work sc bind-off. Work 1 rnd sc in each sc. Fasten off.

RIGHT SLEEVE
Place sts from holder onto size 7 needle (16"). Along underarm, pick up and k7 sts—56 (64, 72) sts. *Next rnd* K9 (5, 9), pm for beg of rnd, k32 (40, 48) sts, pm, k to rnd marker. *Next rnd* Work rnd 1 of Lace pat to last 16 sts. *Sizes XS, M* K8, yo, k2, sl 1-k2tog-psso, k2, yo, k1. *Size S* Yo, k2, ssk, k7, k2tog, k2, yo, k1. *All sizes: Next rnd* Knit. Rep last 2 rnds 3 times more. *Begin Chart D* Work in pat to last 24 sts, pm, work dec rnd 1 of Chart D—2 sts dec'd. Work even in pat, working each dec rnd every 4th rnd until chart complete—40 (48, 56) sts. Lace pat is now continuous. Work even in pat until sleeve measures 10" from underarm. Change to size 8 (5mm) needles and work for 2". Change to size 9 (5.5mm) needles and work for 2". Change to size 10 needles and work for 2". Work sc bind-off (*see illustration*). Work 1 rnd sc in each sc. Fasten off.

LEFT SLEEVE
Work as for right sleeve. Block piece. Work 2 rnds of sc around neck edge.

From the top

Chart A

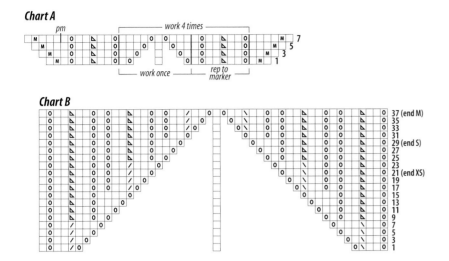

pm
work 4 times
M ... 7
... 5
... 3
... 1
work once
rep to marker

Chart B

37 (end M)
35
33
31
29 (end S)
27
25
23
21 (end XS)
19
17
15
13
11
9
7
5
3
1

Chart C-Size XS, M

4
3
2
dec rnd 1

Chart C-Size S

4
3
2
dec rnd 1

Chart D-Size XS, M

8
7
6
5
4
3
2
dec rnd 1

Chart D-Size S

8
7
6
5
4
3
2
dec rnd 1

□ K on RS, p on WS   ◩ S11-k2tog-psso
◳ Ssk   ○ Yo
◲ K2tog   M M1

Chart Notes
1 Chart A shows RS rows only. Purl all WS rows for Chart A.
Chart B shows odd rnds only. Knit all even rnds for Chart B.
2 Charts C and D are body and sleeve shaping charts. Only the dec rnds are shown. Work other rnds even, by working center underarm or side st as k1.

Single crochet bind-off

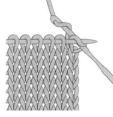 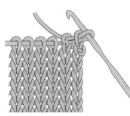

Step 1. Insert hook into first stitch as if to knit, yarn over hook and through stitch, slip stitch off needle—one loop on hook.

Step 2. *Insert hook into next stitch as if to knit, yarn over hook and through stitch and loop on hook, slip stitch off needle—one loop on hook. Repeat from*.

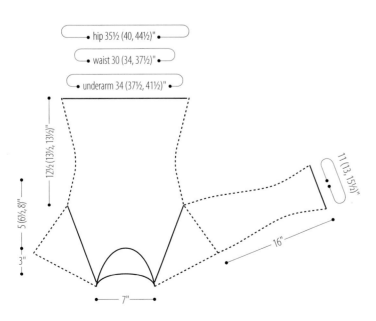

hip 35½ (40, 44½)"
waist 30 (34, 37½)"
underarm 34 (37½, 41½)"
12½ (13½, 13½)"
5 (6½, 8)"
3"
11 (13, 15½)"
16"
7"

FIESTA YARNS CINDY BROOKS & MOLLY CAVIN
Pueblo cape designed by Cindy Brooks

Two skeins of multicolored, double-stranded yarn quadruple the color mix in this quick-to-knit cape.

MATERIALS

Yarn Fiesta *La Boheme* (a 2-stranded yarn) **MC** 4 skeins Bronze, **CC** 2 skeins Aster (each 8oz/228g, 290yds/ 1265m, 1 strand 100% kid mohair, 1 strand 100% rayon).
Needles Size 13 (9mm) circular needle, 29"/74cm long, *or size to obtain gauge.* Size 9 (5.5mm) circular needle, 16"/40cm long.
Extras Three medium clasps. Crochet hook size H/8 (5mm), stitch markers and holders.

NOTES

1 See *Techniques*, p. 228 for M1, cable cast-on, and single crochet (sc). *2* Cape is worked from the neck down with the two strands of La Boheme held together throughout (four strands of yarn). *3* Front bands are worked at the same time as cape using separate balls of yarn. Twist with cape yarn to avoid holes. *4* Change needle lengths as needed. *5* Tweed st pat is worked alternating 2 rows of MC and 2 rows of CC, except on bands. Bands are worked with MC only. *6* Slip first and last stitch of every right-side row knitwise with yarn in back (wyib).

STITCHES USED

Tweed st multiple of 2 sts plus 1
Row 1 (WS) P1, *sl 1 wyib, p1; rep from*. *Row 2* Knit.
Row 3 P2, *sl 1 wyib, p1; rep from*, end p2. *Row 4* Knit.
Rep rows 1–4 for pat.
Double inc worked at seam sts
Work to marker before seam st, M1, sl marker, work seam st, sl marker, M1.

CAPE

With larger needle and 2 strands MC, cast on 39 sts. Knit and place markers (pm) as follows: k2, pm, k1 (seam st), pm, k7, pm, k1 (seam st), pm, k17, pm, k1 (seam st), pm, k7, pm, k1 (seam st), pm, k2. *Begin Tweed st: Rows 1–2* (WS) Change to CC, work rows 1–2 of Tweed st, sl the first and

last st of row 2 (RS). *Row 3* Change to MC, work row 3 of pat. *Row 4* With separate ball of MC (2 strands), cable cast-on 7 sts at beg of row for front band. Sl 1, k6 (front band); with 2nd ball of MC, knit across, working double inc at each seam st; with 3rd ball of MC (2 strands), cable cast-on 7 sts for front band onto LH needle, k6, sl 1—61 sts. *Row 5* With MC, p1, [sl 1 wyib, p1] 3 times for front band; change to CC, work pat row 1 to front band; with MC, p1, [sl 1 wyib, p1] 3 times for front band. *Row 6* Sl 1, k6; with CC, k to front band; with MC, k6, sl 1. *Row 7* P2, [sl 1 wyib, p1] twice, sl 1 wyib; change to 2nd ball MC, work pat row 3 to front band; with 3rd ball MC, [sl 1 wyib, p1] 3 times, p1. *Row 8* Sl 1, k6; with 2nd ball MC, k to front band working double inc at each seam st; with 3rd ball MC, k6, sl 1— 69 sts. Rep rows 5–8 ten times more—149 sts. Continue in pat as established, but work double inc every 8 rows (instead of every 4 rows) 6 times—197 sts. Work even in pat until piece measures 27" from beg.
Bottom band
Working with 1 ball of MC (2 strands) only, work in pat for 2", sl first and last st of every RS row, end with a WS row. Bind off loosely.

FINISHING
Collar
With larger needle and 2 strands MC, cast on 7 sts. With RS facing, pick up and k52 sts evenly around neck, including front bands. Work 1" in Tweed st with MC only, sl first and last st on RS rows. Change to smaller needle, work until collar measures 2". Bind off. With 2 strands MC, work 1 rnd of sc around entire edge of cape, including collar and collar tab. Sew on clasps with the first centered on collar tab (overlap tab onto left front collar for placement of left half of clasp), the next on front bands below collar, and the last 4" down from previous clasp.

Intermediate

Sizes
One size fits most

Finished measurements
Circumference 72½"
Length 31"

Gauge
11 sts and 17 rows to 4"/10cm
over Tweed st using larger
needle with 2 strands held together.

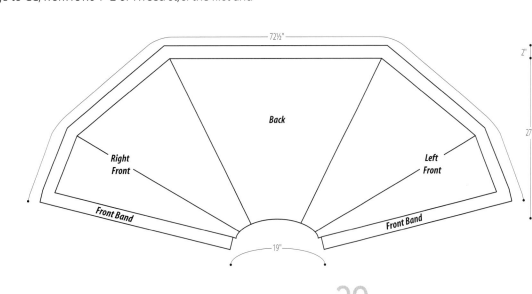

Back

Right Front

Left Front

Front Band

Front Band

72½"

2"

27"

19"

Mountain

We track south from Cheyenne, Wyoming. The Rocky Mountains loom cold and distant to our right, ever advancing as we drive through Denver's rush-hour smog. As the traffic thins and the air begins to cool, we find ourselves winding through foothills at the base of Pike's Peak. We stop in Colorado Springs, awestruck at the eastern edge of the Rockies, an almost vertical backdrop to Judy Ditmore's studio.

INTERLACEMENTS JUDY L. DITMORE

Colorado Springs, Colorado

Judy L. Ditmore

INTERLACEMENTS JUDY L. DITMORE
Colorado Springs, Colorado

One weaver's beginnings Judy Ditmore's "addiction" to fiber began with spinning. "An uncle gave me a spinning wheel and fleece so I did natural colors," she remembers. But for Judy, color was always there; she recalls a turquoise-and-pink kitchen and multicolored doors from her childhood home. It was Rachel Brown (see page 6) who pushed Judy to develop her love of color. Not only did Rachel provide her with pointers involving dye and chemical combinations, but "the other thing is, I'm basically a money person," Judy admits, "and I saw that there was money in selling my hand-dyeds." She met Rachel in 1982, and the very next year she opened Dyelightful Handwovens, a shop specializing in hand-dyed yarns, handwoven garments, and custom art pieces. Soon she began dyeing fibers for customers, the most unusual request being hundreds of pounds of fishing line for a company that made deep-sea fishing lures. During her 13 years there, Judy's shop became a mecca for those searching for instruction in just about everything having to do with fiber.

Clockwise from top: Painted warps drying on racks; hand-dyed textured hanks overhang a mountain vista; the Garden of the Gods inspires Judy.

Judy believes that in those early years she was creative out of necessity. "My creations were eked out then. Now, if I don't have what I need, I buy it. Before, I had to deal with it or make it. Then I had time and no money; now it's the other way," Judy explains. "That's the Catch-22 of success."

Judy recounts the turning point of her life as a fiber artist. She was carrying a stack of mohair shawls to her truck for a trade show when she actually "saw" her first snowflake. She realized that she had become so busy running through life that she couldn't see what was there. "That's when I stopped running the rat race and started walking." In 1996, she closed her thriving store to get on with her art. Of course there was nothing to do but bring

her inventory home. "I'm very compulsive," Judy admits. "I can't live without fiber."

Dyeing outdoors In her back yard, Judy's production studio houses weaving equipment for a business called Interlacements that she shares with partner, Tara Matthews. Together they dye, weave, and sew garments. Adjoining is the dye studio, complete with outdoor burners for custom-made vessels which can hold up to 12 pounds of fiber, and an outdoor stereo system. Here, Judy and Tara dye warps and weft in stock and custom colors.

In Colorado, where the sun shines 320 days a year, dyeing is done outdoors even in winter. "The rule is 30 degrees and sunshine, we work," Judy says. The natural light is wonderful. She hot-processes everything, even cottons, and dries it all outside. "When we are in production, we dye every other day, 6 hours," Judy says. Although they dress for the weather, the real hazard is the wind, which can blow out the gas flames under the dye pots.

Resurrection and the 20% system Today, Judy's most satisfying dye process is one she developed early in her career, called "resurrection dyeing." In the beginning, she could not afford natural dye skeins, so

some of the brightest palettes that are out there, and I think they work because they flow."

Judy loves doing jumbles of solid and semi-solid colors and calls these yarns her "NA's" (not available for reorders). "I like it when I get all the cups out of the chemical room and just pour." She may run 40 or 50 pounds without changing the dye water. She smiles, "We warn people: buy everything you need because this was fun and we don't know how to do it again."

Novelty yarns such as eyelash or boucle are Judy's favorites. The only "plain" yarn she paints is Toasty Toes, a superwash merino that far outsells the others. Other popular yarns include Colorado, a cotton/rayon blend, and Utah, the same blend with more texture. "All of our yarns are available in all the colorways," Judy says. Many can be used successfully for weaving as well as knitting.

To have success with handpainted yarns, Judy advises knitters to understand the difference between handpainted and space-dyed colorways. Commercial space-dyed colorways are produced with color sections of equal length in a repeated sequence, whereas the colors in handpainted yarn move and change. She suggests that knitters use two balls of yarn, switching between them to achieve a consistent spread of color, and that they purchase enough yarn at one time. "If you know these things, you can do anything," she proclaims.

Top: Judy dries all of her yarns outside; Left: Painted warp chains waiting to be threaded on the loom.

she resorted to overdyeing machine-dyed bargain yarns. Now she uses such mill ends to explore an ever-widening monochromatic palette. "I buy ugly-colored yarn cheap and give it life," Judy explains. In order to make designing with colorways more predictable, Judy developed a technique she calls the "20% system" for her standard yarn line. In this technique, a colorway consists of five distinct colors painted in a circle, and each colorway can build diamonds or X's as design motifs when knit. Popular colorways are Café Au Lait, reminiscent of coffee with cream and raspberry sauce, and Chairman of the Board, subdued but beautiful. Judy deviates from this method when working with very bright colors, such as those in the Poppy Fields colorway.

Interlacements' unique colorways are created by placing the colors in an order that flows rather than jumps from one to the next. To Judy, the color created when two colors meet is the most important color in the progression. "If you take five colors and put them in a different order, you're going to get an entirely different look," Judy explains, noting that it took her eight months to develop the sequences for Interlacements. "That is why we call it a color*way*." She adds, "We do

The business of non-promotion Judy and Tara show their Interlacements yarns and handwovens at half a dozen conferences, and have a limited number of wholesale accounts that they support with sample garments. Interlacements sells 17 colorways in 14 yarns (offered in their original dye skeins), painted warps in 14 colorways, accessories, and kits for both weavers and knitters, but no patterns. "We give patterns away!" Judy says. They have no sales representatives because, as Judy says, "Our yarns promote themselves."

Custom dye work for other companies, including everything from hemp roving to silk hankies to exotic yarns, continues to be a significant business area for Judy and Tara. Judy is also part owner of a studio called Fiber

Goddess Gallery, where she shows signature pieces of both wall and wearable art. Her personal line of wearables and interior space art is displayed at Judy L. Ditmore Handwovens, a wearable-art gallery housed at the site of her former yarn shop. How does she keep it all going? "Whichever fire's burning the fastest is the one I'm working on," Judy says.

Future watch Judy recognizes that knitters are looking for ways to combine handpainted yarns with familiar techniques such as slip stitch and Fair Isle to create unique pieces. They also want small, portable projects to fit into their busy lives, and she feels that the sock craze will continue. As knitting gains ever greater popularity, Judy sees more and more men taking up this relaxing and creative pastime.

For the future, Judy plans to travel more. Her love of Harley-Davidson motorcycles allows the kind of touring that inspires new colorways, from the grape harvests of California wine country to the salt-swept beaches of the Florida Keys.

In her personal work, Judy would like to create more wearable art, adding complexity to her designs by incorporating what she has learned from both knitting and weaving. "It doesn't matter if it's on the body or on a wall." In order to focus on her art, she must turn the "meat-and-potatoes stuff" over to Tara.

Because people appreciate the time and effort involved in creating unique products and are willing to pay for them, Judy sees no end to hand-processed yarn as long as supply meets demand. "Keep your business small enough so that you can take care of business," she advises other hand-dyers. Just as her artwork pushes her to grow and learn new techniques, so she believes handpainted yarn can gain broader appeal as long as handdyers stay creative and continue to grow as colorists.

Clockwise from top: A selection of Judy's personal work, some of which is available at her wearable art studio now called Judy L. Ditmore Handwovens and housed in her former yarn shop: an array of hand-dyed silk scarves; a handwoven shawl draped across one of Judy's unique painted chairs; scarves handwoven from Interlacements handpainted yarns; one of Judy's pieces of wall art. Larger juried pieces can be previewed at the Fiber Goddess Gallery, an artist's co-operative downtown.

Opposite: Judy loves to ride her Harley through the Garden of the Gods.

Not every mile is measured by the highway. At the Garden of the Gods, the spires are well over a mile high at the base. Here sunburnt rock formations, shaped by weather and time, stand like monuments against the purple backdrop of the Rockies. Color is everywhere.

Red rocks vest designed by Kara Spitler

Two vests, two very different looks using the same two yarns. In this slip-stitch version, framing the multicolor with a solid emphasizes its range of colors.

MATERIALS

Yarn Interlacements *Colorado MC* 1 (1, 2, 2) skeins Summer Fruit (each 8oz/228g, 700yds/640m, 52% cotton, 48% rayon), and *Utah CC* 2 (2, 3, 3) skeins Violet (each 8oz/228g, 515yds/471m, 68% rayon, 32% cotton).
Needles Sizes 1 and 3 (2.25 and 3.25mm) circular needle, 24"/60cm long, *or size to obtain gauge.* Size 1 (2.25mm) circular needle, 16"/40cm long.
Extras Five ¾"/20mm buttons. Stitch markers and holders.

NOTES

1 See *Techniques*, p. 228 for ssk, 3-needle bind-off, and cutting a steek. *2* Vest is knit circularly from lower edge to shoulders. *3* Steek stitches are used at center front and armholes. Steeks are worked in stockinette stitch, alternating colors of round, and are not included in stitch counts. *4* Change colors in the center of the front steek, knitting the old and new yarns together on this stitch.

STITCH USED

Slip st pat multiple of 8 sts
(***Note*** Slip sts purlwise with yarn in back.)
Rnds 1–2 With MC, sl 2, *k4, sl 4; rep from*, end k4, sl 2.
Rnds 3–4 With CC, knit. ***Rnds 5–10*** Rep rnds 1–4, end with rnd 2. ***Rnds 11–14*** With CC, knit. ***Rnds 15–16*** With MC, k2, *sl 4, k4; rep from*, end sl 4, k2. ***Rnds 17–18*** With CC, knit. ***Rnds 19–24*** Rep rnds 15–18, end with rnd 16. ***Rnds 25–28*** With CC, knit. Rep rnds 1–28 for pat.

VEST

With 24" smaller needle and CC, cast on 230 (254, 278, 302) sts, plus 5 sts for front steek. Place marker (pm) for beg of rnd and join, being careful not to twist sts. Work in k2, p2 rib to 5 steek sts, pm, k5 steek sts. Continue working in rnds in rib for 2", working steek in St st. K 1 rnd, inc 2 sts evenly spaced (not including steek)—232 (256, 280, 304) sts. Change to larger needle. Begin Slip st pat, alternating colors for steek, until piece measures 11½ (12, 13, 13½)" from beg.

Shape armholes and V-neck

Continuing pat, work 48 (54, 60, 66) sts (right front), place next 20 sts on hold (underarm), pm, with both MC and CC held together, cast on 5 sts (steek), pm (marker placed on each side of steek). Join, and continuing pattern, work 96 (108, 120, 132) sts for back, place next 20 sts on hold (underarm), cast on 5 sts (steek) and pm on each side as before. Join, and continuing pattern, work to end— 192 (216, 240, 264) sts. **Next (dec) rnd**

Continuing pattern and steeks, dec 1 st each side of armhole steeks every other rnd 11 times and each side of front steek every 4th rnd 18 (19, 21, 23) times as follows: after steek, k1, ssk, work to 3 sts before steek, k2tog, k1—112 (134, 154, 174) sts. Work even in pat until armhole measures 10½ (11, 11, 11½)", binding off steek sts only on last rnd with MC and CC held tog. Place all sts on hold.

FINISHING

Stitch, then cut through center of each steek. Block lightly. Join shoulders using 3-needle bind-off. Place remaining 36 (38, 42, 46) sts on hold for back neck. Tack steeks to WS. Place markers along left front for 5 buttonholes, with the first 1½" from the bottom, the last at beg of V-neck shaping, and others spaced evenly between.

Front band

With RS facing, 24" smaller needle and CC, pick up and k 83 (88, 94, 99) sts along right front to beg of V-neck shaping, 76 (80, 80, 83) sts along neck edge to shoulder, 36 (38, 42, 46) sts from back neck holder, 76 (80, 80, 83) sts along neck edge to beg of V-neck shaping, and 83 (88, 94, 99) sts along left front—354 (374, 390, 410) sts. Work in k2, p2 rib for ¾". **Next (buttonhole) row** Work in rib and at each buttonhole marker, bind off 4 sts. On next row, cast on 4 sts over each set of bound-off sts. Work even in rib until band measures 1½". Bind off. Sew on buttons.

Armhole bands

With RS facing, 16" smaller needle and CC, k20 sts from holder, pm, then pick up and k152 (160, 160, 168) sts evenly around, pm, join—172 (180, 180, 188) sts. Work in k2, p2 rib for 1½" and AT SAME TIME, work 2 sts tog outside of both underarm markers every other rnd. Bind off.

Slip Stitch Pattern

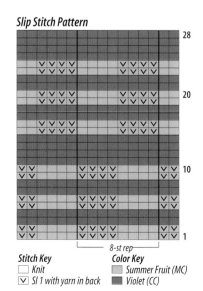

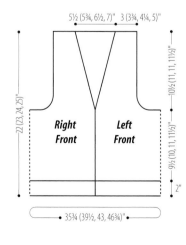

Stitch Key
☐ Knit
☑ Sl 1 with yarn in back

Color Key
▨ Summer Fruit (MC)
▩ Violet (CC)

Diamonds & firs designed by Kara Spitler

In the Fair Isle version, the motif is softened by the texture of the solid yarn. Its dark color reads well against a lighter multicolor.

MATERIALS

Yarn Interlacements *Colorado MC* 2 (2, 3, 3) skeins Summer Fruit (each 8oz/228g, 700yds/640m, 52% cotton, 48% rayon), *Utah CC* 1 (1, 2, 2) skeins Violet (each 8oz/228g, 515yds/471m, 68% rayon, 32% cotton).
Needles Sizes 1 and 3 (2.25 and 3.25mm) circular needle, 24"/60cm long, *or size to obtain gauge.* Size 1 (2.25mm) circular needle, 16"/40cm long.
Extras Four ⁵⁄₈"/1.5cm clasps. Stitch markers and holders.

NOTES

1 See *Techniques*, p. 228 for ssk, 3-needle bind off, and cutting a steek. *2* Vest is knit circularly from lower edge to shoulders. *3* Steek stitches are used at center front and armholes. Steeks are worked in Stockinette stitch, alternating colors of round, and are not included in stitch counts. *4* Change colors in the center of the front steek, knitting the old and new yarns together on this stitch.

VEST

With 24" smaller needle and CC, cast on 222 (254, 286, 318) sts, plus 5 sts for front steek. Place marker (pm) for beg of rnd and join, being careful not to twist sts. Work in k2, p2 rib to 5 steek sts, pm, k5 steek sts. Continue working in rnds in rib for 2", working steek in St st. K 1 rnd, inc 3 sts evenly spaced (not including steek)—225 (257, 289, 321) sts. Change to larger needle. Begin working chart, alternating colors for steek, until piece measures 10 (10½, 11½, 12)" from beg.
Shape armholes and V-neck
Continuing pat, work 46 (54, 62, 70) sts (right front), place next 20 sts on hold (underarm), pm, with both MC and CC held together, cast on 5 sts (steek), pm (marker placed on each side of steek). Join and continuing pat,

work 93 (109, 125, 141) sts for back, place next 20 sts on hold (underarm), cast on 5 sts (steek) and pm on each side as before. Join, and continuing pat, work to end—185 (217, 249, 281) sts. **Next (dec) rnd** Continuing pat and steeks, dec 1 st each side of armhole steeks every other rnd 6 times and each side of front steek every 3rd rnd 23 (26, 28, 30) times as follows: after steek, k1, ssk; work to 3 sts before steek, k2tog, k1—115 (141, 169, 197) sts. Work even in pat until armhole measures 10 (10½, 10½, 11)", binding off steek sts only on last rnd with MC and CC held tog. Place all sts on hold.

FINISHING

Stitch, then cut through center of each steek. Block lightly. Join shoulders using 3-needle bind-off. Place remaining 47 (53, 57, 61) sts on hold for back neck. Tack steeks to WS.
Front band
With RS facing, 24" smaller needle, and CC, pick up and k72 (76, 82, 87) sts along right front to beg of V-neck shaping, 73 (76, 76, 81) sts along neck edge to shoulder, 47 (53, 57, 61) sts from back neck holder, 73 (76, 76, 81) sts along neck edge to beg of V-neck shaping, and 73 (77, 83, 88) sts along left front—338 (358, 374, 398) sts. Work in k2, p2 rib for 1". Bind off. Sew clasps on bands with the first 2½" from the bottom, the last at beg of V-neck shaping, and other 2 spaced evenly between.
Armhole bands
With RS facing, 16" smaller needle, and CC, k20 sts from holder, pm, then pick up and k144 (152, 152, 160) sts evenly around, pm, join—164 (172, 172, 180) sts. Work in k2, p2 rib for 1" and AT SAME TIME, work 2 sts tog outside of both underarm markers every other rnd. Bind off.

Intermediate

Sizes
XS (S, M, L)
Shown in size S.
Directions are for smallest size with
larger sizes in parentheses.
If there is only 1 set of numbers,
it applies to all sizes.

Finished measurements
Underarm 34½ (39, 43½, 48)"
Length 20 (21, 22, 23)"

Gauge
28 sts and 36 rows to 4"/10cm
over chart pat using larger needle.

Diamonds & Firs Chart

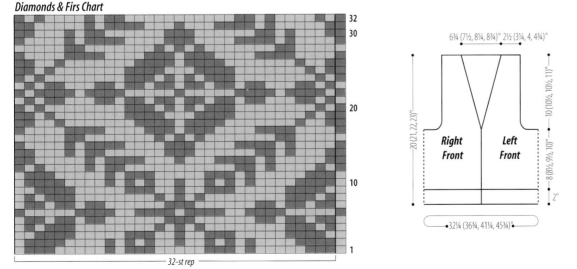

6¾ (7½, 8¼, 8¾)" 2½ (3¼, 4, 4¾)"

20 (21, 22, 23)"

10 (10½, 10½, 11)"

Right Front **Left Front**

8 (8½, 9½, 10)"

2"

32¼ (36¾, 41¼, 45¾)"

32-st rep

Color Key
▨ Summer Fruit (MC)
■ Violet (CC)

Although Cheryl Oberle lives in Denver, Colorado, we catch up with her at the San Geronimo Lodge, a bed-and-breakfast housed in an historic adobe on the outskirts of Taos, New Mexico, and the site of her popular Knitaway retreats.

Cheryl Oberle

CHERYL OBERLE DESIGNS CHERYL OBERLE
Denver, Colorado

It may surprise some people that Cheryl Oberle is a dyer, since she is best known as a teacher, author, and knitwear designer. Her jewel-toned designs incorporating wildflowers, geometric shapes inspired by architecture, and other repeating patterns found in nature are knit in a variety of shawls, vests, pullovers, and other pieces of wearable art.

We meet at the Taos Inn, an historic restaurant Cheryl frequents. Dressed completely in black, her dark hair cascading past the collar of a leather jacket, she looks more the biker chick than the author of *Folk Shawls*. In fact, she does tour the country with her husband on their Harley-Davidson motorcycle. But that's another story.

We ask how she got here. "I am the coloring queen," Cheryl says with a straight face. "I won every coloring contest I entered by the time I was 8." Most notable was a national cereal box coloring competition. "A truck from Pillsbury drove up in front of my house and unloaded a circus tent and every board game ever made," she recalls. This penchant for crayons lingers on. At one of her Knitaway camps, Cheryl encouraged students to color. "They could color any way they wanted," she explains. "It relaxed them so much they didn't think, they just colored."

The chemistry was right Cheryl assures us that she has no other artistic background. Her courses in college included chemistry and architecture. She became a knitting instructor in 1988, at about the same time she met Rachel Brown. "It was a chance meeting—I just walked into her store," Cheryl remembers. At that time, she was exploring her own sense of color, and was inspired by Kaffe Fassett's book, *Glorious Color*, in which he demonstrates how strands of yarn can be combined and changed every row or two to create a blended colorway effect. Rachel's hand-dyed palette of colored and textured fibers opened up new possibilities for Cheryl.

It was not long before she developed her first kit, Wild Flowers, which featured Fair Isle flowers knit with hand-painted yarn on a solid background, a technique she calls Faux Fair Isle. She collaborated with a handpainter in Colorado, and all was fine until Cheryl's first big order came for 20 kits. Her dyer lost interest in production work, and Cheryl had no one to paint the yarn.

Undaunted, Cheryl visited the dyer. "She showed me the dye process, and I realized I had spent three years in a college chemistry lab, and I could do this," Cheryl recalls. "I went right home and I just happened to have the perfect set-up. We have a triplex, and an unoccupied apart-

ment with a small kitchen became my dye kitchen." This was in 1990, and she has never looked back.

Dyeing, a ritual To this day, Cheryl works from a 70-year-old gas stove in that kitchen in the Highland historic district of Denver. Recently, she claimed the apartment on the other side, so now she and painter-husband Gary live sandwiched between rooms of hand-dyed yarn.

Cheryl likens her dye technique to the established ritual of a Japanese tea ceremony. In 1992, after attending her first ceremony, she approached the tea master for instruction. "Studying with her absolutely changed my approach to dyeing yarn," Cheryl explains. "Every movement is prescribed and it's an economy of motion. For me, dyeing is very much a ritual or a meditation."

The saturated colors of the Colorado landscape speak to Cheryl like no other environment. She finds the quality of light that enhances the natural beauty of the mountains "nourishing," and only dyes during hours of the day when the light is right. To keep things simple, she paints just one yarn, a 50% merino/50% mohair blend in 13 colorways, using a space-dye method that features

Clockwise from top: Detail of one of Cheryl's preferred architectural motifs; Dancing Colors yarn; Cheryl does not rewind her yarns but presents the colorways in the skein as they were dyed.

Cheryl would like the knitters to realize that the way yarn looks in the skein is not necessarily the way it's going to look in the sweater. "But, there is a good chance that a yarn you like in a hank will be one you love in a garment, as long as you remain open to its possibilities." She emphasizes swatching because she believes that "handpainted yarn talks to you more than other yarn does."

Future watch Cheryl defines herself as a knitting advocate whose designs integrate color and technique. Her book, *Folk Shawls,* showcases her love for shawls and knitting techniques suited to handpainted yarns. She is currently planning a second book that will draw from her architectural background. "Not many of us approach knitting as architectural construction, but garments are essentially designed to fit the body, which is three-dimensional," Cheryl explains. "A garment must work with the body," she adds, which is one of the reasons she loves shawls.

Top: Many of Cheryl Oberle's designs combine hand- painted yarns with readily available commercially dyed solids. In her small studio, she dyes skeins individually and handpicks yarns for the kits.

Left: Garments against a mission wall.

short color stretches, focusing upon clarity of color. Almost all of her yarn is kitted with a secondary solid color that sets off the multicolored yarns.

Her most popular colorways include Raku, earthtones inspired by a 600-year-old Japanese tea bowl, Amethyst (Cheryl is wearing this one in her photo on page 53) and Azurine, two deep jewel-tone colorways reminiscent of the Rockies.

The complete workshop Teaching is the biggest part of Cheryl's involvement with handpainted yarns. She enjoys demonstrating new techniques that her students may explore more fully in one of her all-inclusive kits. "I'm totally knitter-friendly," Cheryl says.

Cheryl welcomes the mix of handpaints with commercial yarns. These solids showcase her handpaints in a variety of techniques such as framing and Faux Fair Isle. Cheryl believes that knitters who come to her "are looking for jewel-tone colors presented as an integrated kit for a specific garment." As such, each kit is a complete workshop, with detailed instructions that can run up to 30 pages long!

She believes that handpainted yarn is growing in popularity because of the element of surprise. "Handpainted yarn is more challenging." Cheryl smiles. "But I've never met a knitter who didn't step right up to the challenge."

This mission door, fashioned from native wood with willow insets, recalls a rich history we can only imagine. It stands sentry, a passage into the past, a vestige of faith and beauty.

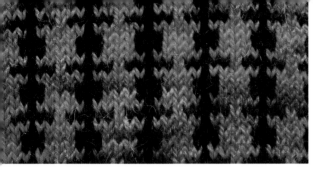

Spools waistcoat designed by Cheryl Oberle

Cheryl makes the most of the hand-dyed yarn by combining it with a commercially dyed solid.

Intermediate

Sizes

S (M, L)

Shown in size M.

Directions are for smallest size with

larger sizes in parentheses.

If there is only 1 set of numbers,

it applies to all sizes.

Finished measurements

Underarm (buttoned) 41 (44½, 49)"

Length 20 (21½, 23)"

Gauge

24 (22, 20) sts and 28 (26, 24)

rows to 4"/10cm over Chart B using

size 3 (4, 5) needles.

MATERIALS

Yarn Cheryl Oberle *Dancing Colors Hand-dyed Yarn* **MC** 1 skein Ruby (8oz/228g, 450yds/412m, 50% mohair, 50% merino); Brown Sheep Company *Naturespun Sport* **CC** 5 skeins #601 Pepper (each 1¾oz/50g, 184yds/168m, 100% wool).

Needles Size 3 (4, 5)/ 3.25 (3.5, 3.75)mm circular needle, 24"/60cm long, *or size to obtain gauge.* Size 2 (3, 4)/ 2.75 (3.25, 3.5)mm circular needle, 24"/60cm long. Size 1 (2, 3)/ 2.25 (2.75, 3.25)mm circular needle, 16"/40cm and 24"/60cm long.

Extras Four ⅝"/15mm buttons. Stitch markers and scrap yarn for holders.

NOTES

1 See *Techniques*, p. 228 for invisible cast-on, ssk, and 3-needle bind-off. *2* Vest is knit circularly from lower edge to shoulders. *3* Steek stitches are used at center front and armholes. Steeks are worked in stockinette stitch, alternating colors of round, and are not included in stitch counts. *4* Change colors in the center of the front steek, knitting the old and new yarns together on this stitch.

WAISTCOAT

Bottom facing

With size 1 (2, 3) 24" needle and CC, invisibly cast on 241 sts. Beg with a k row, work 12 rows of St st. Change to size 2 (3, 4) needle. **Turning ridge** (RS) Purl. Cast on 5 sts at end of row for front steek. Place marker (pm) for beg of rnd and join. K 2 rnds. **Begin Chart A: Rnd 1** Work rnd 1 of Chart A to last 5 steek sts, pm, work steek sts. Complete chart, then with CC, k 2 rnds. Change to size 3 (4, 5) needle and work Rnds 1–5 of Chart B 13 times, alternating colors on steek sts and ending with rnd 4. Piece measures approx 10 (11, 11½)" from turning ridge.

Shape armholes and V-neck

Continuing pat, work 46 sts (right front), place next 29 sts on hold (underarm), pm, with both MC and CC held tog, cast on 5 sts (steek), pm (marker placed on each side of steek). Join and continuing pat, work 91 sts for back, place next 29 sts on hold (underarm), cast on 5 sts (steek) as before and pm on each side. Join and continuing pat, work to end (left front)—185 sts. **Next (dec) rnd** Continuing pat and steeks, dec 1 st each side of armhole steeks every other rnd 6 times and each side of front steek every 4th rnd 16 times as follows: after steek, k1, ssk, work to 3 sts before steek, k2tog, k1—127 sts. Work even in pat until armhole measures approx 10 (10½, 11½)", end with chart rnd 3. Place all sts on hold.

FINISHING

Stitch, then cut through center of each steek (*see illustration*). Join shoulders using 3-needle bind-off. Place remaining 31 sts on hold for back neck. Fold bottom facing to WS at turning ridge and sew live sts to inside of waistcoat. Remove waste yarn.

Front band

With RS facing, size 2 (3, 4) 24" needle and CC, pick up and k46 sts along right front to beg of V-neck shaping, 56 sts along neck edge to shoulder, 31 sts from back neck holder, 56 stitches along neck edge to beg of V-neck shaping, and 46 sts along left front—235 sts. P 1 row, k 1 row. **Begin Chart A** (WS) Reading chart from left to right, work row 1. **Next (buttonhole) row** Working chart row 2, work buttonholes as follows: k3, k2tog, [yo] twice, *k11, k2tog, [yo] twice; rep from* 2 times more, k to end in chart pat. Complete last 2 chart rows, dropping extra yo for each buttonhole on Row 3. With CC, p1 row, k 1 row. **Turning ridge** Knit. **Make facing** Beg with a k row, work 3 rows of St st. **Next (buttonhole) row** (WS) P191, [yo] twice, p2tog, *p11, [yo] twice, p2tog; rep from* 2 times more, p to end. Beg with a k row, work 8 rows of St st, dropping extra yo for each buttonhole on next row. Place sts on scrap yarn to hold. Fold facing to WS at turning ridge and sew live sts to inside of waistcoat, covering cut edge of steek and matching buttonholes. Sew on buttons.

Armhole bands

With RS facing, size 1 (2, 3) 16" needle and CC, k29 sts from holder, then pick up and k86 sts evenly around, pm for beg of rnd and join—115 sts. K 1 rnd. Work Chart A, then with CC, k 2 rnds. **Turning ridge** Purl. **Make facing** K 12 rnds. Place sts on scrap yarn to hold. Fold facing to WS at turning ridge and sew live sts to inside of waistcoat, covering cut edge of steek. Block.

Spools waistcoat

DESIGNER'S TIP

An accurate gauge swatch for stranded circular knitting can be created by knitting a flat swatch. The technique requires double-pointed or circular needles. (**Note** Always knit the first and last stitches of the swatch with both colors to anchor the yarns and produce an even tension.) Cast on 32 sts and work a row of the two-color pattern. At the end of each row, break off the yarn leaving 3-inch tails. Do not turn! Slide all the stitches to the other end of the needle, rejoin the yarns and knit the next row. Repeat this process. Because you are knitting every row you are simulating the gauge that you will have when you are knitting every row on your circular project. Tie the ends of the yarn together on the sides to keep the proper tension. Steam your swatch. Measure the gauge in between, but not including, the two-color edge stitches.

Stitch-and-cut steek

With contrasting yarn, baste down the center stitch of the front and armhole steeks. Make two parallel rows of machine stitching on each side of the basting yarn, stitching down center of stitches and not between. Cut down center stitch through basting yarn.

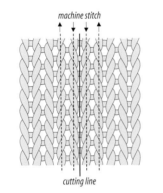

machine stitch

cutting line

Chart A

4

1

12-st rep

End Body

End Front bands & Armhole bands

Chart B

5

1

6-st rep

Color Key
- Ruby (MC)
- Pepper (CC)

Chart A Note

Chart A is worked circularly in stockinette stitch for body and armholes, and back and forth for front band. When working for Front band, row 1 begins with a wrong-side row

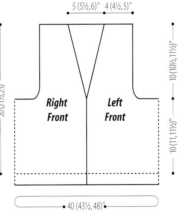

5 (5½, 6)"   4 (4½, 5)"

20 (21½, 23)"

10 (10½, 11½)"

Right Front   *Left Front*

10 (11, 11½)"

40 (43½, 48)"

"*Spools* is sized by changing the stitch gauge rather than by the more conventional method of changing the total number of stitches. Although it seems a bit topsy-turvy, the concept of multi-gauge sizing is basically the same as the regular method. Where a conventional pattern has one gauge and three different sets of instructions, a multi-gauge pattern has one set of instructions worked with three different gauges. In both cases the knitter's gauge determines the finished measurements of the garment. After trying this method for the first time, fellow knitters report that they finally understand the relationship between gauge and size; if the stitch gauge is wrong, the garment won't be just a bit off, it will be the wrong size. With this in mind, taking time to do an accurate gauge swatch has a more immediate meaning. Your swatch is your best friend since it will give you an accurate stitch gauge and a representative sample of the knitted fabric."

Cheryl Oberle

Our journey from Colorado takes us through the grassy plains of Wyoming, dotted with cow ponies and cattle herds, then west into the mountains of Montana. With ears popping from the altitude, we speed north, hugging our lane of the interstate, a lonely road cut from the mountainside. We imagine the pioneers' trek through this rugged country, fragrant with Ponderosa pine. Above us, mountain ranges rise before ghostly, snow-covered peaks. Below, trains chug through the picturesque river valleys. As we descend into the Bitterroot Valley and the town of Stevensville, we can see that Mountain Colors is aptly named.

Stevensville, Montana

Diana McKay and Leslie Taylor

MOUNTAIN COLORS DIANA MCKAY & LESLIE TAYLOR

Stevensville, Montana

Dyeing for space Diana McKay and Leslie Taylor met in California as knitters and spinners with a common interest in expanding their craft. They joined the Foothills Fiber Guild, where they took dyeing, weaving, and knitting classes together. Job changes forced both of them to leave the area, but they reunited a year later in Montana. With small children and a need for flexible work schedules, they decided to become self-employed.

Their part-time "jobs" began when they gave a dye workshop at a local fiber festival and discovered a demand for their yarns. Mountain Colors began in 1992 with dye experiments in Leslie's kitchen. As they attempted to reproduce color combinations, they discovered Huckleberry, one of their first colorways—on Leslie's kitchen floor. They made note of the mixture before mopping it up. "We started with nothing," Diana says. "We literally went to our own yarn stashes and each of us pulled out a pound of mohair." As an alternative to traveling to trade shows, they started a mail-order business.

Clockwise from top: Bitterroot Rainbow; Diana and Leslie prefer the deep, saturated colors of the Rockies; basic yarns combine nicely with novelty yarns.

By the end of 1994, they had reps and wholesale accounts, but still no permanent home for Mountain Colors. In three years, they had dyed themselves out of Leslie's house and into Diana's, from the kitchen to the laundry room, then into the garage, where they were still short on space. Leslie found the room they needed in the old Creamery Building, which had just been renovated into studio spaces. In January 1995, they set up their dye kitchen in a room that had once been the milk cooler. Suddenly, their part-time jobs became a full-time business.

Collaborating with nature The deep, saturated colors of the surrounding Rockies are the inspiration for Mountain Colors. Diana and Leslie do not consciously try to replicate colors in nature, but prefer to make their own combinations. "Say we want to do a great new purple," Diana begins. "We put our heads together and say, 'What if we put this with this?' And we keep putting colors together until it pleases us. Normally at that point we have a color we really like, and say, 'Oh, that reminds me so much of—'…and the name of a color pops up." These experimental musings resulted in popular colorways such as Redtail Hawk, Pine Needle, and Wild Mushroom. "A really good one is Winter Sky," Diana tells us, as she describes a combination of turquoise, blue-purple, and clear blue.

Although both women have taken many fiber classes, neither has formal artistic education. "We have college degrees, but not in art," Leslie notes. Still, color has satisfied them since childhood. Leslie adds, "I always loved my crayons—my 64 Crayolas." She cannot recall a time when she set off for school without her colored pencils and markers. Diana remembers her mother giving her a burlap bag of yarn remnants and a blunt needle for play. She went on to take many art classes, but the fun she had pulling different-colored yarns through the burlap stays in her memory.

Mix and match yarns Diana and Leslie produce large batches of mixed yarns in the same colorway. Because they dye primarily animal fiber (wool, mohair, cashmere, and blends), apply colors in the same predeter-

colorways with names such as Ruby River, Mountain Twilight, and Glacier Teal? Old standbys, such as Moose Creek and Bitterroot Rainbow, are still popular. "Bitterroot Rainbow never died, and it was our first color," Diana notes. But she adds that many of their brighter colorways have been discontinued.

Marketing the mountains According to Diana, the appeal of the Great Northwest helps sell their yarns. "There are an awful lot of people who haven't been to the Northwest but would like to come," she explains, "and I think we somehow give them a piece of that wild, outdoor feel." When knitters buy yarns from Mountain Colors they are looking for colorways that transport them, Diana believes. Diana and Leslie try to convey this sense of the mountains through their whimsical advertisements showing a horse's mane of yarn, and mohair draped from a mountain goat.

A brief stint at retail during their first year led Diana and Leslie to the conclusion that if they wanted to spend time with their children, the wholesale market was best. Now their yarns reach hundreds of stores.

Above: Detail of the textured yarn Moguls.

Center: Most of the colorways in Mountain Colors' palette are derived directly from nature. Here, a colorway named Pine Needles hangs from a pine along a hiking path in the foothills of the Rockies.

Below: Diana and Leslie try to ensure that Mountain Colors' yarn offers an outdoor feel, even if a knitter has never ventured into the Great Northwest.

mined order, and heat-set them together, colorways are very close not only from fiber to fiber, but from batch to batch. "We do the same type of dyeing all the time, for everything," Diana says, noting that both she and Leslie appreciate deep, rich colors that are also vivid and bright.

Except for cashmere, their 32 colorways are available in 14 yarns (their solid-color line varies). "All of our colors are derived from the same six dyes," Diana explains. "So basically, every color we put on yarn is blended." Solid colors are more difficult to achieve, because dyes are rarely used straight from the bottle. "We used to say we were the only people who could put brown and gold together and get purple."

Mountain Colors' best-selling yarn is a basic worsted wool that combines nicely with their novelty yarns for plainer sections such as ribbing and buttonhole bands. Several yarns, including Merino Ribbon and Wooly Feathers, are custom-milled for them. Montana 3-ply is spun from locally grown Targhee sheepswool.

Each year, the colorways with the best appeal vary by region and by what else they are offering. Who can resist

Diana and Leslie also promote kits. "In the last six years we have worked really hard on our pattern design. We have some nice, different styles and we always try to gear them for the beginning to intermediate knitter," Diana says. Kits are designed for knitters who seek a relaxing project and are willing to let the color do the work.

Future watch Finding more studio space is again a priority for Leslie. "When we first moved into our present studio, we thought we had a ton of space," she says. "Now we can see it isn't so huge." Diana's plans to fully explore solids require additional work room. She hopes to train dyers so that yarn can be produced while she and Leslie attend trade shows.

Diana would like to see companies collaborate in the way designers do: they combine different kinds of yarn from several companies in a single project. For example, Mountain Colors' yarns are known for short repeats, "so why not combine ours with a yarn that has a longer repeat?"

As knitters become more sophisticated, they seek new ways to use handpainted yarns, including stranding, using two colorways together, or marrying a colorway to a solid. Leslie is encouraged by the increasing demands of adventurous knitters for creative designs, and feels that hand-dye companies are looking to designers to meet these needs.

"We've had this nice growth pattern that hasn't killed us," Diana says. "We'd like to continue to grow at this rate and have more people know about Mountain Colors." To spread the word, she and Leslie feel they must continue to pull people into the yarn world, through knitting, weaving, guilds, and the media. They support their local guild and feel lucky to have a progressive knitting store with an inspired teacher in their town.

If you're wondering whether you can choose to do something, make a business of it, and be successful at it, Diana assures us, "You can—if you try hard enough and go slow."

Clockwise from right: Wooly Feathers shown in Columbine; Brushed mohair in Bitterroot Rainbow; Ponderosa pine.

Here in the foothills, weather moves rapidly across a landscape vast and beautiful. We feel a sense of immediacy. The air is clear and the sky big; even large distances seem conquerable. Colors slide imperceptibly into each other, a backdrop to our travels.

Moguls designed by Sally Melville

Garter and occasional long stitches keep the featured yarn on the surface of this mostly-stockinette vest.

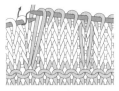

Check stitch pattern

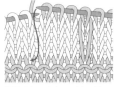

K into st 4 rows below next st on LH needle (a MC st).

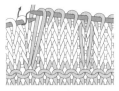

Draw up st to height of current row, then k next st on LH needle (as shown); pass long st over st just knit.

Easy+

Sizes

S (M, L)

Shown in size S.

Directions are for smallest size with larger sizes in parentheses.

If there is only 1 set of numbers, it applies to all sizes.

Finished measurements

Underarm (buttoned) 43 (49, 54½)"

Length 28¼"

Gauge

11 sts and 22 rows to 4"/10cm over Check st pat using size 10½ (6.5mm) needles.

MATERIALS

Yarn Mountain Colors *Moguls MC* 4 (5, 5) skeins Copper King Plum (each 4oz/114g, 65yds/59m, 98% wool, 2% nylon) and *4/8's Wool CC* 4 (5, 5) skeins Mountain Twilight (each 4oz/114g, 250yds/229m, 100% wool).

Needles

One pair size 10½ (6.5mm) needles, *or size to obtain gauge.*

Extras Five 1"/2.5cm buttons. Stitch markers and holders.

NOTES

1 See *Techniques*, p. 228 for ssk. *2* Use CC with 2 strands held together as 1.

STITCH USED

Check st pat multiple of 4 sts plus 3

Rows 1 and 3 (RS) With 2 strands of CC, knit. *Rows 2 and 4* With 2 strands of CC, purl. *Row 5* With MC, *k3, k into st 4 rows below next st on LH needle (a MC st), drawing up st to height of current row, k next st on LH needle; pass long st over st just knit; rep from* across, end k3. *Row 6* With MC, knit. Rep rows 1–6 for pat.

BACK

With MC, cast on 67 (75, 83) sts. K 2 rows. Change to 2 strands of CC, and work rows 1–6 of Check st pat 3 times, then work rows 1–2 once.

Shape sides

Next (dec) row (RS) K1, ssk, k to last 3 sts, k2tog, k1. Continue in pat keeping long MC sts aligned, and rep dec row every 24th row 3 times more—59 (67, 75) sts. Work even in pat until piece measures 18½" from beg, end with pat row 5.

Shape armhole

Next row (WS) Bind off 8 (12, 16) sts, work to end—51 (55, 59) sts. *Next row* (RS) With MC, bind off 8 (12, 16) sts, change to 2 strands of CC and beg with row 1, continue in pat keeping long MC sts aligned—43 sts. Work even until armhole measures 8¾", end with pat row 6.

Shape shoulders

Bind off 4 sts at beg of next 6 rows. Bind off remaining 19 sts for back neck in MC.

RIGHT FRONT

With MC, cast on 35 (39, 43) sts. Work as for back, shaping side only at end of dec rows—31 (35, 39) sts. Continue as for back, shaping armhole at beg of WS row—23 sts. Work even in pat until armhole measures 6½", end with pat row 6.

Shape neck

Next row (RS) With MC, bind off 11 sts, change to 2 strands of CC and beg with row 1, continue in pat—12 sts. Work even in pat until armhole measures same as back to shoulder shaping, end with pat row 1.

Shape shoulders

Bind off 4 sts at beg of next 3 WS rows.

LEFT FRONT

With MC, cast on 35 (39, 43) sts. Work as for Back, shaping side only at beg of dec rows—31 (35,39) sts. Continue as for back, shaping armhole at beg of RS row—23 sts. Work even in pat until armhole measures 6½", end with pat row 5.

Shape neck

Next row (WS) Bind off 11sts, k across—12 sts. Work even in pat until armhole measures same as back to shoulder shaping, end with pat row 6.

Shape shoulders

Bind off 4 sts at beg of next 3 RS rows.

FINISHING

Sew shoulder seams, matching pat.

Neck edging

Row 1 With MC and RS facing, along vertical edge of right front neck, pick up and k1 st for every MC ridge and 2 sts for every 4 rows in CC—approx 10 sts. *Row 2* With MC, bind off all sts in knit. Tack down corners of edgings where necessary. Rep along vertical edge of left front neck.

Armhole edging

Work as for neck edging along vertical edges of each armhole—approx 50 sts. Sew side seams matching pat.

Left front edging

Work as for neck edging along left front—approx 72 sts.

Right front edging

Working from the top down, mark 1st, 5th, 9th, 13th, and 17th CC square along right front edge. Work as for left front edging, and AT SAME TIME, on row 1, cast on 2 sts for buttonhole at each marker instead of picking up 2 sts. Sew on buttons.

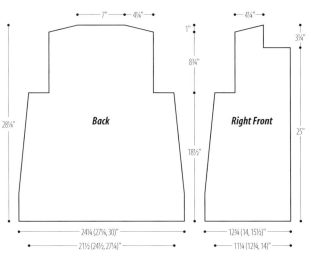

Painted plaid designed by Sally Melville

Doubling a finer yarn can create more color options. Here a strand of the light and the dark create a middle tone.

MATERIALS

Yarn Mountain Colors *Wool Crepe,* **A** 2 skeins Moose Creek, **B** 1 skein Wild Mushroom (each 12oz/343g, 1450yds/1326m, 100% merino wool).
Needles One pair each sizes 6 and 8 (4 and 5mm) needles, *or size to obtain gauge.*
Extras Stitch holders.

NOTES

1 See *Techniques,* p. 228 for intarsia. *2* Work each color section with bobbin or small ball of yarn. *3* Work with 2 strands held together as 1 throughout. *4* Color C is 1 strand A and B held together. *5* To work bands for largest size in A (as shown), an additional skein of A is needed.

BACK

With smaller needles and A (A, C), cast on 99 (109, 119) sts. Work 3" in k1, p1 rib, end with a RS row. *Next row* (WS) Change to larger needles and purl, inc 1 st in center—100 (110, 120) sts. *Begin Gingham pat: Row 1* (RS) K10 (5, 0) A, *k10 C, k10 A; rep from* across, end k10 (5, 0) C. *Row 2* (WS) K10 (5, 0) C, *k10 A, k10 C; rep from* across, end last rep k10 (5, 0) A. *Rows 3–18* Rep rows 1–2 eight times. *Row 19* K10 (5, 0) C, *k10 B, k10 C; rep from* across, end last rep k10 (5, 0) B. *Row 20* K10 (5, 0) B, *k10 C, k10 B; rep from* across, end last rep k10 (5, 0) C. *Rows 21–36* Rep rows 19–20 eight times. Rep rows 1–36 five times more. Work rows 1–12 once. Piece measures approx 28¼".

Shape neck

Continuing in pat, work 35 (40, 45) sts, place center 30 sts on hold, join 2nd ball of yarn and work to end. Working both sides at the same time, dec 1 st at each neck edge every other row twice—33 (38, 43) sts each side. Work even, end with pat row 18. Bind off.

FRONT

(*Note: For M (L) only* Reverse colors A and C in pat rows 1–18 and colors C and B in rows 19–36.)
Work ribbing and inc 1 st as for back. Work rows 19–36 of Gingham pat, then rep rows 1–36 five times. Work rows 1–8 once. Piece measures approx 26" from beg.

Shape neck

Next row (RS) Work 42 (47, 52) sts, place center 16 sts on hold, join 2nd ball of yarn and work to end. Working both sides at the same time, bind off 2 sts at each neck edge once, then dec 1 st each neck edge every other row 7 times—33 (38, 43) sts each side. Work even until piece measures same as back, end with pat row 36. Bind off.

LEFT SLEEVE

With smaller needles and A (A, C) cast on 39 sts. Work ribbing and inc 1 st as for back—40 sts. (*Note* To make color pattern match at armhole, shorten or lengthen sleeves at beg of Gingham pat as follows: to shorten, begin pat within rows 1–18 as desired; to lengthen, begin pat within rows 19–36 as desired.) *Begin Gingham pat and Shaping* Inc 1 st each side (beg on 5th row and working incs into pat) [alternating every 4th row once, then every 6th row once] 15 times—100 sts. AT SAME TIME, work pat as follows: *Row 1* *K10 C, k10 A, rep from*. *Row 2* *K10 A, k10 C, rep from*. *Rows 3–18* Rep rows 1–2 eight times. *Row 19* *K10 B, k10 C; rep from* across. *Row 20* *K10 C, k10 B; rep from* across. *Rows 21–36* Rep rows 19–20 eight times. Rep rows 1–36 three times more. Work rows 1–18 once. Piece measures approx 21" from beg.

RIGHT SLEEVE

Work as for left sleeve, reversing colors A and B in pat for M (L), and reversing colors A and C in rows 1–18 and colors C and B in rows 19–36 in pat for XL.

FINISHING

Sew right shoulder.

Neckband

With RS facing, smaller needles and A (A, C) pick up and k24 sts along left front neck edge, 16 sts from front neck holder, 24 sts along right front neck edge, 5 sts along right back neck edge, 30 sts from back neck holder, 5 sts from left back neck edge—104 sts. Work 1" in k1, p1 rib. Bind off all sts. Sew left shoulder. Place markers 5 squares (10") down from shoulders on front and back. Sew top of sleeves between markers, easing fullness to match squares. Sew side and sleeve seams matching squares.

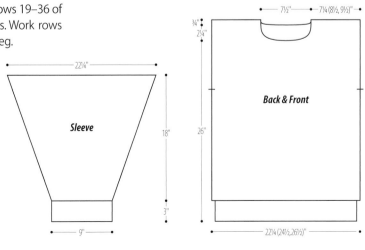

Sleeve
22¼"
18"
9"
3"

¾"
2¼"
7½" — 7¼ (8½, 9½)"
Back & Front
26"
10"
16"
3"
22¼ (24½, 26½)"

Sally's got something up her sleeve: Why do the front and both sleeves start in different places in the pattern? This is necessary to make the pattern continuous at the shoulders and where the sleeves join the body!

Intermediate

Sizes
M (L, XL)
Shown in size M.
Directions are for smallest size with larger sizes in parentheses. If there is only 1 set of numbers, it applies to all sizes.

Finished measurements
Underarm 44½ (49, 53)"
Length 29"

Gauge
18 sts and 36 rows to 4"/10cm over Garter st (knit every row) using larger needles with 2 strands of yarn held together.

Pacific

THE DROP SPINDLE D'ELIN LOHR

Santa Maria, California

It is overcast as we leave San Diego. We drive north on scenic Route 101 to Santa Maria, California, in search of D'Elin Lohr and The Drop Spindle. Rugged hills appear on our right and between the dunes to our left, glimpses of the ocean can be seen. Hours later, we pull up before a Santa Fe-style house in a pleasant subdivision. We glance at the gray sky, hoping it doesn't rain.

D'Elin Lohr

THE DROP SPINDLE D'ELIN LOHR
Santa Maria, California

If there were such a thing as a true "California girl," D'Elin Lohr might have been her. Blonde and blue-eyed, she grew up in Santa Maria at a time when Day-Glo colors, embroidered jeans, and bright beaded necklaces were the height of teen fashion. As a teenager, she became enthralled by beadwork and its endless possibilities for colorful design. Her penchant for unusual combinations of intense colors stayed with D'Elin through the ten years she managed a retail clothing store. "Color has always been important to me, but for a long time, I didn't realize how important," she observes.

D'Elin's enchantment with fiber began as a weaver. She searched for color combinations she could find only by creating them herself as she manipulated the warp and weft of woven fabrics. She describes herself as still evolving as a colorist, always searching for color. "Even when I go to a movie, the first thing I want to talk about afterwards is the clothing and the color and the backgrounds," she admits. Now, with little time for weaving, D'Elin has returned to the more portable world of beads as a medium for experimentation and expression.

Clockwise from above: Mohair boucle from The Drop Spindle glows with saturated color; D'Elin Lohr finds inspiration by the ocean; recently, she has returned to the beadwork of her youth as a means of portable color exploration.

Hand-dyeing as a business began in the 1970s when Canadian Ted Carson introduced D'Elin and fellow dyer Pat Walls to creative dyeing with commercial powders, and their approach to color changed forever. "He had this very free-form way of dyeing with synthetic dyes," D'Elin explains. "Always before that, everything had to be measured perfectly, and you were doing solid colors. Well, he did this thing where you just kind of slapdashed it all together. That really appealed to me." After the birth of her first child, D'Elin bought Pat's mail-order hand-dye business with the mistaken idea that the part-time job would afford her time for weaving. "I tracked myself on my slowest week," D'Elin recalls with a smile. "It was 33 hours."

Every color under the sun The California climate is crucial to the way D'Elin dyes yarn, for she works primarily in her outdoor studio. "I am a weather watcher," D'Elin confirms. "Rain and cold are my enemies." Her optimum dye days are sunny with no wind, no rain, and plenty of warmth. Her work can be especially difficult during the rainy season, when she must bring yarns inside to dry on racks around a woodstove.

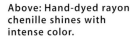

Almost as amazing as D'Elin's well-developed eye is her ability to remember color series. "Everyone I've talked to, they measure, they have formulas." She taps her temple. "Everything's in my head." She measures nothing exactly, but relies upon the way colors look to her practiced eye. Although each skein varies slightly, dye vat lots can range from six to as much as 18 pounds.

Price point is important to D'Elin, whose wholesale company also sells to other wholesalers. "I want my yarns to be affordable," she confides. "I want them out there being used by other people." Economy is just a by-product, however, for Drop Spindle yarns glow with color intensity usually unavailable in yarns such as hand-dyed cotton.

D'Elin works with all kinds of yarn, but favors the novelties. Although her best-selling yarns change with fashion and the season, her rayon chenilles, mohair loop, and rayon boucles are always popular. The jewel tones have the greatest appeal. "I have a series called Winter Nights—deep, rich, jewel-tone colors—that is probably my hottest seller," she says. Winter Nights is not one colorway, but an entire group that she calls a

Above: Hand-dyed rayon chenille shines with intense color.

Left: D'Elin spreads large hanks of brushed mohair to dry in the outdoor studio where she practices her specialized dye-vat technology.

Below: During the rainy season and other times when the weather doesn't cooperate, D'Elin resorts to drying hanks around the woodstove.

D'Elin dyes both animal and plant fibers. On hot days when the sun and heat can produce intense colors, she loves to dye cottons. "If I didn't live where it was sunny most of the time, I couldn't dye, and I definitely couldn't dry anything," she explains. She also dyes with an eye toward the time of day. Mornings produce intense colors, medium colors are best done in the middle of the day, and she saves light colors for afternoons. Her unique set-up includes rescued restaurant dishwashing equipment that has been reconfigured for her outdoor dye process.

Dye-vat technology "Everything I do is variegated or multicolored," D'Elin tells us, adding that she favors self-exhausting dyes applied one at a time to her wools and mohairs. She calls this her "dye-vat technique," which is basically a well-controlled dip-dye method that allows her to achieve clear colors. Cottons and rayons do not get the dye-vat treatment but are space-dyed in the sun. What is most amazing about D'Elin's dye process is her ability to match cottons and rayons to her wools and mohairs. "That's a real challenge," she says.

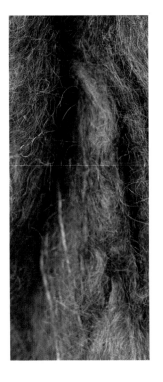

color series. "Anything that comes out dark, intense, and jewel-toned, it's in there," she jokes. D'Elin currently has eight color series, some of which date back from the early days with Pat Walls. But even these she does her own way, putting in additional colors. "I always think more is more, not less is more," D'Elin says.

Because D'Elin comes to hand-dyed fiber from the fashion world, she frequently walks the malls to keep an eye on the latest styles. According to her, the trends over past few years have been "scary." She thinks the younger generation is afraid of color because of the popularity of black, beige, and shades "deadened with brown." In response, D'Elin produces an entire line of soft neutrals, but continues to do her best to fight "dead color."

Future watch The Drop Spindle is not easily accessible, and D'Elin plans to keep it that way. "I don't even have reps," she confesses. Because she sells wholesale only and never under her own name, D'Elin does not produce color cards or tag her yarns; she sells them to retail stores and designers as is. She never reskeins her yarns because she has neither the time nor the resources, and rewinding adds cost. "My yarns aren't for everyone," D'Elin advises. "Because I don't offer pattern support or reskein, they are for the more adventuresome, creative knitter."

With four kids in school, D'Elin finds herself maintaining—neither downsizing nor expanding—the size of her business. She dyes semi-solid colors on a large scale, as well as quantities of custom yarn for kits and clothing, and enjoys the challenge of dyeing yarn to match fabric. Because technology has increased to the point where commercial yarn companies can fake a hand-dyed look, "what we can do is change quickly," she says with a grin.

As D'Elin predicts, the weather does not fail us. The sun dances across the waves as we drive to her favorite ocean park to photograph her yarns. As we walk past beautiful eroded cliffs that drop to the shell-strewn beach, D'Elin shares her creative aspirations. "My goal is to dye better, to grow as an artist."

Clockwise from above: Subtle shading in brushed mohair; The Drop Spindle is known for bright colorways; the Pacific provides a natural backdrop for D'Elin's jewel-toned fibers.

THE DROP SPINDLE D'ELIN LOHR
Surplice blouse designed by Kathleen Power Johnson

To exploit the color changes in space-dyed yarn, try entrelac. Here, it is used for just half of the blouse's front, making it a fine way to get started with the technique.

Experienced

Sizes
S (M, L)
Shown in size S.
Directions are for smallest size with larger sizes in parentheses.
If there is only 1 set of numbers, it applies to all sizes.

Finished measurements
Underarm 36 (40½, 45)"
Length 20 (21, 23½)"

Gauge
22 sts and 34 rows to 4"/10cm over St st using larger needles.

MATERIALS
Yarn Drop Spindle *Rayon Bouclé* 700 (750, 825) yds Ocean Breeze (1000yds/914m per 16oz/457g, 100% rayon).
Needles One pair size 4 (3.5mm) needles, *or size to obtain gauge.* Size 2 (2.75mm) double-pointed needles (dpn) and circular needle, 24"/60cm long.
Extras 1 hook and eye, small amount of matching perle cotton yarn for assembly, stitch marker and holders.

NOTES
1 See *Techniques*, p. 228 for ssk, ssp, M1, and 3-needle bind-off, and *Getting Started* on p. 79 for entrelac. *2* Entrelac charts are worked in tiers of rectangles and triangles. Follow chart for placement of each rectangle or triangle. For ease in working, place ruler under each tier (solid line for right-side tiers and dotted line for wrong-side tiers). *3* When instructed to work M1, work M1-knit on right-side rows and M1-purl on wrong-side rows.

BACK
With larger needle, cast on 100 (112, 124) sts. Work in St st until piece measures 11 (11, 13½)" from beg, end with a WS row.
Shape sleeves
Cast on 2 sts at beg of next 4 rows, then 1 st at beg of next 6 rows—114 (126, 138) sts. Work even until piece measures 19 (20, 22™)" from beg, end with a WS row.
Next row (RS) Bind off 73 (82, 94) sts for right shoulder and back neck, put remaining 41 (44, 44) sts on hold for left shoulder.

LEFT FRONT
Work as for back until piece measures 2½", end with a RS row.
Shape front edge
(WS) Dec 1 st at beg of every WS row 52 (61, 72) times, then bind off every 4th row 3 sts 0 (2, 3) times, then 2 sts 7 (4, 3) times. AT SAME TIME, when piece measures 11 (11, 13½)" from beg, cast on 2 sts at beg of every RS row twice, then 1 st at beg of every RS row 3 times for sleeve. Work until all decs complete and piece measures same as back. Place remaining 41 (44, 44) sts on hold for left shoulder.

RIGHT FRONT
(**Note** Turn work after every tier has been completed unless otherwise indicated.)
With larger needle, cast on 72 (81, 90) sts.
Tier 1 (RS) [Work BT] 8 (9, 10) times. **Tier 2** Work T1, [work R1] 7 (8, 9) times, work T2. **Tier 3** [Work R2] 8 (9, 10) times. **Tier 4** Work T1, [work R1] 6 (7, 8) times, work R4. **Tier 5** [Work R2] 7 (8, 9) times. **Tier 6** Work T1, [work R1] 5

(6, 7) times, work R4. **Tier 7** [Work R2] 6 (7, 8) times. **Tier 8** Work T1, [work R1] 4 (5, 6) times, work R4. **Tier 9** [Work R2] 5 (6, 7) times. **Tier 10** Work T1, [work R1] 3 (4, 5) times, work R4. **Tier 11** [Work R2] 4 (5, 6) times. **Tier 12** Work R5 (R5, T1), [work R1] 3 (3, 4) times, work T2 (R4, R4). **Tier 13** [Work R2] 4 (4, 5) times, [work T6] 1 (1, 0) time. **Tier 14** [Work R5] 0 (0, 1) time, [work R1] 4 times. **Tier 15** Work T3, [work R2] 3 (3, 4) times, work T6. **Tier 16** [Work R1] 3 (3, 4) times, work R4. **Tier 17** [Work R2] 3 (3, 4) times, work T6. **Tier 18: Size S** Work 3 T7, fasten off (Size S ends here). **Sizes M, L** [Work R1] 3 (4) times, work T2. **Tier 19: Size M** [Work T5] 3 times, work T4 (Size M ends here). **Size L** [Work R2] 4 times, work T6. **Tier 20** [Work R1] 3 times, work R4. **Tier 21** [Work T5] 3 times, work T4 (Size L ends here).

FINISHING
Block. Join left shoulders using 3-needle bind-off. Using matching perle cotton thread, sew right shoulder seam. Sew sides and underarm seam, lapping right front over left and sewing in place.
Bottom band
With smaller circular needle, RS facing and beg at left side seam, pick up and k170 (196, 210) sts around lower edge of back and right front, leaving lower edge of left front free, place marker for beg of rnd and join. Work circularly for 1" in k1, p1 rib. Bind off. Loosely sew lower edge of left front in place at top of ribbing.
Front edging
With dpn, cast on 4 sts. Beg in lower most corner of right front edge and working around to lower most corner of left front edge (behind right front), work as follows: With RS facing, k4, pick up and k1 st from front edge, turn. P5, turn. *K3, ssk, pick up and k1 st from edge, turn. P4, turn. Rep from* around entire front opening, binding off at lower most corner of left front edge. Sew cast-on and bound-off edges in place. Sew on hook and eye invisibly between fronts where front neck edges meet.

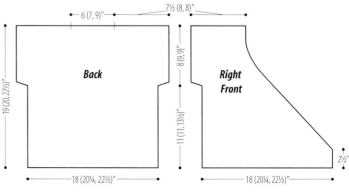

Surplice blouse

TRIANGLES
(***Note*** Turn work after every row unless otherwise indicated.)
Base triangle (BT)
Row 1 (RS) K1. ***Row 2*** P1. ***Row 3*** Sl 1, k1. ***Row 4*** P2. ***Row 5*** Sl 1, k2. ***Row 6 and all WS rows*** P all sts worked on last row. ***Row 7 and all RS rows*** Sl 1, k all sts worked on last row plus 1 more. Continue until 9 sts have been worked, ending with a RS row. Do not turn.
Triangle 1 (T1)
Row 1 (WS) P1. ***Row 2*** M1, k1. ***Row 3*** P1, p2tog. ***Row 4*** K1, M1, k1. ***Row 5*** P2, p2tog. ***Row 6*** K2, M1, k1. ***Row 7*** P3, p2tog. ***Row 8*** K3, M1, k1. ***Row 9*** P4, p2tog. ***Row 10*** K4, M1, k1. ***Row 11*** P5, p2tog. ***Row 12*** K5, M1, k1. ***Row 13*** P6, p2tog. ***Row 14*** K6, M1, k1. ***Row 15*** P7, p2tog. ***Row 16*** K7, M1, k1. ***Row 17*** P8, p2tog. Do not turn.
Triangle 2 (T2)
Row 1 With WS facing, pick up and p9 sts along side of triangle or rectangle. ***Row 2 and all even rows*** Knit. ***Row 3*** Sl 1, p6, p2tog. ***Row 5*** Sl 1, p5, p2tog. ***Row 7*** Sl 1, p4, p2tog. ***Row 9*** Sl 1, p3, p2tog. ***Row 11*** Sl 1, p2, p2tog. ***Row 13*** Sl 1, p1, p2tog. ***Row 15*** Sl 1, p2tog. ***Row 17*** P2tog. The remaining st becomes the first picked-up st of the next triangle or rectangle.

Triangles 3–7
See p. 82.

RECTANGLES
(***Note*** Turn work after every row unless otherwise indicated.)
Rectangle 1 (R1)
Row 1 With WS facing, pick up and p9 sts along side of triangle or rectangle, sl last st to LH needle, p2tog. ***Row 2*** K9. ***Row 3*** Sl 1, p7, p2tog. ***Rows 4–17*** Rep last 2 rows 7 times more. Do not turn.
Rectangles 2–5
See p. 82.

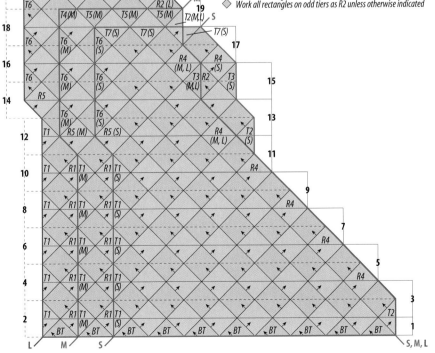

↗ *Direction of knitting on even tiers*
↖ *Direction of knitting on odd tiers*

◇ *Work all rectangles on even tiers as R1 unless otherwise indicated*
◈ *Work all rectangles on odd tiers as R2 unless otherwise indicated*

GETTING STARTED Entrelac

Entrelac is worked in tiers of triangles and rectangles. The shapes are worked one at a time and attached to their neighbors as you knit.

Start work here with last cast-on stitch.

1a *Start Tier 1 with a Base Triangle (BT) worked on first 9 stitches of cast-on.*

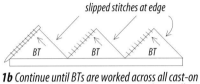

slipped stitches at edge

1b *Continue until BTs are worked across all cast-on stitches. All live stitches are on circular needle.*

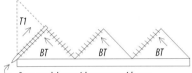

Start work here with a wrong-side row.

2a *Start Tier 2 with a T1 triangle.*

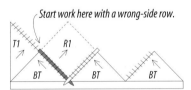

Start work here with a wrong-side row.

2b *For R1 rectangle, with shaded end of circular needle pick up stitches along slipped edge of BT. At end of every wrong-side row, work together last stitch and first stitch from white end of circular needle.*

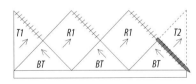

2c *End Tier 2 with T2 triangle.*

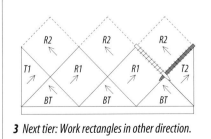

3 *Next tier: Work rectangles in other direction.*

Entrelac to suit designed by Kathleen Power Johnson

The simple lines of this jacket let the space-dyed colors tell the story of multi-directional entrelac.

Experienced

Sizes
S (M, L)
Shown in size S.
Directions are for smallest size with larger sizes in parentheses. If there is only 1 set of numbers, it applies to all sizes.

Finished measurements
Underarm (buttoned) 42 (46, 48)"
Length 21 (25, 27)"

Gauge
19 sts and 29 rows to 4"/10cm over St st using size 5 (3.75mm) needle.

MATERIALS
Yarn Drop Spindle *8-cut Rayon Chenille* 1250 (1350, 1450) yds Ocean Breeze (920 yds/841m per 16oz/457g, 100% rayon).
Needles Size 5 (3.75mm) circular needle, 29"/60cm long, *or size to obtain gauge.*
Extras 1"/25mm button. Small amount of matching perle cotton yarn for assembly, size G/6 (4.5mm) crochet hook.

NOTES
1 See *Techniques*, p. 228 for ssk, ssp, M1, chain (ch), and single crochet (sc), and *Getting started* on p. 79 for entrelac. *2* Jacket is worked in one piece to underarms, then divided for fronts and back. *3* Entrelac charts are worked in tiers of rectangles and triangles. Follow chart for placement of each rectangle or triangle. For ease in working, place ruler under each tier (solid line for right-side tiers and dotted line for wrong-side tiers). *4* When instructed to work M1, work M1-knit on right-side rows and M1-purl on wrong-side rows.

BODY
(*Note* Turn work after every tier has been completed unless otherwise indicated.)
Bottom facing
Cast on 200 (218, 228) sts. Work 1" in St st, ending with a RS row. *Turning ridge* (WS) Knit, dec 56 (58, 68) sts evenly spaced—144 (160, 160) sts. *Tier 1* (RS) Work 16 (20, 16) BT. *Tier 2* Work T1, [work R1] 15 (19, 15) times, work T2. *Tier 3* [Work R2] 16 (20, 16) times. Rep Tiers 2–3 three (five, four) times more.
Divide for fronts and back
Tier 10 (14, 12) (WS) Work T1, [work R1] 2 (3, 2) times, work R4 (do not cut yarn; the remaining st becomes the first picked-up st of the next triangle), work T7, [work R1] 6 (8, 6) times, work R4 (do not cut yarn; the remaining st becomes the first picked-up st of the next triangle), work T7, [work R1] 3 (4, 3) times, work T2.

RIGHT FRONT
Tier 11 (15, 13) (RS) [Work R2] 3 (4, 3) times. *Tier 12 (16, 14)* Work T1, [work R1] 2 (3, 2) times, work T2. *Next tier* Rep Tier 11 (15, 13).
Shape neck
Tier 14 (18, 16) Work T1, [work R1] 1 (2, 1) times, work R4. *Tier 15 (19, 17)* [Work R2] 2 (3, 2) times. *Tier 16 (20, 18)* Work T1, work R1, [work R4] 0 (1, 0) times. *Size M: Tier 21* [Work R2] twice. *Size M: Tier 22* Work T1, work R1. *All Sizes: Last tier* Work T3, then T5. Fasten off.

BACK
(*Note* See chart for placement of first R2.)

Tier 11 (15, 13) [Work R2] 6 (8, 6) times. *Tier 12 (16, 14)* Work T1, [work R1] 5 (7, 5) times, work T2. Rep last 2 tiers 2 (3, 2) times more. *Last tier* [Work T5] 6 (8, 6) times. Fasten off.

LEFT FRONT
(*Note* See chart for placement of first R2.)
Tier 11 (15, 13) [Work R2] 3 (4, 3) times. *Tier 12 (16, 14)* Work T1, [work R1] 2 (3, 2) times, work T2.
Shape neck
Tier 13 (17, 15) [Work R2] 2 (3, 2) times, work R3. *Tier 14 (18, 16)* [Work R1] 2 (3, 2) times, work T2. *Tier 15 (19, 17)* [Work R2] 1 (2, 1) times, work R3. *Tier 16 (20, 18)* [Work R1] 1 (2, 1) times, work T2. *Size M: Tier 21* Work R2, work R3. *Tier 22* Work R1, work T2. *All Sizes: Last tier* Work T5, work T4.

SLEEVES
Bottom facing
Cast on 40 (42, 44) sts. Work 1" in St st, ending with a RS row. *Turning ridge* (WS) Knit. Beg with a k row, work in St st and AT SAME TIME, when piece measures 1" from turning ridge, inc 1 st each side every 6th row 18 times—76 (78, 80) sts. Work even until piece measures 17" from turning ridge.
Shape cap
Bind off 4 sts at beg of next 2 rows, then dec 1 st each side every other row 3 (3, 6) times, then every 4th row 5 (5, 2) times. Bind off remaining 52 (54, 56) sts.

FINISHING
Block pieces. Using matching pearl cotton thread, sew shoulders. Set in sleeves. Sew side and sleeve seams. Fold bottom facings of body and sleeves to WS at turning ridge and sew to inside. With RS facing, yarn, and crochet hook, begin at lower right front corner and work 2 (3, 3) rows sc along front and neck edges. On the 1st (2nd, 2nd) row, at beg of neck shaping on right front, ch 4, skip 4 sts for buttonhole. On next row, work 4 sc into ch-4 space. Sew on button so that fronts overlaps about 2" at neckline.

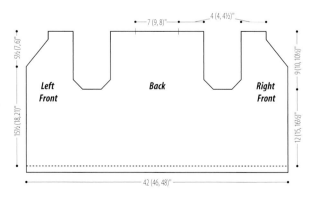

Entrelac jacket

See p.82.

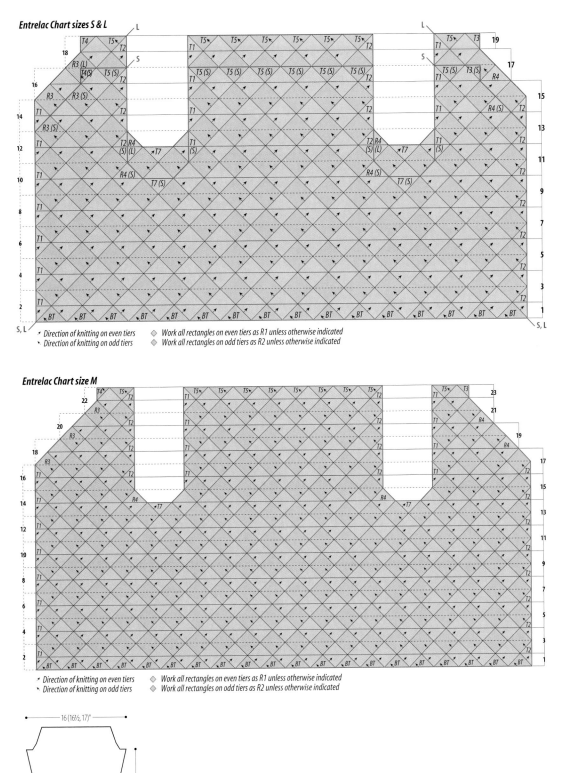

Entrelac Chart sizes S & L

⬩ Direction of knitting on even tiers
⬩ Direction of knitting on odd tiers
◇ Work all rectangles on even tiers as R1 unless otherwise indicated
◇ Work all rectangles on odd tiers as R2 unless otherwise indicated

Entrelac Chart size M

⬩ Direction of knitting on even tiers
⬩ Direction of knitting on odd tiers
◇ Work all rectangles on even tiers as R1 unless otherwise indicated
◇ Work all rectangles on odd tiers as R2 unless otherwise indicated

Sleeve

16 (16½, 17)"

17"

8½ (8¾, 9¼)"

Note When a st remains on needle at end of a triangle or rectangle, it counts as the first picked-up st or cast-on st for the next rectangle or triangle.

TRIANGLES

(**Note** Turn work after every row unless otherwise indicated.)

Base triangle (BT)

Row 1 (RS) K1. **Row 2** P1. **Row 3** Sl 1, k1. **Row 4** P2. **Row 5** Sl 1, k2. **Row 6 and all WS rows** P all sts worked on last row. **Row 7 and all RS rows** Sl 1, k all sts worked on last row plus 1 more. Continue until 9 (8, 10) sts have been worked, ending with a RS row. Do not turn.

Triangle 1 (T1)

Row 1 (WS) P1. **Row 2** M1, k1. **Row 3** P1, p2tog. **Row 4** K1, M1, k1. **Row 5** P2, p2tog. **Row 6** K2, M1, k1. **Row 7** P3, p2tog. **Row 8** K3, M1, k1. **Row 9** P4, p2tog. **Row 10** K4, M1, k1. **Row 11** P5, p2tog. **Row 12** K5, M1, k1. **Row 13** P6, p2tog. **Row 14** K6, M1, k1. **Row 15** P7, p2tog (Size M ends here; do not turn). **Row 16** K7, M1, k1. **Row 17** P8, p2tog (Size S ends here; do not turn). **Row 18** K8, M1, k1. **Row 19** P9, p2tog. Do not turn.

Triangle 2 (T2)

Row 1 With WS facing, pick up and p9 (8,10) sts along side of triangle or rectangle. **Row 2 and all even rows** Knit. **Row 3** Sl 1, p6 (5, 7), p2tog. **Row 5** Sl 1, p5 (4, 6), p2tog. **Row 7** Sl 1, p4 (3, 5), p2tog. **Row 9** Sl 1, p3 (2, 4), p2tog. **Row 11** Sl 1, p2 (1, 3), p2tog. **Row 13** Sl 1, p1 (0, 2), p2tog. **Row 15: Size M** P2tog. **Sizes S, L** Sl 1, p0 (1), p2tog. **Row 17: Size S** P2tog. **Size L** Sl 1, p2tog. **Row 19** P2tog. **All sizes** The remaining st becomes the first picked-up st of the next triangle or rectangle

Triangles 3–7

See p.82.

RECTANGLES

(**Note** Turn work after every row unless otherwise indicated.)

Rectangle 1 (R1)

Row 1 With WS facing, pick up and p9 (8,10) sts along side of triangle or rectangle, sl last st to LH needle, p2tog. **Row 2** K9 (8, 10). **Row 3** Sl 1, p7 (6, 8), p2tog. **Rows 4–17 (4–15, 4–19)**. Rep last 2 rows 7 (6, 8) times more. Do not turn.

Rectangles 2–5

See p.82.

Entrelac jacket

TRIANGLES 3–7
(**Note** In Triangles 3–7, definitions are for both the jacket and blouse. Jacket figures are given first, blouse figures follow in brackets. If there is only 1 figure or set of instructions, it applies to all sizes of jacket and blouse.)

Triangle 3 (T3)
Jacket size S only: Row 1 K1. **Row 2** M1, p1. **Row 3** K1, ssk. **Row 4** P1, M1, p1. **Row 5** K2, ssk. **Row 6** P2, M1, p1. **Row 7** K3, ssk. **Row 8** P3, M1, p1. **Row 9** K4, ssk. **Row 10** P4, M1, p1. **Row 11** K2, pass first st over 2nd, k3, ssk. **Row 12** P5. **Row 13** Ssk, k2, ssk. **Row 14** P4. **Row 15** Ssk, k1, ssk. **Row 16** P3. **Row 17** [Ssk] twice, pass the first st over the 2nd. Do not turn.

Jacket size M only Work rows 1–8 as for Size S. **Row 9** K2, pass first st over 2nd, k2, ssk. **Row 10.** P4. **Row 11** Ssk, k1, ssk. **Row 12** P3. **Row 13** [Ssk] twice. **Row 14** P2. **Row 15** Ssk. Do not turn.

Jacket size L only Work rows 1–10 as for Size S. **Row 11** K2, pass first st over 2nd, k3, ssk. **Row 12** P5. **Row 13** Ssk, k2, ssk. **Row 14** P4. **Row 15** Ssk, k1, ssk. **Row 16** P3. **Row 17** [Ssk] twice. **Row 18** P2. **Row 19** Ssk. Do not turn.

Blouse only Work rows 1–10 as for Size S Jacket. **Row 11** K5, ssk. **Row 12** P5, M1, p1. **Row 13** K6, ssk. **Row 14** P6, M1, p1. **Row 15** K7, ssk. **Row 16** P7, M1, p1. **Row 17** K8, ssk. Do not turn.

Triangle 4 (T4)
Row 1 With RS facing, pick up and k9 (8, 10) [9] sts along side of rectangle. **Row 2 and all even rows** Purl. **Row 3** K2, pass first st over 2nd st, k5 (4, 6) [5], k2tog. **Row 5** Ssk, k3 (2, 4) [3], k2tog. **Row 7** Ssk, k1 (0, 2) [1], k2tog. **Jacket size M only** Pass first st over 2nd st and fasten off. **Row 9: Jacket size S and blouse** Sl 1-k2tog-psso and fasten off. **Jacket size L** Ssk, k2tog; **Row 11** Ssk and fasten off.

Triangle 5 (T5)
Row 1 With RS facing, pick up and k9 (8, 10) [9] sts along side of triangle or rectangle. **Row 2 and all even rows** Purl. **Row 3** K2, pass first st over 2nd st, k7 (6, 8) [7]. **Row 5** Ssk, k6 (5, 7) [6]. **Row 7** Ssk, k5 (4, 6) [5]. **Row 9** Ssk, k4 (3, 5) [4]. **Row 11** Ssk, k3 (2, 4) [3]. **Row 13** Ssk, k2 (1, 3) [2]. **Row 15** Ssk, k1 (0, 2) [1]. **Jacket sizes S, L, and blouse: Row 17** Ssk, k0 (1)[0]. **Jacket size L: Row 19** Ssk. **Jacket and blouse all sizes** Do not turn. The remaining st becomes first picked-up st of next triangle or rectangle.

Triangle 6 (T6) (Blouse only)
Row 1 With RS facing, pick up and k9 sts along side of triangle or rectangle. **Row 2 and all even rows** Purl. **Row 3** K7, k2tog. **Row 5** K6, k2tog. **Row 7** K5, k2tog. **Row 9** K4, k2tog. **Row 11** K3, k2tog. **Row 13** K2, k2tog. **Row 15** K1, k2tog. **Row 17** K2tog. The remaining st becomes the first picked-up st of the next triangle or rectangle.

Triangle 7 (T7)
Row 1 With WS facing, pick up and p9 (8, 10) [9] sts along side of triangle or rectangle, sl last st to LH needle, p2tog. **Row 2 and all even rows** Knit. **Row 3** P2, pass first st over 2nd st, p6 (5, 7) [6], p2tog. **Row 5** Ssp, p5 (4, 6) [5], p2tog. **Row 7** Ssp, p4 (3, 5) [4], p2tog. **Row 9** Ssp, p3 (2, 4) [3], p2tog. **Row 11** Ssp, p2 (1, 3) [2], p2tog. **Row 13** Ssp, p1 (0, 2) [1], p2tog. **Jacket sizes S, L, and blouse: Row 15** Ssp, p0 (1) [0] p2tog. **Jacket size L: Row 17** Ssp, p2tog. **Jacket and blouse all sizes: Row 17 (15, 19) [17]** Sl 1, p2tog, psso. Do not turn. The remaining st becomes the first picked-up st of the next triangle or rectangle.

RECTANGLES 2–5
(**Note** In Rectangles 2–5, definitions are for both the jacket and blouse. Jacket figures are given first, blouse figures follow in brackets. If there is only 1 figure or set of instructions, it applies to all sizes of jacket and blouse.)

Rectangle 2 (R2)
Row 1 With RS facing, pick up and k9 (8, 10) [9] sts along side of triangle or rectangle, sl last st to LH needle, ssk. **Row 2** P9 (8, 10) [9] sts. **Row 3** Sl 1, k7 (6, 8) [7], ssk. **Rows 4–17 (4–15, 4–19) [4–17]** Rep last 2 rows 7 (6, 8) [7] times more. Do not turn.

Rectangle 3 (R3) (Jacket only)
Rows 1–16 (1–14, 1–18) Work as for Rectangle 2. **Row 17 (15, 19)** Bind off, working ssk over last 2 sts before binding them off. Fasten off, unless otherwise indicated.

Rectangle 4 (R4)
Rows 1-16 (1–14, 1–18) [1-16] Work as for Rectangle 1. **Row 17 (15, 19) [17]** Bind off, working p2tog over last 2 sts before binding them off. Fasten off, unless otherwise indicated.

Rectangle 5 (R5) (Blouse only)
Cast on 9 sts, turn. **Row 1** (WS) P8, p2tog. **Rows 2–17** Work as for R1.

THE DROP SPINDLE D'ELIN LOHR
Boucle skirt designed by Kathleen Power Johnson

The texture and drape of hand-dyed boucle add life to a simple skirt.

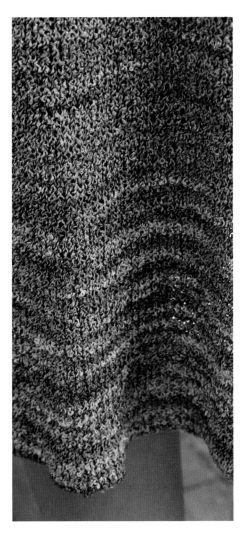

MATERIALS
Yarn Drop Spindle *Rayon Bouclé* 925 (1025, 1125) yds Ocean Breeze (1000yds/914m per 16oz/457g, 100% rayon).
Needles Size 4 (3.5mm) circular needle, 24"/60cm and 40"/100cm long, *or size to obtain gauge.*
Extras 1 yd of ¾" waistband elastic, stitch markers, small amount of matching perle cotton yarn for assembly.

NOTES
1 Skirt is worked circularly from the bottom to waist. *2* Change needle lengths as needed.

SKIRT
(*Note* Use a different color of marker to distinguish rnd marker from others.)
Bottom facing
Cast on 330 (350, 370) sts. Place marker (pm) for beg of rnd and join, being careful not to twist sts. Work 1" in St st. **Turning ridge** Purl. **Next rnd** K33 (35, 37), [pm, k33 (35, 37)] 9 times. K 8 (8, 12) rnds. **Next (dec) rnd** [K to 2 sts before marker, k2tog] 10 times. Work even, rep dec rnd every 13th rnd 10 times more—220 (240, 260) sts. Work even until piece measures 16" from turning ridge.
Shape hips
Rep dec rnd every 10th (8th, 8th) rnd 6 (7, 8) times—160 (170, 180) sts. Work even until piece measures 26" from turning ridge.
Waistband facing
Turning ridge Purl. Work 1" in St st. Bind off.

FINISHING
Fold bottom facing to WS at turning ridge and using matching perle cotton yarn, sew to inside. Fold waistband facing to inside and sew to inside, leaving 2" unsewn for inserting elastic. Cut elastic 2" longer than desired waist measurement. Thread through casing. Overlap ends 1" and machine stitch. Sew unsewn facing to inside.

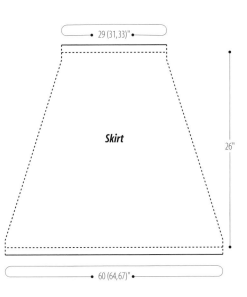

29 (31, 33)"

Skirt

26"

60 (64, 67)"

Intermediate

Sizes
S (M, L)
Shown in size S.
Directions are for smallest size with larger sizes in parentheses.
If there is only 1 set of numbers, it applies to all sizes.

Finished measurements
Waist 29 (31, 33)"
Hips 40 (43½, 47¼)"
Length 26"

Gauge
22 sts and 34 rows to 4"/10cm over St st using size 4 (3.5mm) needle.

Even in the pouring rain, the wine country north of San Francisco is lush and gorgeous. Redwoods stand brick red and intensely green against the gray day. As we drive on, Douglas fir and Ponderosa pine take over the rolling hills. From Willits, we follow soggy roads to the crest of a rise called Hilltop. There angora bunnies and alpacas peek out from a shed shrouded in mist. We arrive at a contemporary house with a studio at the front entrance, the home of Chasing Rainbows Dyeworks and Nancy Finn.

CHASING RAINBOWS DYEWORKS NANCY FINN

Willits, California

Nancy Finn

CHASING RAINBOWS DYEWORKS NANCY FINN
Willits, California

Top: 100% Tussah silk dyed in the colorway Merlot is inspired by the California wine country where Nancy Finn has lived for the past 27 years.

Right: Small skeins of cultivated silk spinning fiber adorn a moss-covered stump at the site of Nancy's new dye studio.

In one way or another, Nancy Finn has been involved with textiles all her life. She took up knitting at the age of seven and mastered the sewing machine by the time she was twelve. In college, she earned a degree in clothing and textiles, and her postgraduate studies led her to weaving and spinning. She credits Max Lenderman, her weaving teacher, as a major influence, for it was through him that she discovered her color sense and the important role it would play in her life. She remembers particularly an exercise in which she had to match colors in yarn to objects, and how this was not unlike matching thread colors to the sewing fabrics of her childhood. Her first fiber-related business involved selling hand-spun, handknit sweaters, but she soon moved on to hand-dyed spinning fiber and yarns.

In 1990, Nancy founded Chasing Rainbows Dyeworks. "I've always had a studio," she tells us, "even if it was my kitchen." She built her present studio nearly ten years ago. Nancy's studio caters to the handspinner, weaver, and knitter. She dyes roving and top to match her yarns, so that spinners can add their own handspun yarn in her colorways to their knitted or woven piece. She also dyes fabric for specific projects.

Having lived in California for 27 years, Nancy believes that the lush environment has everything to say about her color inspiration. One of her oldest color combinations, Madrona, which she describes as "sort of goldy brown and salmony red and purple," is named after an indigenous tree. Many of her colors are inspired by nature but just as often she looks to art, both contemporary and classical, and her favorite artists are the Impressionists. She also pages through what she calls "girlie magazines, like Vogue and Elle," to keep abreast of current fashions and colors.

Finger paints Nancy does not exactly "paint" yarn; in fact, she finds it difficult to describe her unusual technique. She colors huge skeins with subtle, almost undetectable repeats and then splits these skeins into smaller hanks, so that it is nearly impossible to discern where one color ends and another begins. She calls her approach "mooshing," which is performed with gloved hands. "Mooshing is a big part of what I do," she laughs, likening it to finger painting. She achieves her subtle color changes by working and then reworking the yarn.

Her finished product does not look "mooshed," however. She dyes yarns in analogous color groups, for example, blues and purples, or various shades of brown. She finds that many knitters are comfortable with a palette that contains tonal variations of one or two colors. Her personal favorites are high-contrast combinations, and she occasionally sneaks them into the mix. Subtle striping or stacking may occur when knitting with yarn dyed in this manner, but rather than see it as a problem, "I've kind of gone the other way with it," Nancy says. "What's wrong with stacking? It's a design all in itself."

Although she is able to dye 12 pounds at once, she usually packages her yarns in sweater amounts so that there is no need for dye lots. Her main advice for knitters is: "Buy enough yarn for your project, or be willing to improvise."

Nancy has never had a business plan. Her dyeing began as a hobby that grew on its own; sometimes she feels that it has grown ahead of her. For 12 years, she has

what they have before them," she notes. She cites space-dyed yarn as an example: it has been knit up in stockinette stitch for so long that she is afraid knitters tend to ignore other possibilities, like mosaic and Fair Isle. She urges knitters to take a fresh look at handpainted yarns and experiment with stitch patterns and techniques to bring out the best in these yarns. Trends are not so important to her, although she has noticed that colors seem to be getting brighter, and she is encouraged that a wider range of colors has appeared in the marketplace.

Future watch Nancy and her husband are building a new, larger studio complete with a house on land they purchased nearby. She plans for expansion in her business as well. Nancy enjoys trunk shows and would like to do more of them. Pattern support and kits are in the works because "I understand that that's what people really want," Nancy says. Because she is a spinner at heart, she can never give up dyeing roving and top, and hopes to dye more fabric

Clockwise from above: Chasing Rainbows' new home is situated in a lush, old forest. Here, handspun singles in colorway Crocus drapes mossy rocks; kid mohair boucle overhangs an ancient stump.

exhibited her yarns at fiber festivals and conferences. She also sells yarn via trunk shows, mail order, and to wholesale customers. Although she straddles the line between retail and wholesale, she feels that there is no conflict because her selling areas are so far-flung. She is not a self-promoter and rarely advertises. Instead, she relies upon word of mouth and persistence in showing her fibers and handing out her business cards.

Touch appeal Nancy favors exotic yarns, like angora and silk blends, some of which are spun by hand. Her curly kid mohair is her best seller. A recent addition to her line is Mendocino Homespun, a 100% Targhee wool yarn that is spun at a domestic mill. She offers six different yarns in about 25 colorways, as well as non-repeatable mill ends. She also dyes both microfiber and silk fabric ribbon, which is actually fabric that she treats as yarn.

In terms of fiber content, customers "want a new animal," according to Nancy. Or at least spinners do, she adds, referring to the current craze for fiber from exotic creatures. "But even knitters tend to think they've done it all and they want something brand new—when, really, they haven't even begun to plumb the depths of

in the future as well.

Nancy feels that the market for handpainted yarn has reached a saturation point. "We're not going away, but our customers may go away from it for awhile," she cautions. To keep the movement alive, she believes that it is the job of hand-dyers to show knitters interesting and innovative ways to create with handpainted yarn.

Chevron bag designed by Rick Mondragon

This bag is an exercise in practical knitted luxury. From a flat bottom to strong twisted handles, it is made to be used, not just admired.

MATERIALS

Yarn Use leftover yarn from Billy the Kidd Jacket on page 90: Chasing Rainbows *Kid Mohair A* Peacock Plume (8oz/228g, 500yds/457m, 84% kid mohair, 12% wool, 4% nylon); *Mendocino Homespun B* Peacock Plume (8oz/228g, 325yds/297m, 100% wool); *Silk Textured C* Lime Green (8oz/228g, 500yds/455m, 100% silk).

Needles Size 7 (4.5mm) circular needle, 16"/40cm long, *or size to obtain gauge.*

Extras Size 2 steel crochet hook, size D/3 (3.25mm) crochet hook, stitch marker, 6 D-rings, 1 yd black gabardine fabric for lining.

NOTES

1 See *Techniques*, p. 228 for ssk, M1, single crochet (sc), and half-double crochet (hdc). *2* When using color C, use 2 strands held together as 1 unless otherwise indicated.

STITCHES USED

Chevron pat multiple of 75 sts
Rnds 1–3 Knit. *Rnd 4* [K15, M1, k28, ssk, k2tog, k28, M1] twice. Rep rnds 1–4 for pat.
Seed st over even number of sts
Row 1 *K1, p1; rep from* across. *Row 2* P the knit sts and k the purl sts. Rep row 2 for pat.

BAG

Bottom

With circular needle and 1 strand A and C held together as 1, cast on 60 sts. Continuing with 2 strands, work back and forth in Seed st for 4". Do not turn.

Sides

With 2 strands C, pick up and k15 sts along short edge, 60 sts along cast-on edge, 15 sts along other short edge, and k60—150 sts. Place marker (pm) for beg of rnd. K 6 rnds. **Tuck rnd** *Pick up next st 6 rnds below and working on the wrong side, place on LH needle. Knit picked-up st tog with next st. Rep from* around. **Begin Chevron pat** Work Chevron pat in following color sequence: [10 rows B, 4 rows C, 10 rows A, 4 rows C] twice, 10 rows B. End Chevron pat. K 4 rnds D. Rep Tuck rnd, picking up st 4 rnds below. K 6 rnds A. Rep Tuck rnd picking up st 6 rnds below. K 4 rnds A. Rep Tuck rnd, picking up st 4 rnds below. Bind off.

FINISHING

Lining

For bottom, cut a rectangle with slightly rounded corners 15" long and 4" wide, not including seam allowance. Using bag as pattern, lay flat and cut 2 lining sides, including a seam allowance, with top ½" below top of C tuck rnd. Sew sides tog. Sew sides to bottom piece. With RS facing, steel crochet hook, and 1 strand C, work 1 rnd sc through lining ½" down from top edge, working sc ¼" apart. With B and size D crochet hook, work 3 rnds hdc. With WS together, place lining inside bag. Sew last hdc rnd of lining to bag directly under C tuck rnd. Working inside bag, sew 2 sets of 3 D-rings to last hdc rnd as follows: center 1 D-ring above lining seam and place 1 ring approx 3" on either side of it.

Handle

Cut 10 strands of each yarn (30 strands total) 6 yds long. Make a twisted cord (*see below*) and thread through D-rings. Adjust to preferred length. Knot ends together and trim.

Intermediate

Finished measurements
15" long x 4" wide x 12" tall

Gauge
18 sts and 28 rows to 4"/10cm
over St st using size 7 (4.5mm) needle
with yarn A.

Making a twisted cord

Knot strands of yarn together at each end. Hold 1 end (close in a door or have someone hold it); insert a pencil through other end, or attach it to a hand mixer as follows: loop a short piece of yarn between the strands of yarn and tie to 1 beater on a hand mixer; remove other beater. Stand back far enough so yarn is taut, turn on mixer or turn pencil clockwise until strands are tightly twisted (1). Keeping strands taut, fold in half and allow cord to twist onto itself (2). Remove from holders (pencil or beater) and knot ends together.

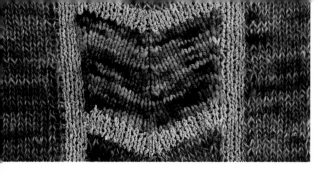

This graphic jacket has come a long way from its Western roots: silk solids outline each handpainted column and chevron.

Intermediate

Sizes

S (M, L)

Shown in size S.

Directions are for smallest size with larger sizes in parentheses.

If there is only 1 set of numbers, it applies to all sizes.

Finished measurements

Underarm (buttoned) 42 (46, 50)"

Length 23"

Gauge

18 sts and 28 rows to 4"/10cm over St st using larger needles with yarn A.

MATERIALS

Yarn Chasing Rainbows *Kid Mohair A* 2 skeins Peacock Plume (each 8oz/228g, 500yds/457m, 84% kid mohair, 12% wool, 4% nylon); *Mendocino Homespun B* 1 skein Peacock Plume (8oz/228g, 325yds/297m, 100% wool); *Silk Textured C* 1 skein Lime Green (8oz/228g, 500yds/455m, 100% silk).

Needles One pair each sizes 5 and 7 (3.75 and 4.5mm) needles, *or size to obtain gauge.* Size 5 (4.5mm) circular needle, 36"/90cm long.

Extras Five ¾"/19mm buttons, stitch markers.

NOTES

1 See *Techniques*, p. 228 for ssk, M1, intarsia knitting, and short-row wraps. *2* Use a separate bobbin or small ball of yarn for each block of color. *3* Twist yarns at color change to avoid holes.

STITCHES USED

(**Note** Work Right and Left front bias pat, and Center chevron pat in following color sequence:*20 rows B, 4 rows C, 20 rows A, 4 rows C; rep from* once, end rep with 20 rows A. For Sleeve, rep from* once, then work 20 rows B.)

Right front bias pat over 10 sts

Row 1 (RS) K10. *Row 2* P10. *Row 3* K2tog, k7, M1, k1. *Row 4* P10. Rep rows 1–4 for pat.

Left front bias pat over 10 sts

Row 1 (RS) K10. *Row 2* P10. *Row 3* K1, M1, k7, ssk. *Row 4* P10. Rep rows 1–4 for pat.

Center chevron pat over 20 sts

Row 1 (RS) K20. *Row 2* P20. *Row 3* K1, M1, k7, ssk, k2tog, k7, M1, k1. *Row 4* P20. Rep rows 1–4 for pat.

Bobble

With A, (k1, yo, k1) in same st. Sl 3 sts back to LH needle, with C, k3tog.

BACK

With smaller needles and A, cast on 90 (100, 110) sts. Work 1" in k1, p1 rib. Change to larger needles and C. Beg with a k row, work 4 rows St st, inc 8 sts evenly spaced on first row—98 (108, 118) sts. **Set up pat as follows:** (RS) K0 (0, 5) C, k5 (10, 10) A, k3 C, k15 A, k3 C, k10 A, k3 C, with B work 20 sts in Center chevron pat, k3 C, k10 A, k3 C, k15 A, k3 C, k5 (10, 10) A, k0 (0, 5) C. **Next row** P across in appropriate colors. Work as established in St st, working center 20 sts in Center chevron pat until piece measures approx 13" from beg and 10 rows Center chevron pat in A have been worked.

Shape armholes

(RS) Bind off 14 (19, 21) sts at beg of next 2 rows, then dec 1 st each side every other row 4 times—62 (62, 68) sts. Center chevron pat completed. Fasten off

yarns. **Begin Chart A** Work Chart A as indicated for back for your size through row 44.

Shape shoulders

Continuing in chart pat, bind off 7 (7, 8) sts at beg of next 2 rows, then 6 (6, 7) sts at beg of next 4 rows. Bind off remaining 22 sts for neck.

RIGHT FRONT

With smaller needles and A, cast on 45 (50, 55) sts. Work 6 rows in k1, p1 rib. Change to larger needles and C. Beg with a k row, work 4 rows St st, inc 4 sts evenly spaced on first row—49 (54, 59) sts. **Set up pat as follows:** (RS) With A, work 10 sts in Right front bias pat, k3 C, k10 A, k3 C, k15 A, k3 C, k5 (10, 10) A, k0 (0, 5) C. **Next row** P across in appropriate colors. Work as established in St st, working first 10 sts in Right front bias pat until piece measures approximately 13" from beg and 11 rows Right front bias pat in A have been worked.

Shape armhole

(WS) Bind off 14 (19, 21) sts, then dec 1 st every other row 4 times—31 (31, 34) sts. Right front bias pat completed. Fasten off yarns.

Shape neck

Begin Chart A Work Chart A as indicated for right front for your size through row 45. Shape shoulder at armhole edge as for back.

LEFT FRONT

Work as for right front to pat set-up. **Set up pat as follows:** K0 (0, 5) C, k5 (10, 10) A, k3 C, k15 A, k3 C, k10 A, k3 C, with A work 10 sts in Left front bias pat. Continue as for right front, working last 10 sts in Left front bias pat until piece measures approx 13" from beg and 10 rows Left front bias pat in A have been worked. Shape armhole as for back.

Shape neck

Work Chart A as indicated for left front for your size through row 44. Shape shoulder at armhole edge as for back.

SLEEVE

With smaller needles and A, cast on 48 (48, 60) sts. Work 1½" in k1, p1 rib. Change to larger needles and C. Beg

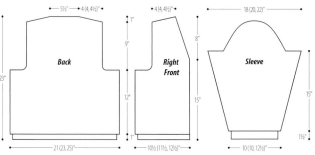

Chart A

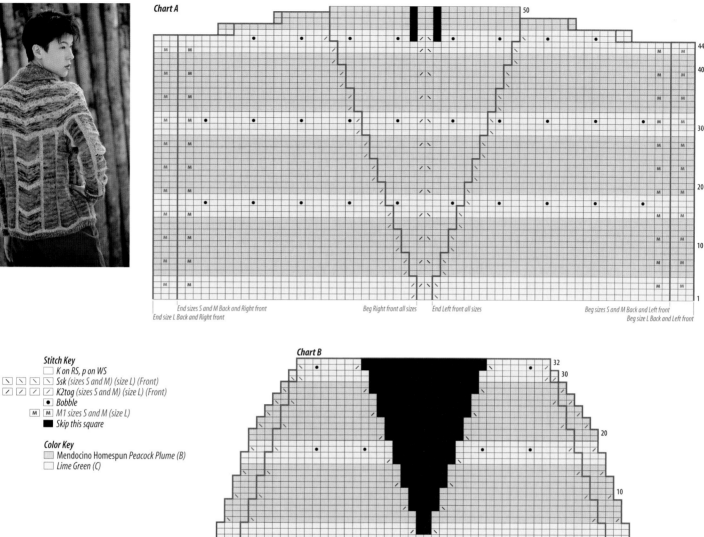

End sizes S and M Back and Right front
End size L Back and Right front

Beg Right front all sizes

End Left front all sizes

Beg sizes S and M Back and Left front
Beg size L Back and Left front

Chart B

End size L

End sizes S and M

Beg sizes S and M

Beg size L

Stitch Key
- ☐ K on RS, p on WS
- ↖ ↖ ↖ ↖ Ssk (sizes S and M) (size L) (Front)
- ↗ ↗ ↗ ↗ K2tog (sizes S and M) (size L) (Front)
- • Bobble
- M M1 sizes S and M (size L)
- ■ Skip this square

Color Key
- ☐ Mendocino Homespun *Peacock Plume (B)*
- ☐ Lime Green (C)

with a k row, work 4 rows St st, inc 4 sts evenly spaced on first row—52 (52, 64) sts. **Set up pat as follows:** (RS) K0 (0, 6) A, k3 C, k10 A, k3 C, work 20 sts in Center chevron pat, k3 C, k10 A, k3 C, k0 (0, 6) A. **Next row** P across in appropriate colors. Work as established in St st, working center 20 sts in Center chevron pat and AT SAME TIME, inc 1 st each side on next row, then every 4th row 0 (12, 9) times, then every 6th row 14 (7, 9) times, working new sts in A—82 (92, 102) sts. Work even in pat until piece measures approx 16½" from beg and 10 rows Center chevron pat in B have been worked.

Shape cap

(RS) Continuing in pat, bind off 14 (19, 21) sts at beg of next 2 rows, then dec 1 st each side every other row 4 times—46 (46, 52) sts. Center chevron pat completed. Fasten off yarns. Work Chart B as indicated for your size. Bind off remaining 16 sts.

FINISHING

Block pieces. Sew shoulders. Set in sleeves matching stripes. Sew side and sleeve seams matching stripes.

Front bands

With RS facing, circular needle, and A, begin at lower right front edge and pick up and k80 sts to beg of V-neck shaping, 46 sts along neck edge to shoulder, place marker (pm), 22 sts along back neck, pm, 46 sts along neck edge to beg of V-neck shaping, 80 sts along left front to lower edge—274 sts. **Next 2 rows** Work in k1, p1 rib; on 2nd row work a yo, k2tog buttonhole on right front at each of 5 C stripes from lower edge to beg of V-neck shaping.

Shape collar: Begin short rows (WS) Work in rib to 2nd marker (right shoulder), wrap next st and turn (W&T). Work 22 sts to marker (left shoulder), W&T. Work 28 sts hiding wrap, W&T. Work 34 sts hiding wrap, W&T. Continue in this manner, working 6 more sts each row to 64 sts, W&T. **Next (inc) row** (RS) Work to first marker, M1 (in pat) each side of next st, work 10 sts, M1 (in pat) each side of next st, work to 1 st before marker, M1 (in pat) each side of next st, work to 6 sts past last worked st of previous row, W&T—76 sts worked. Work 82 sts hiding wrap, W&T. Continue in this manner, working 6 more sts each row to 112 sts. Then work 6 less sts each row to 28 sts, W&T. Work across sts hiding wraps, to end. **Next row** (RS) Work across all sts, hiding wraps. Work 3 more rows across all sts. Bind off. Sew on buttons along left front band pick-up row.

Central

Early-morning traffic thickens as we approach St. Louis, bypassing arteries that branch toward Chicago. The radio promises record-breaking high temperatures and crowds of holiday travelers as we creep through the pre-Labor Day traffic. Rising above the haze, no sight is finer that the silver arch of St. Louis. We exit into Lafayette Square, an historic district of brick Victorian houses on the edge of urban renewal.

It is in this changing residential area that we find Rosalie Truong and Exquisitely Angora. Behind her narrow Victorian stands Rosalie's studio, a brick outbuilding that once served as the detached kitchen and later, a garden shed. There Rosalie set up her dye studio, complete with rooftop drying racks.

EXQUISITELY ANGORA ROSALIE TRUONG

St. Louis, Missouri

A block away, where houses like hers sit vacant, waiting to be renovated or torn down, Rosalie has started a community garden. It is here that we photograph her yarns.

Rosalie Truong

EXQUISITELY ANGORA ROSALIE TRUONG

St. Louis, Missouri

Clockwise from top:
A highly textured hank hangs at the community garden; flowers adorn Rosalie Truong's handspun angora; handspun yarn and herbs.

Starting from scratch Rosalie Truong lived in Vietnam until she was seven, when her parents, both doctors, fled to Paris. She remained in France for seven years. Then she and her two brothers were sent to Los Angeles to complete their educations. A multicultural transplant, she took root in California.

It was a long time before Rosalie discovered her creative side. After taking a handspinning course in college, she began raising Angora rabbits. Following the French tradition of creating from scratch, she did it all—harvested the fiber, spun the yarn, and designed the sweaters.

Rosalie got hooked on dyeing at a fiber guild workshop. When she found it impossible to achieve the solid colors shown on the dye packets, she began doing variegateds. Her first success came with angora, which she rainbow-dyed in roasting pans in the oven.

At her first show, a small fair in Columbia, Missouri, in 1991, Rosalie sold so much fiber and so many rabbits that she knew she had found her calling. Soon she was dyeing custom yarns to sell all over the country. In 1994, when the *St. Louis Post Dispatch* ran an article about her unique techniques, Rosalie was discovered and Exquisitely Angora was born. These days she sells fiber only, although six Angora bunnies still have a home in her basement.

As she completed college and entered medical school, Rosalie continued to dye fiber in her spare time. Because she found medical research bland, fiber arts became the color in her life. Conversely, fiber could not give Rosalie the intellectual challenge she craved, so the unlikely duo of yarn and medicine developed. Today, Rosalie specializes in emergency medicine because it allows her blocks of off-duty time for dyeing.

Memorable colors Rosalie's color sense developed when she was a young girl in France, a place where art and fashion dictate everyday life. Her ability to coordinate colors was innate. Now, combining colors is like a child's game, in which she creates colorways such as the turquoise and burgundy Sultan from *1001 Nights* or Carmen from the opera.

Many of her color references come from cross-cultural experiences—for example, the tropical storms in California remind her of monsoons in the rain forests of Vietnam. Travel inspires her palette, whether it's driving through sorghum fields in Minnesota or recalling the stands of wheat strewn with poppies from her French childhood.

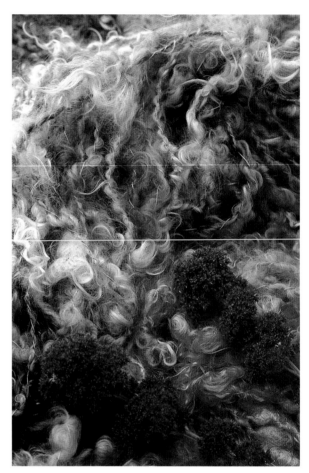

Exquisitely Angora is best known for highly textured yarns with a wild spread of colors. What makes Moira, her handspun mohair available in nearly 20 colorways, unique is the tailspinning technique Rosalie developed. Mohair fleeces are scoured and dried outside her backyard studio, then Rosalie spins directly from the fleece, explaining, "I don't card, I spin from the locks, leaving the tip of the mohair lock unspun. That is what gives it beauty." Another distinctive handspun is Sophie, otherwise known as "lumpy bumpy," an angora yarn that uses all parts of the rabbit's fleece, including neck and belly hair.

Rosalie has dual goals: to please the public and herself. "I would be miserable if I didn't," she confesses. She loves to combine space-dye techniques with loads of texture for exotic results. For example, she rainbow-dyes mohair locks then tailspins them to her own whims, creating colorways as she goes. She also experiments with natural dyes and textured commercial yarns, blending all to broaden her distinctive look.

Sophisticated savage? Piled-on primitive? Richly rustic? Whatever the name, when knitters buy from Exquisitely

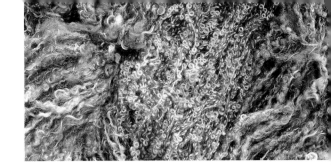

Angora, they get unique yarns with incredible texture, higher loft, and a soft hand.

When Rosalie selects machine-spun yarns for dyeing, she chooses carefully, seeking textured fiber—the thicker, the better. "I'm always on a quest for thicker yarns," Rosalie says, adding that she has recently begun working with cotton chenille, a popular yarn with a thick, plush texture she loves. She admits, "I'm a short-reward type of person, so I like fat needles and fat yarns."

Coast-to-coast colors When she was single, Rosalie used to dye fiber in her kitchen. "I figured that I couldn't poison anybody but myself," she says with a laugh. After marrying and moving to the Midwest, Rosalie abandoned the sprinkle dyes of her early years in favor of liquid dyes that she pours over fiber. "I have a medical background, so I think that inhaling dye dust is the worst thing you can do to your lungs."

When asked which colors have the best appeal, Rosalie responds, "To whom?" When she moved from California to Missouri, Rosalie found that the bright range of colors she had developed had to be toned down. "The yarn is unique in terms of its texture alone," she explains, observing that adding a lot of color can overwhelm some people. "I have to curtail my palette for people who live around here," she says, with a grin. "Midwesterners don't particularly like yellow or orange, so I introduce them to new choices and combinations."

Generally, she dyes navies, burgundies, and browns for the Midwest; for the West Coast, she revels in high-contrast brights, from yellows and cobalt blues, to greens, reds, and oranges. For the East Coast, she chooses a different set of brights. "The West Coast is more playful, the East Coast more sophisticated," she notes.

"Knitters want something new every year," Rosalie says, remarking that trends seem to alternate between classic and novelty yarns. To preview color trends, Rosalie window-shops at the malls. Recently she has seen a '70s revival that allows her to explore the greens and golds she so loves. As color trends revert to the muted shades of previous years, she is glad she kept her line of Classic Colors.

The soft sell These days, Rosalie finds that she is less production-oriented. She attends three or four retail shows each year and relies on mail order and word of mouth for additional business. Staying small and specialized allows her to serve the needs of individual customers and retain the personal contact that is so necessary to her art.

Rosalie resists kits because she likes customers to choose from her wide range of unique yarns. She designs her own garments, and often looks to sewing patterns for construction. She finds it is more important to fit the pattern to the yarn, than the yarn to the pattern. And because she is limited to two skeins per pot, Rosalie has no dye lots. Although she uses repeatable color combinations, "they don't always turn out the same way," she cautions.

When considering the cost of her yarns, knitters need to realize how much physical labor is involved in the spinning and dyeing process, "Then there's the work that goes into the design of the colors," she adds, as well as the "little tweakings" it takes to make the colorway fit. Rosalie may do five batches to get one custom color, for example.

Future watch Soon, Rosalie will need to hire help and find a commercial studio. After finishing her doctoral degree, she "jumped right back into a clinical clerkship," and has yet to begin her medical residency. She has started a family (Ernie was born in March 2001) and knows that something has to give. "For now, this means that I sleep less."

Rosalie dreams of owning a farm across the river in Illinois, where she could have 300 rabbits. She imagines weekend retreats and workshops, and a large studio in a natural setting.

"As artists we are visionaries. The vision is absolutely necessary to carry out our work. Without it, we won't get anywhere." Rosalie says softly, "You have to have a dream."

Top: A chunky mixture of hand-dyed boucles. Rosalie favors thick yarns that knit quickly without sacrificing texture.

Bottom: Her studio is located in a small brick kitchen detached from the house, where a trap door decorated with a cowhide motif leads to drying space on the roof.

EXQUISITELY ANGORA ROSALIE TRUONG
Curly locks designed by Rosalie Truong

When both color and texture are at play as in this amazing jacket, keep everything else simple.

MATERIALS
Yarn Exquisitely Angora *Handspun Moira* **A** 5 (7) skeins The New Yorker (each 10½oz/300g, 100yds/91m, 99% mohair, 1% cotton binder) **B** 500 (700)yds/457 (640)m sport-weight wool in matching color.
Needles Sizes 13 and 15 (9 and10mm) circular needles, 24"/61cm long *or size to obtain gauge.*
Extras Four 2"/50mm horn buttons. Stitch holder.

NOTES
1 See *Techniques,* p. 228 for grafting, M1, and short-row wraps. *2* Work with 1 strand A and 1 strand B held together as 1 throughout. *3* Fronts are reversible. Turn left front over so that the wrong side becomes the right side. *4* Coat may stretch in length due to weight.

STITCH USED
Seed st over even number of sts
Row 1 (RS) *K1, p1; rep from* across. *Row 2* K the purl sts and p the knit sts. Rep row 2 for pat.

BACK
With 1 strand A and B and larger needle, cast on 34 (37) sts. Work 3" in Garter st (k every row). Mark next row as RS and work in Seed st, dec 1 st each side when piece measures 4" and 8" from beg. Work even until piece measures 14 (16)" from beg, end with a WS row. Change to smaller needles and dec 1 st each side once—28 (31) sts. Mark each end of row for armhole. Work even in pat until piece measures 24½ (28)" from beg. Bind off.

FRONT make 2
With 1 strand A and B and larger needle, cast on 14 (16) sts. Work as for back, shaping side only at end of RS rows through last dec—11 (13) sts. Mark end of RS row for armhole. Work even in pat for 3 rows.

Shape neck
(RS) Dec 1 st at beg of this row (neck edge) once, then every 10th row 1 (2) times—9 (10) sts. Work even until piece measures same as back. Bind off all sts.

SLEEVES
With 1 strand A and B and smaller needle, cast on 14 (16) sts. Work 3" in Garter st. Change to larger needles. Work in Seed st and AT SAME TIME, inc 1 st each side (working incs into pat) every 8th row 4 (5) times—22 (26) sts. Work even in pat until piece measures 18" from beg. Bind off all sts.

FINISHING
Sew shoulders. Mark center back neck. Place 4 markers along right front for buttonholes, with the first 1" below first neck dec, the last 3" above bottom, and 2 others spaced evenly between.
Right front shawl collar
(*Note* Sew band to coat as you knit, stretching slightly to fit.)
Beg at lower edge, with 1 strand A and B and smaller needle, cast on 6 sts. Mark next row as RS and work in Garter st to beg of neck shaping, working buttonhole at each marker as follows: k3, yo, k2tog, k1. Continue in Garter st and at beg of neck shaping, inc on next RS rows as follows: K1, M1, k to end. Rep inc every 6th row 0 (1) time, then every 4th row 7 (8) times—14 (16) sts. K 10 (12) rows more. *Begin short rows: Row 1* (RS) K12, wrap next st and turn (W&T). *Row 2* K12. *Row 3* K8, W&T. *Row 4* K8. *Row 5* K4, W&T. *Row 6* K4. *Row 7* K14 (16), hiding wraps. Work even in Garter st until center back neck is reached. Place sts on hold.
Left front shawl collar
Work as for right front shawl collar, omitting buttonholes and working shaping on WS rows. Graft open sts of shawl collars tog. Sew sleeves between markers. Sew side and sleeve seams. Sew on buttons.

Pockets make 2
With 1 strand A and B and larger needles, cast on 12 sts. Work 6 (7)" in Seed st. Work 2" in Garter st. Bind off all sts. With bottom of pockets 4" above bottom of fronts and next to front bands, sew pocket sides and bottom to fronts.

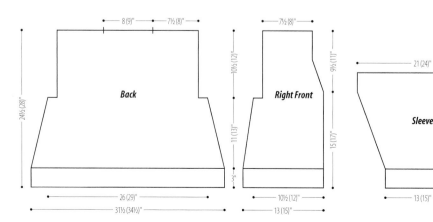

JOSLYN'S FIBER FARM JOSLYN SEEFELDT

Milton, Wisconsin

As the sun burns through the sweltering haze of mid morning, we are already hours into the midwestern leg of our journey. Ribbons of highway stretch across the Great American Plains, cutting through rectangular fields of corn and soybeans crisped by the summer drought. Here, distances between towns are marked by hours more than miles. The landscape greens as we reach the Mississippi and the rolling hills that lead us from Minnesota into Wisconsin. Waves of heat shimmer above the road as we turn toward Joslyn's Fiber Farm in the tiny town of Milton.

Joslyn Seefeldt

JOSLYN'S FIBER FARM JOSLYN SEEFELDT
Milton, Wisconsin

Large, fluffy Samoyeds bound toward us as we approach the house, while Angora rabbits watch from shaded hutches in the barn. On her wraparound deck, Joslyn Seefeldt waits with tubs of yarn destined for our photo shoot.

Starting out A relative newcomer to the world of hand-dyed fiber, Joslyn can see yarn with fresh eyes, and this is reflected in her clear, bright colorways. She began working with fiber in 1996, primarily as a handspinner of Samoyed dog hair. Then she acquired two Angora rabbits as pets. As they quickly multiplied to 60, she tried blending angora with other fibers, and soon realized that it was difficult to sell only naturally colored yarn. Thus, her hand-dyeing career was born of necessity.

Joslyn decided to dye solid colors because she assumed they would be easy to reproduce. When she learned that they were not, she quickly switched to handpaints. In the same amount of time that it took to carefully kettle-dye two pounds of solids, she could process ten pounds of handpaint. "That really opened up a lot more avenues for me," Joslyn says.

Ironically, she finds her technique coming full circle as her customers ask for hand-dyed solids to accent her growing line of handpaint yarns. This approach is less intimidating for Joslyn, because the solids are complements to her colorways, rather than focal points. "Now I can attack it from a different angle," she adds.

Although Joslyn has no artistic training—she was a business major in college and spent years on the production line at General Motors before starting a family, she has been a knitter since she was 8 and is lucky enough to list Meg Swansen as her mentor. "Meg has been so helpful to me. She's very supportive and truly, if there is anyone who has given me a helping hand, it is her," Joslyn says. She first attended Meg's annual knitting camp in 1998 as a student. Now she is a vendor at all four sessions each summer.

Her first big market was the TKGA National Convention in Milwaukee in 1998. Joslyn laughs about how little yarn she had to show then. "I didn't know any better,""she says with a smile. "I basically had two colorways at that time." However, the positive response to her colors, coupled with the fact that she quickly sold everything, gave her the confidence to continue.

Everyday inspiration Even while studying business, Joslyn knew color would play a big part in her life. "I've always been intrigued with color." She acknowledges that even during her lean college days, when she could not afford fine yarns, she had to have the perfect color for every project.

One of her favorite colorways is Clear Lake, a lovely combination of multicolored blues and greens. As we drive to this colorway's namesake to photograph her yarns, Joslyn discusses environment, both in terms of her colorways and her physical workspace.

Color inspiration comes to Joslyn from everyday life: the mulberry tree in her backyard, her picnic spot at Clear Lake, the piñata used for her daughter's 6th birthday party. She remembers looking at the piñata and thinking, "If I could capture that, it would be really cool." The resultant colorway, called Party, is still her best seller,

Clockwise from top: A handpaint vest is knit and then felted; Joslyn developed this colorway, called Party, for her daughter's birthday.

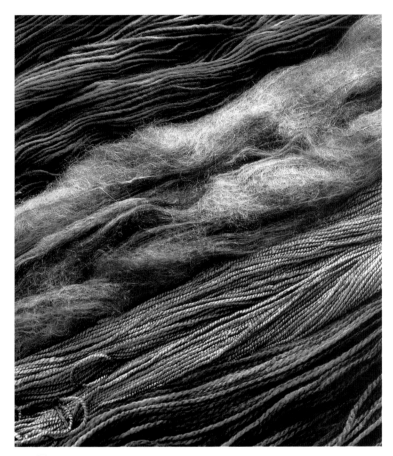

certain shades like yellow. "I detest squishing the dyes around with gloves," she adds. Her penchant for clear, bright hues leads her to dye what she considers "full-strength" colors rather than grays, blacks, and subdued shades.

When asked what her favorite colorways is, Joslyn replies, "Any new colorway is my absolute favorite until I dye a couple hundred pounds of it!" Currently, she rewinds and tags her skeins for the retail market. Because all of her fibers are available in all colorways, knitters can mix and match texture as well as color.

Each hand-dyer imprints his or her personal stamp on a colorway, Joslyn believes. And it is this particular use of color that knitters look for when purchasing handpainted yarns. "You either like the way I do yarn or you prefer somebody else's interpretation."

Building a business Joslyn is developing all aspects of her business—selling at festivals and conferences, expanding her mail-order clientele, and sending out a regular newsletter. Referrals are growing, her Web site is up and running, and although she mostly sells retail, she is beginning to invite wholesale accounts.

What is it like, to have a young, growing company? "Scary," says Joslyn. After the excitement of her reception into the hand-dye world, she feels that now she must live up to certain expectations. She is already meeting with designers and selecting yarns for new patterns and knitting kits. To keep from feeling overwhelmed, she reminds herself that the entire process is a series of small steps.

Knitter to knitter One of the appeals of Joslyn's fiber is its innate "knitability." An avid knitter, she selects yarns that she enjoys working with herself. She dyes a variety of textures and weights, and encourages knitters to "let the yarn do the talking." She also chooses to work with less common animal fibers; much of her yarn is a blend of angora or dog hair. Her best-selling yarn, Mohair Myst, is a luminous blend of 50% kid mohair and 50% merino.

Clockwise from top: Felted vest is knit in the colorway "Party"; hanks hang from a boat launch at Clear Lake; the colorway Clear Lake uses only two dyes.

incorporating seven colors that range from bright yellow to deep purple.

Like many new fiber artists, Joslyn's work environment is becoming ever more important as she experiences growing pains. Her dyeworks has expanded from the confines of her kitchen to the garage and finally to the basement, which she is currently remodeling. "I need a work space and a home space," Joslyn says, "And that's the hardest thing to juggle." She dyes fiber in spurts, depending upon the time of year, finding herself most productive in spring.

Less is more Joslyn's current palette consists of 18 colorways on animal fibers only. With names like Claret, Mulberries, and Denim, they incorporate from two to seven colors. "Two?" I ask incredulously. Joslyn shrugs. "If it works, why put any more on it?"

Because Joslyn recognizes that the various striping effects that space-dyeing can produce have given painted yarns a "bad rep" with some knitters, she alternates short and long stretches of color in the skeins. She avoids dip-dyeing, and instead favors blending techniques that segue colors into each other, except with

Below: The colorway Claret shown in several yarns and a knitted shawl is a testimony to Joslyn's belief that if a simple color progression works, there is no need to add any more dyes.

Right: By accident, our rowboat goes adrift on Clear Lake, laden with hundreds of Joslyn's handpaints. As repeated attempts to reach it with oars and hook it with fishing poles fail, Joslyn jumps in fully clothed to swim after the boat.

Painted yarn is not for everyone, cautions Joslyn. "The neat thing about hand-dyed yarn is that each skein is unique," she says, "but I think that is also the thing that gives people fits!" She adds that because she never dyes skeins of yarn exactly alike, she recommends knitting from two balls to maintain a consistent depth of color in any knitting project.

"Knitters are looking for a project that they can complete. They want to create something nice," Joslyn tells us, as we load skein after skein of handpainted yarn into a rowboat for the next photograph. "You can do anything with this yarn." As we slide the boat into Clear Lake, the late afternoon sun streaks the shadowed waters rippling around the bow, ringing the yarn with ever-changing patterns. The scene is so soothing and breathtakingly beautiful that we stand mesmerized—until we realize that someone has dropped the rope. Always ready for a challenge, it is Joslyn who plunges into the water to retrieve her precious cargo.

Future watch Joslyn's primary concern is how much more yarn she can paint within her limitations of space and time. To keep her current customers satisfied, she plans to let her business expand slowly. Her trade show experience has taught her that handpainted yarn is not a passing fad. Joslyn sees more knitters trying handpaints, "even in small hanks they can use for the yoke of a sweater."

Part of the increased popularity of handpainted yarns can be attributed to knitters becoming more educated about what to do with handpainted yarns, and Joslyn credits publications like *Sally Melville Styles* for making this possible. In *Styles,* Sally introduced a whole new way of knitting with many types of yarns. "Knitting like that opens people's eyes about what can be done with painted yarn."

After her new studio is complete, Joslyn hopes to return to her first love of knit and design. "I don't want to have to give up the knitting to do the dyeing," she says. "Right now, it's either/or, because there's just not enough time in the day to do both."

Felted friends designed by Bev Galeskas

Knitting is only half the fun of these vests. Fun to knit, fun to felt.

Intermediate

Sizes
3/4 (5/6)
Shown in size 3/4 (V-neck vest)
and 5/6 (Zippered vest).
Directions are for smallest size with
larger sizes in parentheses.
If there is only 1 set of numbers,
it applies to all sizes.

Finished measurements
Underarm 26 (30)"
Length 13½ (15½)"

Gauge
Before felting: 13 sts and 18 rows to
4"/10cm over St st using size
10½(7mm) needle.

MATERIALS
Yarn Joslyn's Fiber Farm *Midwest Shepherd's Blend* **MC** 2 (3) skeins Party, **CC** 1 skein Royal Blue (4oz/114g, 200yds/180m, 100% wool).
Needles Size 10½ (7mm) circular needle, 24"/60cm long, *or size to obtain gauge*. Spare circular needle in smaller size.
Extras Stitch holders, fine cotton yarn (for basting), large mesh laundry bag, washing machine, liquid dish-washing detergent; *for zippered vest:* 14"/35cm separating zipper cut to appropriate length.

NOTES
1 See *Techniques*, p. 228 for M1, short-row wraps, and 3-needle bind-off. *2* Work neck and armhole shaping as full-fashioned decreases. *3* Finished measurements will vary with the amount of felting. Size may be adjusted by amount of felting.

Full-fashioned decs
At beg of RS rows K1, ssk; *at end of RS rows* Work to last 3 sts, k2tog, k1.

V-NECK VEST
With MC, cast on 100 (116) sts. *Row 1* (WS) P94 (110), wrap next st and turn (W&T). *Row 2* K88 (104), W&T. *Row 3* P to st that was wrapped on last row, pick up the wrap and purl it tog with the next st, W&T. *Row 4* K to st that was wrapped on last row, pick up the wrap and knit it tog with the next st, W&T. Rep rows 3–4 four times more. (The last two wraps will be made on the edge sts.) *Next row* P to end. Beg with a k row, work even in St st until there are 46 (54) rows from beg.
Divide for fronts and back
Next row (WS) P23 (26) (left front), bind off 4 (6) sts (armhole), p until there are 46 (52) sts for back, bind off 4 (6) sts (armhole), p to end (right front). Mark this row with a pin in each of the 3 sections. Place left front and back on hold.

RIGHT FRONT
Shape neck and armhole
(RS) Dec 1 st at armhole edge every RS row five times, then at neck edge every 4th row 11 (12) times—7 (9) sts. Work even in St st until there are 54 (60) rows above marked underarm row. Cut yarn and place sts on hold.

LEFT FRONT
With RS facing, join yarn to left front at underarm. Work as for right front.

BACK
With RS facing, join yarn to back at underarm. Dec 1 st each side every RS row 5 times—36 (42) sts. Work even in St st until there are 51 (57) rows above the marked underarm row.
Shape neck
Next row (WS) P8 (10), bind off 20 (22) sts, p to end. *Next row* Working right shoulder only, knit, dec 1 st at neck edge. *Next row* Purl. Join right shoulders using 3-needle bind-off. With RS facing, join yarn to left shoulder at neck. Work as for left shoulder.

FINISHING
Outer band
(*Note* Before felting, the front edges of vest will gather into the band. This is necessary because St st loses more length than width when felted.)
With RS facing, join CC at right shoulder. Pick up and k22 (24) sts across back neck, 27 (30) sts along neck to base of neck shaping (1 st for every 2 rows), 3 sts close tog at base of neck shaping, 18 (22) sts along left front to beg of bottom shaping, 100 (116) sts along curved edge to end of bottom shaping (1 st in every st), 18 (22) sts along right front to base of neck shaping, 3 sts close tog at base of neck shaping, 27 (30) sts along neck to shoulder, place marker (pm) for beg and join—218 (250) sts. P 6 rnds (rev St st).
Join and bind off band
(*Note* Sts may be picked up in groups of 20 or more and worked off before next group is picked up.)
With the WS facing and spare circular needle, pick up the back loops of the pick-up row (CC loops). With WS facing, work 3-needle bind-off.
Armhole band
With RS facing, join CC at underarm. Pick up and k59 (67) sts around armhole, pm for beg of rnd and join. P 6 rnds (rev St st). Join and bind off as for outer band. Weave in all ends.

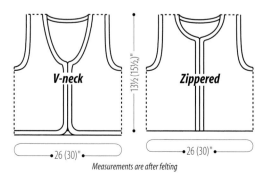

V-neck · 13½ (15½)" · *Zippered*

26 (30)" · 26 (30)"

Measurements are after felting

Felted friends

ZIPPERED VEST

Cast on 81 (94) sts. *Rows 1–3* Knit. *Row 4* (WS) Purl. *Row 5* K5, M1, *k4, M1; rep from* to last 4 (5) sts, k4 (5)—100 (116) sts. *Row 6* Purl. Work even in St st until there are 45 (53) rows from beg, end with a RS row.

Divide for fronts and back
Next row (WS) P23 (26) (left front), bind off 4 (6) sts (armhole), p until there are 46 (52) for back, bind off 4 (6) sts (armhole), p to end (right front). Mark this row with a pin in each of the 3 sections. Place left front and back on hold.

RIGHT FRONT
Shape armhole
(RS) Dec 1 st at armhole every RS row 5 times—18 (21) sts. Work even in St st until there are 24 (26) rows above marked underarm row, end with a WS row.
Shape neck
(RS) Dec 1 st at neck edge every RS row 11 (12) times—7 (9) sts. Work even in St st until there are 54 (60) rows above marked underarm row. Cut yarn and place sts on hold.

LEFT FRONT
With RS facing, join yarn to left front at underarm. Work as for right front.

BACK
Work as for back of V-neck vest.

FINISHING
Front and neck band
(*Note* Before felting, the front edges of vest will gather into the band. This is necessary because St st loses more length than width when felted.)

With RS facing, join CC at lower right front. Pick up and k35 (40) sts along right front to base of neck shaping, 3 sts close tog at base of neck shaping, 16 (18) sts along neck to shoulder, 22 (24) sts across back neck, 16 (18) sts along neck to base of neck shaping, 3 sts close tog at base of neck shaping, 35 (40) sts along left front—130 (146) sts. Beg with a WS knit row, work 6 rows of rev St st (p on RS, k on WS). Join and bind off band as for V-neck vest.
Armhole bands
Work as for V-neck vest. Weave in all ends.

FELTING VESTS
Prepare for felting
Using a fine cotton, baste fronts and sleeve openings closed using long sts. This will help the edges to felt to the same length.

Felting
Place vest in a large mesh bag. (This protects your washer's pump from the excess fiber that washes out during felting.) Set your washer for a delicate cycle, hot water, and maximum water level. Add a small amount (slightly less than a tablespoon) of a liquid dish detergent. Start machine and check progress every 5 minutes. Set washer back to agitate longer as needed. Do not let it drain and spin, as this may set a permanent crease in the felt. At each check, remove vest from the bag completely so it does not remain folded in the same position. As vest nears the desired size, begin checking more frequently. Basting cotton can be removed at this time. When correct size is reached, remove from washer. To remove soap, rinse in a sink, by hand, using water the same temperature used for felting. Agitation while rinsing may cause further shrinkage. Use several towels to remove as much water as possible. Lay vest on a flat surface and pull into shape, checking measurements. Allow to dry completely, away from heat and sunlight. For zippered vest, adjust length of zipper to match fronts and sew in place.

"Quick and easy to knit, these felt vests are the perfect hand knit garments for small children. No stitches to snag on little fingers and the multicolored handpainted yarn will help to hide the dribbles and spills that are a daily event at that age.

Handpainted yarn will take on a more subtle and muted appearance when felted, as shown in our before and after picture. Be sure to consider this when choosing colors. This is the time to be bold with your colorway choice."

Bev Galeskas

We fight the Labor Day traffic from St. Louis to Kansas City in the rising heat and humidity. The sky darkens. We try to ignore the claps of thunder that accompany us to Lawrence, Kansas. Sprinkles of rain smear the windshield by the time we pull up to the brick building that houses Traci Bunkers' new studio. A freight elevator takes us to the third floor and the 2600-square-foot loft destined to house Bonkers, Traci's hand-dye company.

Traci Bunkers

BONKERS HANDMADE ORIGINALS TRACI BUNKERS
Lawrence, Kansas

Top and right: Prepared batts ready for spinning; Traci Bunkers spins hand-dyed fiber into yarn for one of her many projects.

Below: A selection of current works-in-progress. In addition to her talents as a dyer, Traci designs knitwear for magazines and produces one-of-a-kind art pieces. Spare time finds her creating huge urns at a local arts center.

We find Traci Bunkers in transition, moving from a smaller studio downtown. It is a stone's throw from Yarn Barn, where she learned to knit and later to spin. Dyeing fleece began as a way to acquire colored spinning fiber, but soon Traci found herself dyeing for other spinners. She was heavily into experimentation. "I dyed my first fleece on a barbecue grill," Traci relates with a smile. "I never took a dye class."

Traci's unconventional approach extends to other media. Yarn fills pottery urns originally intended for houseplants, and a mosaic coffee table she crafted from flea-market dinnerware became a study in free-form color theory. For Traci, her pottery and mosaics are creative outlets not intended for the marketplace.

Traci researches her craft by reading and taking classes as often as she can. She particularly admires the knitting of Kathryn Alexander and the wild crochet techniques of Sylvia Cosh, both of whom stimulated her appetite for exploration. "Everything we experience in life, whether it's looking at a painting or talking to someone, I think it affects us," Traci observes. She enjoys what she calls "free-form work," a mixture of knit and crochet in all directions that she uses to produce signature hats, bags, and home décor items.

Going Bonkers Traci has reinvented her business through several moves over the past ten years. After the barbecue phase, she began designing one-of-a-kind machine-knit garments from commercial yarns in the privacy of her home basement. She also developed a random-dye technique to paint the cotton clothing she sold at art fairs. "It wasn't like tie-dyeing because I didn't tie anything. It's hard to explain," Traci admits.

Her desire to have her work be taken seriously coincided with a flood that drove her from the basement, and she rented a small studio downtown. Although she was dyeing more fiber, it was all going into her garments. Finally she decided to cut back on shows and drop machine knits altogether. From there, exploration and experimentation took her everywhere. At one point, she tried hand-dyed felt hats festooned with toy lobsters and snakes. This venture failed financially, but it opened

doors for her at an art gallery and also taught her lessons in mixed-media marketing. "Sometimes you have to make something that doesn't work so that you can understand why it didn't work. Then you know what to do the next time," she acknowledges.

Gradually, Traci rented more space to house fiber and a dye kitchen. Her dyeing became more production-oriented as she refocused on hand knits, custom-dyed fiber, and kits. In addition, she began designing for yarn companies and magazines. Once again, space considerations forced a move. She hopes the move to the brick warehouse is all Bonkers needs for the future.

Unusual fibers, extraordinary results These days, Traci estimates that she dyes as much yarn as spinning fiber. She custom-cards batts, which are wide sheets of parallel fibers arranged to provide easy drafting for the handspinner, in one of two ways. Either she thoroughly blends various fibers for a variegated look, or for more of a challenge, she cards "Mulligan Stew," in which the colors are arranged but are not blended. "I'll throw on some red wool and then some purple nylon—whatever I want," Traci explains. This batt spins into a funkier yarn. Traci

niques, most discovered though trial and error. She has been known to solar-dye fiber in fish aquariums, zap it in the microwave, or simply let it take over the sinks. Generally, she paints cotton and prefers to sprinkle powdered dye on wools. Sometimes she resorts to the dye pot to force color separation by fiber resists or to work with unconventional blends. For example, with a merino and tencel blend, the merino absorbs the dye but the tencel is only stained, which creates a beautiful watercolor effect.

Not surprisingly, when carding fiber, Traci does whatever appeals to her, blending nylon with wool, or cotton with mohair and wool, and using various staple lengths to promote color and textural complexity. The classes she teaches, such as Custom Carding and Knitting Socks From The Toe Up, emphasize this kind of exploration in what Traci hopes is a very freeing way. "When I first started teaching, it amazed me—people are so afraid to experiment and try things," Traci says. "Always, even as a little kid, I tried whatever I wanted to."

Clockwise from top: Traci created this mosaic table from odd pieces of old china; a Kansas cornfield in fall; combed top hand-dyed and ready for spinning.

often dyes yarn and fiber together for coordinating projects that may require felted or handspun accents.

Traci has found that the challenge in working with her favorite fibers—yak down, camel, and dog hair—is acquiring them. Sources shift with changes in the geopolitic. In contrast, color is easy; her combinations are organic and innate. Spinners come to her searching for exotic fibers and a wilder look. "I never really worry about whether colors are going to go together." Traci laughs. "I use all colors together all the time, and I think that looks great."

Inspiration comes to Traci both from city life and nature. "Although I live in Kansas, and people think of that as farm land, I live in a college town where people are really colorful in what they wear," she explains. Her downtown studio was a window on that urban world, and she also frequented a local garden nursery where she acquired many of the plants that fill her home. Whenever she's feeling out of sorts, she stops by the greenhouse "for a pick-me-up."

Anything goes Traci uses synthetic dyes on plant, animal, and manmade fibers. She employs a range of tech-

Business with Bunkers and Bonkers Bonkers, the fiber end of Traci's business, is split equally between retail and wholesale, between yarn and spinning fiber. In addition to selling at fiber festivals and from her studio, Traci markets Bonkers via the Internet and mail order and provides pattern support for knitters. To make it easier for customers to place orders, she recently started working on reproducible colorways.

When asked what she thinks knitters need to know about hand-dyed yarns, Traci laughs. "Not to be afraid to try different colors ... I have never held two yarns together that I wouldn't use in the same project." She feels hand-dyed yarns also produce a "fuller" look born of subtle shading within dramatic color variations. Ever the free spirit herself, she encourages knitters to be adventurous in choosing colors and to try different hand-dyed yarns within the same project.

Traci feels that her wild color sense paired with her sometimes funky designs add to the Bonkers appeal. The fact that knitters can begin a sweater by handspinning painted roving also holds a special attraction.

"Handspun garments have a lot more life to them," Traci says, "because the spinner/knitter has more input along the way in terms of weight, color, and texture."

When it comes to yarn, Traci dyes "all kinds, anything I can find!" In addition to naturals, she loves to over-dye commercial yarns. Her current best seller is a sport-weight wool she dyes for sock kits. She has found that knitters are becoming educated about hand-dyed yarns. "For a long time, people assumed that it was expensive," Traci says. "A lot of my yarns are less expensive than some of the commercial yarns."

Future watch Traci sees a trend of increased diversity in the fiber market. Not only has the quality of fiber risen, but colors have become brighter, and more multi-colored yarns are available. Commercial yarn companies have begun to produce natural fiber yarns with a hand-dyed look, in contrast to the acrylic space-dyes of years past. Traci welcomes this as a way to reach more knitters and open their minds to possibilities.

As we wander around the stacks of boxes and piles of bags and garments yet to be unpacked at Bonkers, it is obvious that no one would move this amount of equipment and inventory unless they had to. Traci nods. "The whole point of moving was to have more space so that I could have a better dye area," which will help Bonkers expand in terms of efficiency and the ability to carry inventory. Although she is not yet ready to send out color cards, Traci is working toward expanding her line of repeatable colorways.

And although she calls pattern writing her "bread and butter," Traci gets a much bigger charge out of dyeing,

and would like to place more emphasis on it as time goes on. We leave knowing Traci will continue her adventure with fiber and color, wherever it takes her and Bonkers.

Clockwise from top:
Batts on cornstalks; a batt opened to show subtle shading; a field of sunflowers; Traci wears her favorite hat among the flowers.

Mulligan stew pillow designed by Traci Bunkers

Everything but . . . is in this playful patchwork pillow.

MATERIALS

Yarn (Available as handspun yarn or as spinning fiber) Bonkers Handmade Originals *Handspun Merino 'n Rayon* 1 skein of yarn or bag of roving **A** Vinland Grape (1¾oz/50g, 80yds/73m handspun yarn or 4oz/114g roving, 70% merino, 30% rayon); *Handspun Mulligan Stew* 1 skein of yarn or spinning batt **B** Tomato, 2 skeins of yarn or 1 batt **C** Green Bean (1¾oz/50g, 75yds/68m skein or 3oz/85g batt, miscellaneous fibers).

Needles One pair size 7 (4.5mm) needles, *or size to obtain gauge.*

Extras Size F/5 (3.75 mm) crochet hook, cable needle (cn), 12" pillow form.

NOTES

1 See *Techniques*, p. 228 for sl 2-k1-p2sso, chain (ch), and double crochet (dc). *2* Each side is made up of 2 strips sewn together. *3* Pick up all stitches with right side facing.

STITCHES USED

Sand st even number of sts
Row 1 (RS) *K1, p1; rep from* across. *Row 2* (WS) Knit. Rep rows 1–2 for pat.

Seed st even number of sts
Row 1 *K1, p1; rep from* across. *Row 2* P the knit sts and k the purl sts. Rep row 2 for pat.

3/3 LC Sl 3 sts to cn, hold to front, k3, k3 from cn.

Make bobble (MB)
(K1, yo, k1) in same st, turn. P3, turn. Sl 2-k1-p2sso.

Bobble pat multiple of 4 sts plus 2
Rows 1–4 Work 4 rows St st. *Row 5* K2, [MB, k3] across. *Row 6* Purl. *Row 7* K4, [MB, k3] 4 times, k2. *Row 8* Purl. Rep rows 1–8 for pat.

SIDES make 2

Strip 1

Step 1: With B, cast on 22 sts. Work in Sand st until piece measures 3", end with a WS row. Change to C. *Row 1* (RS) Knit. *Row 2* K8, p6, k8. *Rows 3–8* Rep rows 1 and 2 three times. *Row 9* K8, 3/3 LC, k8. *Row 10* K8, p6, k8. Rep rows 1–10 until C section measures 4½", end with a WS row. Change to A. Work 8 rows of Bobble pat, then work in St st until piece measures 9" from beg. Bind off. Piece measures approx 5" by 9".

Step 2: With B, pick up and k42 sts along right edge. (WS) Beg with a p row, work 3 rows St st. Change to A. K 1 row, then work in Seed st until section measures 2" (7" total). Bind off.

Step 3: With C, pick up and k32 sts along edge with bobbles. *Beg with a p row, work 4 rows St st, then k 2 rows (1 garter ridge); rep from* once, then work 2 rows St st. Change to B. Work 2 rows St st, then k 2 rows. Bind off. Piece measures approx 12" by 7".

Strip 2

Step 1: With C, cast on 22 sts. Work in St st for 2", end with a WS row. Change to A. K 6 rows (3 garter ridges). Change to B. Work 8 rows of Bobble pat, then work in St st until piece measures 4½" from beg, end with a WS row. K 4 rows. Bind off. Piece measures approx 5" by 5".

Step 2: With A, pick up and k22 sts along left edge. Work in Sand st for 1". Change to B and work 14 rows as for Strip 1, Step 3 to color change. Change to C and k 8 rows (4 garter ridges). Change to A and work 4 rows St st. Bind off.

Step 3: With C, pick up and k22 sts along opposite edge of strip. Work in St st until piece measures 12" long. Bind off.

ASSEMBLY

With B bound-off edge of Strip 1 and C bound-off edge of Strip 2 at top, sew strips tog.

FINISHING

With WS of both pieces facing tog, join A in any corner with a sl st through both pieces. Ch 3 (counts as 1 dc), working through both pieces, work 2 more dc in same st, dc evenly around, working 3 dc in each corner, until 4th corner has been worked, leaving last side open. Insert pillow form. Continue dc pieces tog to beg. Join with a sl st in top of beg ch-3. Fasten off.

Intermediate

Finished measurements
12" square

Gauge
22 sts and 30 rows to 5"/12.5cm over St st using size 7 (4.5mm) needles.

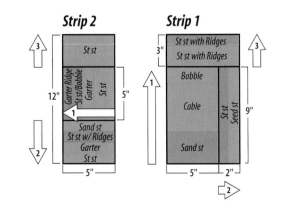

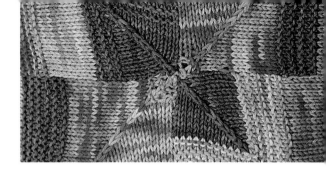

Mitered pillow designed by Traci Bunkers

Fractured miters lend a mosaic appeal to this punchy pillow.

MATERIALS

Yarn Bonkers Handmade Originals *Cotton 'n Merino* 1 skein each *A* Dorothy's Dream, *B* Indigo, *C* Konza Prairie (each 3½oz/100g, 215yds/195m, 80% pima cotton, 20% merino).

Needles One pair size 6 (4mm) needles, *or size to obtain gauge.*

Extras Size F/5 (3.75mm) crochet hook, 16" pillow form.

NOTES 1 See *Techniques*, p. 228 for sl 2-k1-p2sso, sl 2-p1-p2sso, chain (ch), and double crochet (dc). **2** Each side is made up of Squares 1–4.

STITCHES USED

St st pat

Row 1 (RS) K to 1 st before center st, sl 2-k1-p2sso, k to end—2 sts dec'd. *Row 2* (WS) P to 1 st before center st, sl 2-p1-p2sso, p to end—2 sts dec'd. Rep rows 1–2 for pat.

Garter st pat

Row 1 (RS) K to 1 st before center st, sl 2-k1-p2sso, k to end—2 sts dec'd. *Row 2* (WS) Knit—1 garter ridge made. Rep rows 1–2 for pat.

SIDES make 2

Square 1

With C, cast on 81 sts. *Begin Garter st pat* as follows: *Row 1* K39, sl 2-k1-p2sso (center st), k to end—79 sts. *Row 2* Knit. *Row 3* K38, sl 2-k1-p2sso, k to end—77 sts. *Row 4* Knit. *Rows 5–8* Work 4 more rows in Garter st pat (4 ridges total)—73 sts. *Rows 9–18* Work 10 rows in St st pat—53 sts. *Rows 19–30* With B, work 12 rows in Garter st pat—41 sts. *Rows 31–46* With A, work 16 rows in St st pat—9 sts. *Rows 47–52* With C, work 6 rows in Garter st pat—3 sts. *Row 53* Sl 2-k1-p2sso. Fasten off.

Square 2

With B, work as for Square 1 through row 8. *Rows 9–10* Work 2 more rows in Garter st pat (5 ridges total)—71 sts. *Rows 11–16* Work 6 rows in St st pat—59 sts. *Rows 17–26* With A, work 10 rows in Garter st pat—49 sts. *Rows 27–36* With C, work 10 rows in St st pat—29 sts. *Rows 37–42* With B, work 6 rows in Garter st pat—23 sts. *Rows 43–52* Work 10 rows in St st pat—3 sts. *Row 53* Sl 2-k1-p2sso. Fasten off.

Square 3

With A, work as for Square 1 through row 8. *Rows 9–14* Work 6 more rows in Garter st pat (7 ridges total)—67 sts. *Rows 15–26* With C, work 12 rows in St st pat—43 sts. *Rows 27–34* With B, work 8 rows in Garter st pat—35 sts. *Rows 35–48* With A, work 14 rows in St st pat—7 sts. *Rows 49–52* Work 4 rows in Garter st pat—3 sts. *Row 53* Sl 2-k1-p2sso. Fasten off.

Square 4

Work as for Square 2 through row 16. *Rows 17–18* Work 2 more rows in St st pat—55 sts. *Rows 19–24* With A, work 6 rows in Garter st pat—49 sts. *Rows 25–32* Work 8 rows in St st pat—33 sts. *Rows 33–42* With C, work 10 rows in Garter st pat—23 sts. *Rows 43–52* With B, work 10 rows in St st pat—3 sts. *Row 53* Sl 2-k1-p2sso. Fasten off.

ASSEMBLY

Sew squares tog in order clockwise with cast-on edges at outside and last sts at center.

FINISHING

With WS of both pieces tog, matching corner colors, and using crochet hook, join matching yarn in any corner with a sl st through both pieces. Ch 3 (counts as 1 dc), working through both pieces, work 2 more dc in same st, dc in each st across to last st before center seam. Change color (*see illustration*). Dc in each st across to corner, work 3 dc in corner st. Continue dc pieces tog as established until 4th corner has been worked, leaving last side open. Insert pillow form. Continue dc pieces tog to beg. Join with a sl st in top of beg ch-3. Fasten off.

Double crochet color change

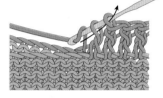

1 In last st before changing to new color, work until 2 loops remain on hook. With new color, yarn over and draw through last 2 loops on hook

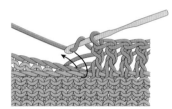

2 Continue with new color.

Intermediate

Finished measurements
16" square

Gauge
21 sts and 28 rows to 4"/10cm
over St st using size 6 (4mm) needles.

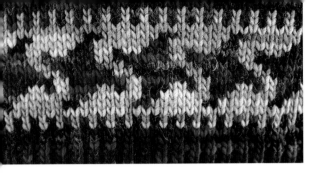

Nightshade designed by Traci Bunkers

Two skeins of one colorway of handpainted yarn are alternated to get the widest spread of colors in this mostly-stockinette stitch sweater.

Intermediate

Sizes

S (M, L, XL)

Shown in size M.

Directions are for smallest size with larger sizes in parentheses. If there is only 1 set of numbers, it applies to all sizes.

Finished measurements

Underarm 38 (42, 46, 50)"

Length 21 (22½, 24, 26½)"

Gauge

17 sts and 26 rows to 4"/10cm over St st using larger needles.

MATERIALS

Yarn Bonkers Handmade Originals *Worsted Wool* **MC** 5 (6, 7, 8) skeins Eudora Nightshade, **CC** 1 (1, 2, 2) skeins De Soto Sage (each 4oz/114g, 190yds/174m, 100% wool).

Needles One pair each sizes 6 and 8 (4 and 5mm) needles, *or size to obtain gauge.* Size 6 (4mm) circular needle, 16"/40cm long.

Extras Cable needle (cn), stitch holders.

NOTES

1 See *Techniques*, p. 228 for ssk and grafting. *2* To maintain continuity of hand-dyed yarn, alternate between 2 skeins, changing every 2–6 rows. Do not fasten off when alternating skeins; carry unused yarn along side edge.

STITCHES USED

2/2 LC Sl 2 to cn and hold to front, k2, k2 from cn.

Cable and eyelet pat over 26 sts

Rows 1 and 3 (RS) P2, [k4, p1, k1, yo, k2tog, p1] twice, k4, p2. *Row 2 and all WS rows* K2, [p4, k1, p3, k1] twice, p4, k2. *Row 5* P2, [2/2 LC, p1, k1, yo, k2tog, p1] twice, 2/2 LC, p2. *Rows 7–8* Rep rows 1–2. Rep rows 1–8 for pat.

Full-fashioned decs

At beg of RS rows K1, ssk; *at end of RS rows* Work to last 3 sts, k2tog, k1.

BACK

With smaller needles and MC, cast on 82 (90, 98, 106) sts. Work in k1, p1 ribbing for 2". Change to larger needles and beg with a k row, work 2 rows in St st. Work 16 rows of Houndstooth chart for body, then continuing with MC, work in St st until piece measures 11½ (13, 14, 16)" from beg, end with a WS row. Work rows 1–3 of Houndstooth chart. Fasten off CC. *Next row* (WS) With MC, purl.

Shape armholes

(RS) Bind off 6 sts at beg of next 2 rows—70 (78, 86, 94) sts. *Begin Cable and eyelet pat: Row 1* (RS) K22 (26, 30, 34), place marker (pm), work row 1 of Cable and eyelet pat over next 26 sts, pm, k to end. *Row 2* P to marker,

work row 2 of Cable and eyelet pat to marker, p to end. Continue working even in pat, working sts outside of markers in St st, until armhole measures 9 (9, 9½, 10)", end with a WS row. Place all sts on hold.

FRONT

Work as for back until armhole measures 7", end with a WS row.

Shape neck

(RS) K to marker, p2, sl next 22 sts onto holder for front neck, join a second ball of yarn and p2, k to end—24 (28, 32, 36) sts each shoulder. Working both sides at the same time, and working full-fashioned decs, dec 1 st each neck edge every RS row 6 (6, 7, 8) times—18 (22, 25, 28) sts each shoulder. Work even until armhole measures same as back. Place sts each side on hold.

SLEEVES

With smaller needles and MC, cast on 34 (36, 38, 40) sts. Work as for back and AT SAME TIME, inc 1 st each side (working incs into chart pat) on chart row 3, then every 4th row 12 (11, 12, 15) times more, then every 6th row 8 (8, 8, 6) times—76 (76, 80, 84) sts. Work even until piece measures 18½" from beg, ending with a WS row. Work rows 1–3 of Houndstooth chart. *Next row* (WS) With CC, purl. With CC, bind off all sts. Mark each side 1½" down from top of sleeve.

FINISHING

Graft shoulder seams, leaving 34 (34, 36, 38) sts on hold for back neck. With RS facing, circular needle, and CC, pick up and k34 (34, 36, 38) sts from back neck holder, 12 (12, 14, 16) sts along left neck edge, 22 sts from front neck holder, and 12 (12, 14, 16) sts along right neck edge—80 (80, 86, 92) sts. Pm for beg of rnd. Work in rnds in k1, p1 rib for 1". Bind off. Sew top of sleeves to armholes. Sew straight portion at top of sleeves (above markers) to bound-off armhole sts. Sew side and sleeve seams.

Cable and eyelet chart

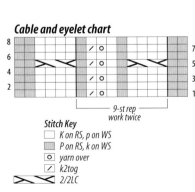

Stitch Key
☐ K on RS, p on WS
▨ P on RS, k on WS
◯ yarn over
╱ k2tog
✕ 2/2LC

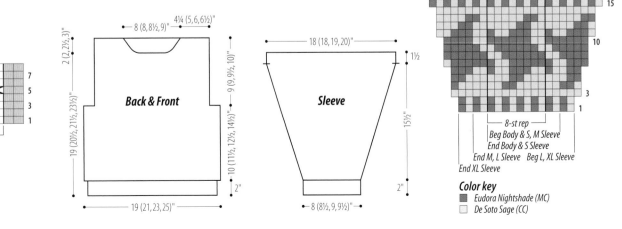

Back & Front
Sleeve
Houndstooth chart

8-st rep
Beg Body & S, M Sleeve
End Body & S Sleeve
End M, L Sleeve Beg L, XL Sleeve
End XL Sleeve

Color key
■ Eudora Nightshade (MC)
☐ De Soto Sage (CC)

Medusa de... Bunkers

*Frequent color ch...ple on this no-darn beret. Just leave
those long ends ...ation.*

MATERIALS

Yarn Bonkers Handmade Ori... 1 skein
each Cranberry, Emerald Fo... Amber
(each 1¾oz/50g, 184yds/168m, 100% wool).
Needles Size 3 (3.25mm) needles, *or size to obtain
gauge.* One pair straight needles, 16"/40cm long circular needle, and 2 double-pointed needles (dpn).
Extras Small crochet hook for chain stitching on top,
yarn needle.

NOTES

1 See Techniques p. 228 for short-row wraps, chain (ch),
I-cord, cable cast-on, and grafting. *2* Hat is made up of
4 panels with triangles that form the top. *3* Leave
approximately 6-10" tails when changing colors. These
will be worked as I-cord or decorative stitching when
hat is finished.

STITCH USED

Nop pat multiple of 6 sts plus 4
Row 1 (RS) K2, *[k3, turn; p3, turn] 4 times, wrapping next
st before turning at end of every k side and once at end
of 2nd p side, k6 (3 sts you've been working and then
next 3 sts—one nop completed); rep from* across, end
k2. *Row 2* Purl. *Row 3* K5, *[k3, turn; p3, turn] 4 times
wrapping next st before turning at end of every p side
and once at end of 2nd k side, k6; rep from* across, end
last rep with k5. *Row 4* Purl. Rep Rows 1–4 for pat.

PANEL make 4

(*Note* For each panel, shift color sequence by 1. *See
Sequence chart.*)

Side section

With A, cast on 42 sts. **Row 1** (WS) Purl. **Row 2** (RS) K2 A,
k2 B, k2 A; rep from across. **Row 3** P2 A, *p2 B, p2 A; rep
from* across. **Rows 4–7** Rep rows 2 and 3 twice more. K
2 rows C, k 2 rows D (2 garter ridges). **Next row** (RS)
With A, knit, inc 4 sts evenly spaced—46 sts. **Next row**
Purl. **Begin Nop pat** Work rows 1–4 of Nop pat twice,
then rows 1–2 once, changing colors randomly after
any completed nop.

Make flap

(RS) With A, beg with a k row, work 4 rows St st. **Next
row: turning ridge** (RS) Purl. Beg with a p row, work 4
rows St st. With dpn and WS facing, pick up each st of
row before flap. **Joining row** (WS) Fold at turning ridge,
and with both needles parallel to each other, k first st of
each needle tog across.

I-cord fringe

First I-cord (RS) *K5, sl sts back to LH needle; rep from*
7 times more. Cut yarn. Thread through yarn needle,
draw yarn through sts and pull tightly. Insert yarn needle down through center of I-cord and pull yarn

through. Cut yarn at base of I-cord. *2nd I-cord* With any
color, *k next 4 sts, sl sts back to LH needle; rep from*
desired number of times. Finish off as for first I-cord.
Continue across as for 2nd I-cord, working last I-cord
over last 5 sts.

Make top triangle

With A and WS facing, pick up 45 sts along I-cord base
at flap joining row. **Row 1** (RS) K1, k2tog, k to last 3 sts,
k2tog, k1—2 sts dec'd. **Row 2** Knit. Rep last 2 rows until
5 sts remain, changing colors randomly during any row
as desired, end with a WS row. **Next row** K1, k3tog, k1.
Next row Knit. **Next row** K3tog. Fasten off.

FINISHING

Sew panels tog in order made along sides and top triangle edges, leaving ends of flaps open.

Side section I-cords

On each side section, pull the tails through to RS and
work I-cord as follows: With RS facing and dpn, pick up
2 sts where tail is pulled through, work I-cord over 2 sts
for desired length. Thread through yarn needle, draw
yarn through sts and pull tightly. Insert yarn needle
down through center of I-cord and to WS. Pull yarn
through and cut.

Top

Pull tails through to RS. Using tails, randomly work 2-st
I-cord as for side sections and with crochet hook, work
chain stitch (*see illustration*) as desired. While working
chain st, randomly work picot as follows: ch 3, sl st in
first ch, continue working chain st on hat.

I-cord band

With circular needle, cranberry and RS facing, pick up
and k40 sts per panel along cast-on edge—160 sts.
Using cable cast-on, cast on 5 sts onto LH needle. Work
attached I-cord as follows: *k4, k2tog tbl, sl 5 sts from RH
needle back to LH needle; rep from* around until 5 sts
remain. Graft 5 edging sts to cast-on sts.

Embellishing with chain stitch

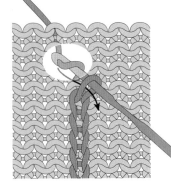

Intermediate

Size
One size fits all

Finished measurements
circumference 21"
Height 4"

Gauge
28 sts and 28 rows to 4"/10cm
over Garter st (k every row) using
size 3 (3.25mm) needles.

Sequence chart
Panel

1	2	3	4	
A	B	C	D	Cranberry
B	C	D	A	Emerald forest
C	D	A	B	Plum
D	A	B	C	Burnt amber

Chart note:
*For each side panel, follow each letter
over to the right to determine color.*

To reach Nebraska, we drive west into the sunset, losing an hour of time over the windswept prairies of South Dakota. As we cross the Missouri River, the topography changes almost immediately. We pass Wall Drug, a landmark since the dust bowl days of the Depression. As we approach the Badlands, the sandstone shapes banded with subtle colors of striated rock remind us of handpainted hanks. From there, it is a southerly journey through prairie dotted with cattle to Mitchell, Nebraska and Brown Sheep Company.

BROWN SHEEP COMPANY PEGGY WELLS

Mitchell, Nebraska

The Browns

BROWN SHEEP COMPANY PEGGY WELLS
Mitchell, Nebraska

A family enterprise Brown Sheep is widely known for high-quality, all-purpose yarns available in a variety of weights and solid colors. But unlike most major yarn companies, Brown Sheep sells only the yarns it spins at a small factory beside the home of Harlan and Janet Brown. The Browns are unpretentious people with well-deserved pride in the company they founded just over 20 years ago. In those days, they were sheep ranchers seeking a way to add value to their product. Now, like many yarn manufacturers, they are riding the current wave of handpaint popularity by offering their version as a sideline.

Brown Sheep's handpainted yarns are dyed on-site by Bev Ross, who joined the company more than 12 years ago. Although handpainted yarn represents less than 2% of Brown Sheep's sales, Peggy Wells, the Browns' daughter and company manager since 1999, sees it as an important collaborative effort within the company.

Clockwise from top:
A selection of Kaleidoscope, a handpainted cotton/wool blend; wheel from a covered wagon at Chimney Rock; a wagon laden with hand-painted yarn; Forest Floor, a colorway used in Beth Brown-Reinsel's gansey.

Always the "practical pragmatist," Peggy is aware that her recent arrival at Brown Sheep brings advantages and disadvantages. "We didn't get to create everything," she admits, "but the advantage is, we can ask a lot of questions." She recalls a time when Harlan began "messing with handpaint" in the late '80s. On weekends, Peggy would "dabble in the back room" with him, painting as many skeins as possible when no one was around to see their mess. "We had a wonderful time," Peggy remembers. "Dad and I both enjoy lots of bright, clear colors." And the results? "Our technique was not very good," she says with a laugh. "We hadn't learned yet that we had to use heat to set the color."

When it came time to lay down the actual colorways, Michelle Wiplinger, a colorist, was consulted. With her help, Brown Sheep's first set of colorways was developed, with names like Tropical Water, Forest Floor, and Strawberry Patch. Soon after, Peggy and Bev decided to expand their line to cottons. "We had lots of trial and error, lots of rejects," Bev says, remembering those early days.

One batch at a time Bev processes all of the hand-paints in the back room of Brown Sheep Company, an area that started out as play space, but is now known as "the lab." Here, she has an array of modified commercial dye equipment at her disposal, from an extractor that spins the yarn damp-dry to an autoclave that steam-sets the yarn. And although she paints with commercial dyes, she doesn't have to mix them. Brown Sheep's dye-master pours the colors she needs from the bulk dyes used on the production line. To her, following a dye recipe is "much like baking cookies."

that with the addition of handpainted yarn, "Brown Sheep can now offer it all: the combination of handcraft with beautiful colors and the feel of good fiber." When knitters buy Brown Sheep Paints, they are looking for consistent quality in both spinning and dyeing, as well as the brighter, more brilliant colors from the Brown Sheep line.

Brown Sheep is a wholesale company with sales reps across the United States and Canada. In addition to selling yarns in hundreds of stores, Brown Sheep sells to rug makers of the Navajo Nation and clothing manufacturers such as Ralph Lauren, and even to handpaint competitors. "I don't see other hand-dyers as competitors; I want to see them using a good product," Peggy asserts.

The handpaints are marketed along with the rest of Brown Sheep's line through national advertising and existing accounts. The growing demand for handpainted yarns has prompted Peggy to increase their pattern support. Rather than using the yarn only as an accent, she plans to show garments knit entirely in painted yarn.

Clockwise from top: Close-up of Handpaint Originals, a handpainted mohair/wool blend; an afghan knit from Brown Sheep yarn displayed on the back of an historic wagon; hanks of Kaleidoscope hang from the wagon.

Along the way, Bev has developed her own technique. She begins by dyeing large yarn reelings in a light base color. The hanks are then stretched over a wheel, where she applies diamond and patchwork patterns with each of the colors in the colorway until the yarn is completely painted. These reelings are then dried and broken down into small retail hanks like any other Brown Sheep yarn. Allowing an hour for each dye skein, Bev can produce just over twenty pounds a day. She has never had a back order.

Although Brown Sheep mills a variety of natural-fiber yarns, their handpaint line consists of just two. The first and most popular is Handpaint Originals, a 70% mohair/30% wool blend available in nine variegated colorways and ten new handpainted solids. Peggy points out that the high percentage of mohair adds sheen to the yarn, lending eye appeal along with a soft hand. A more recent addition is Kaleidoscope, an 80% cotton/20% wool blend in six colorways. Available in 50-gram mini-hanks, both variegated yarns sell well year-round and have built-in color coordination with the solids in Brown Sheep's standard line.

Rounding out the business The year 2000 marked Brown Sheep's 20th anniversary, and Peggy believes

Future watch Bev Ross would like a dyeing assistant so that she can experiment with more yarns and colors. She has her eye on Fantasy Lace, a wool boucle that Brown Sheep already produces in solids. As for handpainted yarn, "I love it," she says. "I hope everybody tries it at least once." With every reel of yarn, she tries to create a unique color repeat. This adds excitement to each skein. "You never know what kind of pattern you're going to have until you've knit it."

Peggy feels that some colorways have run their course and that it is time to develop new ones that will better support Brown Sheep's main line of solids. The handpainted yarn is just now taking off. She is fascinated by the number of people who want to paint yarn as well as knit with it. Handpainted yarn appeals to the individual who desires to be different, Peggy observes. "There is a uniqueness there that is almost unspoken."

Great Plains socks designed by Beth Brown-Reinsel

A little color goes a long way in handpainted socks sparked with coordinating solids.

MATERIALS
Yarn Brown Sheep *Handpaint Originals* **MC** 2 (3, 3) skeins HP70 Forest Floor; **A** 1 skein HP75 Cross-country Green; **B** 1 skein HP55 Ink Blue (1¾oz/50g, 88yds/80m, 70% mohair, 30% wool).
Needles One pair each sizes 2 and 4 (2.75 and 3.5mm) needles, *or size to obtain gauge.* Four size 4 (3.5mm) double-pointed needles (dpn).
Extras Cable needle (cn), stitch marker, bobbins.

NOTES
1 See *Techniques,* p. 228 for intarsia knitting, ssk, and grafting. *2* Leg is worked flat, then joined for heel and worked in rounds. *3* Work cables in A and B with a separate bobbin; twist yarns at color change to avoid holes. Work MC across entire row, carrying across the back of cables. *4* Slip all stitches purlwise.

STITCHES USED
2/2 LC worked over 4 sts
Sl 2 sts to cn, hold to front, k2; k2 from cn.
2/2 RC worked over 4 sts
Sl 2 sts to cn, hold to back, k2; k2 from cn.

LEG
With smaller needles and MC, cast on 46 (50, 54) sts. *Row 1* (WS) *P1, k1; rep from* across. *Row 2* *P1, k1 through back loop (tbl); rep from* across. Rep rows 1–2 three times more. Change to larger needles. *Next row* (WS) P10 (11, 12); join A and p4; continuing with MC, p18 (20, 22); join B and p4; continuing with MC, p10 (11, 12). Work 2 rows in St st in established colors. *Next row* With MC, k10 (11, 12); with B, work 2/2 RC; continuing with MC, k18 (20, 22); with A, work 2/2LC; continuing with MC, k10 (11, 12). Continue in colors as established in St st, twisting yarn at color changes to avoid holes and crossing cables every 4th row, until piece measures 7" from beg, end with a WS row. *Next row* (RS) K2tog, k to first cable, ssk, k2tog, k to next cable, ssk, k2tog, k to last 2 sts, ssk—40 (44, 48) sts. Fasten off A and B.

Begin working in rnds
Evenly distribute the sts on 3 dpns and join. With MC, knit for ½". *Next rnd* K to last 10 (11, 12) sts.

Heel flap
Onto empty dpn, k last 10 (11, 12) sts, then k10 (11, 12) sts of beg of rnd onto same dpn—20 (22, 24) sts for heel flap. Turn. Fasten off MC. With A, work heel sts only as follows, leaving remaining sts for instep unworked. *Row 1* (WS) Sl 1 with yarn in front (wyif), p19 (21, 23). *Row 2* *Sl 1 with yarn in back (wyib), k1; rep from* across. Rep rows 1–2 until heel flap measures 2¼ (2¼, 2½)", end with a WS row.

Turn heel
Row 1 (RS) K12 (14, 15), ssk, turn. *Row 2* Sl 1wyif, p4 (6, 6), p2tog, turn. *Row 3* Sl 1 wyib, k4 (6, 6), ssk, turn. Rep rows 2–3 until 6 (8, 8) sts remain, end with a WS row.

Heel gusset
With MC, k6 (8, 8) heel sts, pick up and k10 (12, 14) sts along edge of heel flap. With 2nd needle, k20 (22, 24) instep sts. With 3rd needle, pick up and k10 (12, 14) sts along other edge of heel flap, then k3 (4, 4) from 1st needle. Rnd now begins here (center of heel)—46 (54, 60) sts. Place marker for beg of rnd. *Rnd 1* K to last 3 sts on 1st needle, k2tog, k1; on 2nd needle, k across; on 3rd needle, k1, ssk, k to end—2 sts dec'd. *Rnd 2* Knit. Rep rnds 1–2 two (four, five) times more—40 (44, 48) sts.

Foot
Work even in St st until foot measures 6 (7, 7½)" long—or 2¼ (2¼, 2½)" less than desired length. Fasten off MC.

Toe
Rnd 1 With B, on 1st needle, k to last 3 sts, k2tog, k1; on 2nd needle, k1, ssk, k to last 3 sts, k2tog, k1; on 3rd needle, k1, ssk, k to end. *Rnd 2* Knit. Rep rnds 1–2 until 16 sts remain. K4 sts from 1st needle onto 3rd needle. Graft sts tog. Sew leg seam. For second sock, reverse the colors of the cables.

Intermediate

Sizes
S (M, L)
Shown in size M.
Directions are for smallest size with larger sizes in parentheses.
If there is only 1 set of numbers, it applies to all sizes.

Finished measurements
Foot circumference 8 (8¾, 9½)"

Gauge
20 sts and 28 rnds to 4"/10cm over St st on larger needles.

Great Plains gansey designed by Beth Brown-Reinsel

Intarsia cables help give a handpaint twist to the traditional gansey.

MATERIALS
Yarn Brown Sheep *Handpaint Originals MC* 10 (11, 13, 15) skeins HP70 Forest Floor, **A** 4 (5, 5, 6) skeins HP75 Cross-country Green, **B** 3 (4, 4, 5) skeins HP55 Ink Blue (each 1¾oz/50g, 88yds/80m, 70% mohair, 30% wool).
Needles One pair each sizes 4 and 6 (3.5 and 4mm) needles, *or size to obtain gauge.* Size 4 (3.5mm) circular needle, 16"/40cm long.
Extras Cable needle (cn), stitch markers, bobbins.

NOTES
1 See *Techniques*, p. 228 for M1, intarsia knitting, ssk, and sl 2-k1-p2sso. *2* Work cables in A and B with a separate bobbin; twist yarns at color change to avoid holes. Work MC across entire row, carrying across the back of cables.

STITCHES USED
3/3 LC worked over 6 sts
Sl 3 sts to cn, hold to front, k3; k3 from cn.
3/3 RC worked over 6 sts
Sl 3 sts to cn, hold to back, k3; k3 from cn.
4/4 LC worked over 8 sts
Sl 4 sts to cn, hold to front, k4; k4 from cn.
4/4 RC worked over 8 sts
Sl 4 sts to cn, hold to back, k4; k4 from cn.
Seed St over odd number of sts
Row 1 *K1, p1; rep from* across. *Row 2* P the knit sts and k the purl sts. Rep row 2 for pat.

BACK
Bottom welt
With smaller needles, cast on 90 (100, 110, 120) sts. Work in Seed st for 1¾", end with a WS row. Change to larger needles. *Set up pats: Row 1* (RS) Work 7 sts in Seed st, place marker (pm), k to last 7 sts, pm, work 7 sts in Seed st. *Row 2* Work 7 sts in Seed st, p to marker, work 7 sts in Seed st. *Row 3* Work 7 sts in Seed st, k9 (12, 13, 14), M1, k1, M1, [k13 (14, 16, 18), M1, k1, M1] 4 times, k10 (13, 14, 15), work 7 sts Seed st—100 (110, 120, 130) sts. *Row 4* Rep row 2. *Row 5* Work 7 sts Seed st, k8 (11, 12, 13), pm, work 3/3 LC, pm, k9 (10, 12, 14); join A and work 4/4 LC; continuing with MC, k9 (10, 12,14), pm, work 3/3 LC, pm, k9 (10, 12, 14); join B and work 4/4 RC; continuing with MC, k9 (10, 12, 14), pm, work 3/3 LC, pm, k8 (11, 12, 13), work 7 sts Seed st. *Row 6* Continuing in colors as established, work in St st with first and last 7 sts in Seed st, crossing cables every 8th row, until piece measures 5" from beg. Continue working in pat, working 1 less st in Seed st every row (and 1 more st in St st) at beg and end, tapering toward edges. When Seed st tapering is complete, cast on 1 st each edge for selvages—102 (112, 122, 132) sts. Continue working in St st and cables until piece measures 12", end with a WS row. *Next row*

Removing all markers, work to first cable, ssk, k2, k2tog, work across to last cable, ssk, k2, k2tog—98 (108, 118, 128) sts, and all 3/3 cables ended (work in St st). Work even in pat for 6 rows. Change to smaller needles.

UPPER BODY
Next row (WS) Work 8 rows, working MC in garter st (k every row) and A and B in established pat. *Next row* (WS) K to cable, p8 B, k to cable inc 1 (dec 1, dec 1, dec1) st, p8 A, k to end—99 (107, 117, 127) sts. Fasten off MC. Change to larger needles. With A, k28 (32, 35, 38), p1, join B, k4 sts; with A, k4 sts; with B, p1, k23 (23, 27, 31), p1; join A, k4; with B, k4; with A, p1, k28 (32, 35, 38). *Begin charts: Row 1* (WS) With A, p3 (2, 5, 5), work 17 sts of Chart A row 1, p8 (13, 13, 16), k1; with B, p4 sts; with A, p4; with B, k1, p23 (23, 27, 31), k1; with A, p4; with B, p4; with A, k1, p8 (13, 13, 16), work 17 sts of Chart A row 1, p3 (2, 5, 5). *Row 2* With A, k3 (2, 5, 5), work 17 sts of Chart A row 2, k8 (13, 13, 16), p1; with A and B, work 4/4 LC; with B, p1, k1 (1, 3, 5), work 21 sts of Chart B row 1, k1 (1, 3, 5), p1; with A and B, work 4/4 RC; with A, p1, k8 (13, 13, 16), work 17 sts of Chart A row 2, k3 (2, 5, 5). Continue in pats as established working Chart A in outer sections, Chart B in center section, and colors A and B in 4/4 cable pats until Chart A complete. *Next row* (RS) With A, k9 (12, 15, 16) sts, work Chart A row 1, k2 (3, 3, 5) sts, continue in pats across to outer section, k2 (3, 3, 5) sts, work Chart A row 1, k9 (12, 15, 16) sts. Continue in pats, working Chart C above completed Chart B, then Chart B again; and working third Chart A as for first. When all charts completed, continue 4/4 cable pats and work areas above charts A and B in St st until piece measures 26" from beg. Bind off all sts in established colors.

FRONT
Work as for Back omitting Chart C and working Chart B twice through row 32. Continue last 4 rows of chart and dec both cables as follows: *Row 33* Ssk, k4, k2tog; *Row 35* Ssk, k2, k2tog—4 sts each cable section. When second chart B completed, continue working in pat, working area above Chart B in St st until piece measures 23" from beg, end with a RS row.
Shape neck
Next row (RS) Work 28 (32, 35, 38) sts in pat, bind off 35 (35, 39, 43) sts, work across in pat. Continue working even in Chart A until piece measures same as Back. Bind off all sts.

SLEEVES
With smaller needles and MC, cast on 44 (44, 48, 48) sts. *Row 1* (WS) Work in Seed st. *Row 2* Work 18 (18, 20, 20) sts in Seed st; pm, join A and k4, join B and k4, pm; continuing with MC, work across in Seed st. *Row 3* Work

Great Plains gansey

in Seed st to marker; p4 A, p4 B; continuing with MC, work across in Seed st. **Row 4** Work in Seed st to marker; with A and B, work 4/4 LC; continuing with MC, work across in Seed st. Continue in colors and pats as established, crossing cables every 8th row, until piece measures 3 (3, 3½, 3½)" from beg, end with a WS row. Change to larger needles. **Next row** (RS) With MC, knit inc 2 sts evenly to marker, with A and B, work 4/4 LC; continuing with MC, knit inc 2 sts evenly across—48 (48, 52, 52) sts. Continue as established, AND AT SAME TIME, inc 1 st each side every 3rd row 0 (0, 0, 5) times, then every 4th row 11 (11, 5, 19) times, then every 5th row 8 (8, 14, 0) times—86 (86, 90, 100) sts. Work even until piece measures 16 (16, 17, 17)" from beg. **On next 2 RS rows**, dec 1 st in each half of 4/4 LC as for front—82 (82, 86, 96) sts. Work even until piece measures 17 (17, 18, 18)" from beg. Bind off in pat.

FINISHING

Block pieces. Sew shoulder seams. Place markers 8½ (8½, 9, 10½)" down from shoulders on front and back. Sew top of sleeves between markers with cable at shoulder seam. Sew sleeve seams. Sew side seams leaving bottom open at Seed st for slits.

Neckband

With circular needle and MC, pick up and k35 (35, 39, 43) sts across back neck, 17 sts down front neck, 35 (35, 39, 43) sts across front neck, 17 sts up front neck—104 (104, 112, 120) sts. Join and work in rnds as follows: **Rnds 1, 3, and 5** Knit. **Rnds 2, 4, and 6** Purl, working sl 2-k1-p2sso at each corner. **Rnd 7** Knit, working sl 2-k1-p2sso at each corner. Bind off.

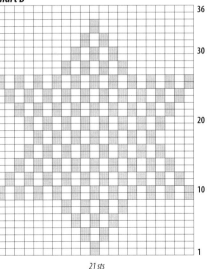

Chart A

17 sts

Chart B

21 sts

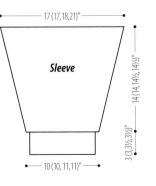

Back & Front

Sleeve

Stitch Key

☐ K on RS, p on WS
▨ P on RS, k on WS

Chart Notes

Charts may beg with a RS or WS row. Follow instructions carefully.

Chart C

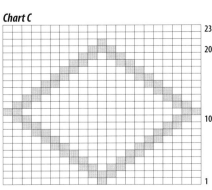

21 sts

Northern

To reach our next stop, we fly to Toronto and rent a car. As we drive north and west of the city, the urban landscape almost immediately gives way to rolling fields. Soon we are passing through the Canadian countryside. Brick farmhouses stand beside the remains of ancient barns, separated from distant neighbors by stone walls and rail fences. Victorian houses and churches with tall steeples adorn the towns. Just when we fear we are lost, Koigu Wool Designs, or Koigu, as it is popularly known, appears on our left.

At the pond, we pause for reflection.
As we gaze at the stilled waters,
our thoughts pool. A slight breeze
ripples the surface. As the doubled
image washes over us, we are
reminded that the ability to see
begins with stillness.

KOIGU WOOL DESIGNS MAIE & TAIU LANDRA
Maritime mates designed by Maie Landra

A special highlighting technique used in this handpainted yarn prevents stacking. For a nautical look, add stripes in a coordinating solid.

MATERIALS
Yarn Koigu *Painter's Palette Premium Merino* (each 1¾oz/50g, 175yds/160m, 100% wool) #P513 **Toddler set, turtle:** 4 (5) skeins, **Leggings:** 3 skeins; **Pullover: MC** 6 (6, 6, 7) skeins. *Premium Merino* **Pullover: CC** 6 (6, 6, 7) skeins #2170 Navy.
Needles One pair size 3 (3.25mm) needles, *or size to obtain gauge*.
Extras Crochet hook size B/1 (2.5mm). *For toddler set:* Stitch holders and markers, ¾yd of ¾" waistband elastic.

NOTES
1 See *Techniques*, p. 228 for chain (ch), single crochet (sc), ssk, and short-row wraps.

PULLOVER
BACK
With MC, cast on 126 (140, 154, 168) sts. Work 12 rows in St st (k on RS, p on WS). Change to CC, work 12 rows in St st. Continue alternating colors every 12 rows until piece measures 21 (21, 21, 23)" from beg, end with a WS row.
Shape neck
Next row (RS) K49 (53, 58, 63), bind off next 28 (34, 38, 42) sts for neck, join a second ball of yarn and k to end. Working both sides at the same time, at each neck edge, dec 1 st every row 7 times—42 (46, 51, 56) sts each shoulder. Bind off all sts.

FRONT
Work as for back until piece measures 20½ (20½, 20½, 22½)", end with a WS row.
Shape neck
Next row (RS) K49 (53, 58, 63), bind off next 28 (34, 38, 42) sts for neck, join a second ball of yarn and k to end. Working both sides at the same time, at each neck edge, dec 1 st every row 4 times, then every other row 3 times—42 (46, 51, 56) sts each shoulder. Work even until piece measures same as back. Bind off all sts.

SLEEVES
Cast on 60 sts. Work in 12-row stripe pat as for back and AT SAME TIME, inc 1 st each side every other row 15 times, then every 4th row 25 times—140 sts. Work even until piece measures 16" from beg. Bind off all sts.

FINISHING
Block pieces. Sew right shoulder seam.
Neckband
With MC and WS facing, pick up and k84 (96, 104, 112) sts evenly around neck edge, picking up underneath bound-off sts at center of front and back neck. Work in Rev St st (p on RS, k on WS) for 12 rows. Bind off loosely. Sew left shoulder and neckband seam. Fold neckband in half and sew to inside along pick-up row. Place markers 10" down from shoulders on front and back. Sew top of sleeves between markers. Sew side and sleeve seams, matching stripes.
Edging
With MC and crochet hook, work 4 rnds of sc around bottom of pullover and sleeves.

TODDLER TURTLE
Back
Cast on 84 (91) sts. Work in St st (k on RS, p on WS) for 8 (9)", end with a WS row.
Shape armhole
(RS) Bind off 5 sts at beg of next 2 rows—74 (81) sts. Work even in St st until armhole measures 4½ (5)", end with a WS row.
Shape neck
Next row (RS) K25, place next 24 (31) sts on hold for neck, join a second ball of yarn and k to end. Working both sides at the same time, at each neck edge, dec 1 st every row 5 times—20 sts each shoulder. Bind off all sts.

FRONT
Work as for back until armhole measures 2½ (2)", end with a WS row.
Shape neck
Next row (RS) K30 (33) sts, place next 14 (15) sts on hold for neck, join a second ball of yarn and k to end. Working both sides at the same time, dec 1 st at each neck edge every RS row 10 (13) times as follows: Work to 3 sts before neck edge, ssk, k1, then at other neck edge, k1, k2tog, work to end—20 sts each shoulder. Work even until armhole measures same as back. Bind off all sts.

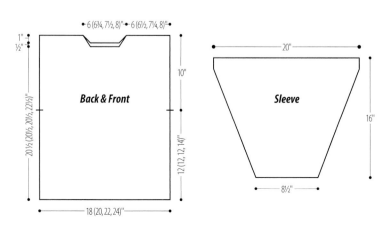

6 (6¾, 7½, 8)" — 6 (6½, 7¼, 8)"
1"
½"
10"
Back & Front
20½ (20½, 20½, 22½)"
12 (12, 12, 14)"
18 (20, 22, 24)"

20"
Sleeve
16"
8½"

Maritime mates

SLEEVES

Cast on 50 (54) sts. Work in St st and AT SAME TIME, inc 1 st each side every 6th row 10 (12) times—70 (78) sts. Work even until piece measures 8 (9½)" from beg. Bind off all sts. Mark each side ¾" down from top.

FINISHING

Block pieces. Sew right shoulder seam.

Turtleneck

With RS facing, pick up and k16 (22) sts along front neck to holder, k14 (15) sts from holder, pick up and k20 (26) sts to back neck holder, k24 (31) sts from holder, pick up and k4 sts to end—78 (98) sts. Work in k1, p1 rib for 2½ (3)". Bind off loosely. Sew left shoulder and turtle-neck seam. Sew top of sleeves to armholes. Sew straight portion at top of sleeves (above markers) to bound-off armhole sts. Sew side and sleeve seams.

Edging

Work edging around bottom of pullover, sleeves, and around neck as follows: with crochet hook and yarn, work 1 rnd single crochet. **Next (picot) rnd** Ch 1, *sc in next sc, in next sc work (sc, ch 3, sc), sc in each of next 2 sc; rep from* around. Fasten off.

TODDLER LEGGINGS

Left leg

Cast on 46 (52) sts. Work in St st and AT SAME TIME, inc 1 st each side every 4th row 21 (22) times—88 (96) sts. Work even in St st until piece measures 11 (12)" from beg, end with a WS row.

Shape crotch

(RS) Bind off 3 sts at beg of next 2 rows, then dec 1 st each side every 8th row 6 (8) times—70 (74). Work even until piece measures 18 (20)" from beg.

Shape back

Begin short rows: Rows 1–2 (RS) K5 (8), wrap next st and turn (W&T), p to end. **Rows 3–4** K20 (23) hiding wrap, W&T, p to end. **Rows 5–6** K35 (38) hiding wrap, W&T, p to end. **Rows 7–8** K50 (53) hiding wrap, W&T, p to end. **Rows 9–10** K65 (68) hiding wrap, W&T, p to end. **Row 11** K across all sts hiding wrap. Bind off all sts.

RIGHT LEG

Work as for left leg, reversing back shaping by working short rows on WS.

FINISHING

Block pieces. Fold each leg in half and sew inseams up to crotch. Sew legs to each other along back, crotch and front seams. Fold waist to inside 1" down and sew to inside, leaving 2" unsewn for inserting elastic. Cut elastic to desired waist measurement. Thread through casing. Overlap ends 1" and machine stitch. Sew unsewn facing to inside. Work edging around cuffs as for turtle.

Toddlers love the colorful leggings and turtle in smooth Merino wool.

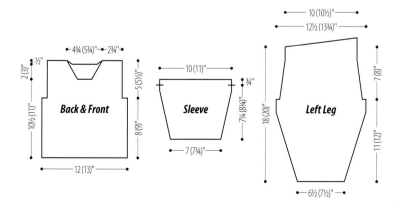

Driving through the tiny towns and back roads of upstate New York, it is easy to miss the turn to Patti Subik's, and we do. The driveway leading to The Great Adirondack Yarn Company is practical and unpretentious. At the end of the lane, we find Patti and the hand-dye company she created 12 years ago from nothing but imagination, help from a friend, and several packets of Kool Aid.

THE GREAT ADIRONDACK YARN CO. PATTI SUBIK

Amsterdam, New York

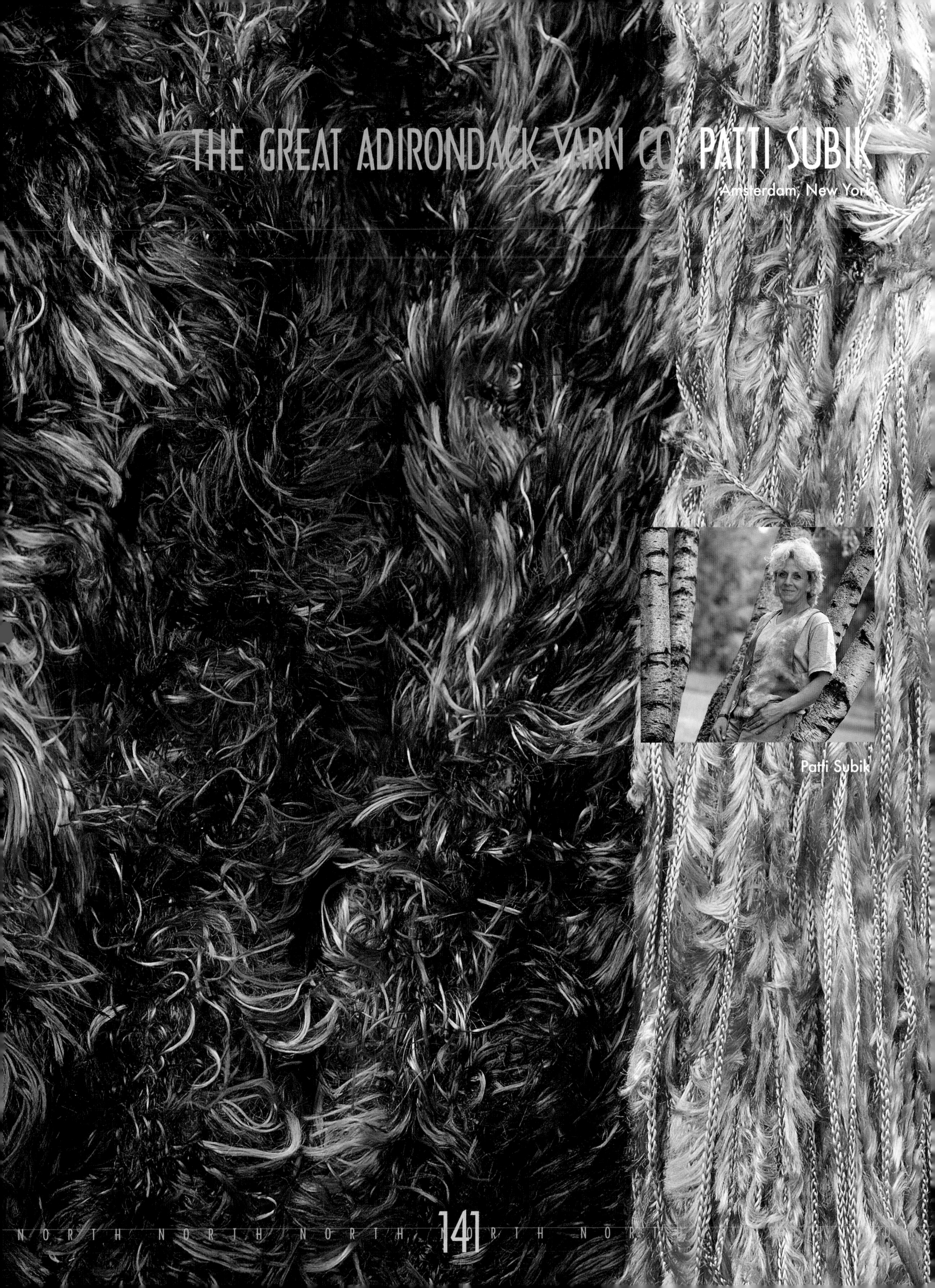

Patti Subik

THE GREAT ADIRONDACK YARN CO. PATTI SUBIK
Amsterdam, New York

Clockwise from above: Yarn and fabric dyed in the same colorway; we are invited to a handpaint picnic before the pumphouse; at Great Adirondack, even the birds have a handpainted house.

A sense of place As we survey Patti Subik's well-equipped studio and a showroom boasting dozens of colorways applied to over 50 kinds of yarn, Kool Aid origins are difficult to imagine. Even Patti can only chuckle. "Although our efforts were less than stellar," she admits, "the yarn smelled great!"

In an effort to recreate the landscape of her childhood, Patti and her husband searched out their 34-acre farm 13 years ago. The rutted drive gives way to a shingled farmhouse with a new addition that is Patti's dye studio. Beyond that lie a horse barn, various outbuildings housing pumps and garden tools, woods, fields, and a pasture. Inside Patti's studio, the two dominant features are the large windows on the back wall and a Vermont Castings Vigilant wood stove. The windows provide a view of Patti's seven horses (weekends often find her riding competitively). The stove keeps the house warm and the yarns dry through the long winter.

Although the whiffs of Kool Aid cherry and grape are long gone, Patti's easy-going, down-to-earth demeanor remains, and it colors everything she does. Evidence of her boundless energy is everywhere. Blue eyes sparkling, she darts here and there, casually throwing together handpainted buttons that almost coincidentally coordinate with her hand-dyed silk garments and color-matched hanks of fabric and trim. The studio is a riot of color, from the hand-dyed flowers and painted floor cloths to the whimsically painted furniture, not to mention the polymer clay beads, painted rocks, and diachroic glass that serve as her touchstones. Drying racks laden with space-dyed hanks and cubbyholes stacked floor to ceiling overflow with finished yarn. Outside, a handpainted birdhouse graces one of the birches.

Discoveries Like many hand-dyers, Patti's romance with fiber began while running a retail yarn store. From there, her love of colorful garments led her to the ready-to-wear market, where she created handpainted silk shawls and scarves from stamped velvet as well as a variety of handknit originals. When it became obvious that the response to the painted yarns in her cardigans and jackets threatened to overcome the popularity of the garments themselves, Patti knew that her life was about to take yet another creative turn.

Her big break came in 1991 at Stitches in Valley Forge, Pennsylvania, where she was "discovered" by Tahki Yarns. Tahki immediately seized upon her unique line, Ribbons and Bows—strips of fabric tied end-to-end, interspersed with stretches of yarn, all dyed in the same colorway. This line progressed to an even more popular muslin version, Rags to Riches, and finally to a silk version, Silky Rags. As for the rest of her fibers? "They took off by themselves," Patti says, with a shrug and a smile.

Breaking the rules Serendipity and simplicity play essential roles in Patti's approach to the handpaint process. Often on a whim, her creative twists and turns become tangents that lead her to the discovery of a new way to dye fiber or new fibers to dye

Keeping it simple All of Great Adirondack's yarns have deceptively uncomplicated names, the most popular being "Fluff," which you might mistake for fur on a core. Patti calls a similar yarn "Pouf," the length of the "fur" being the only difference, or as Patti explains: "Pouf is the buzz-cut of Fluff." Another slinky, soft yarn, aptly named "Chamois," sells itself on touch appeal. "It's yummy to knit with," says Patti. Chamois is very knitter-friendly and an easy selection for the beginning novelty yarn knitter.

Inspiration for her seemingly countless colorways come to Patti from everyday experiences: the calico cat grooming itself, her flower garden blooming in the spring, the waning light catching the neighbor's house, a visit to her parents out West, or even the displays at the grocery store. The names of her colorways are enticing. Who can resist a color sequence called Verry Berry, Firefly, Wild Birch, or Potpourri? Patti and two other hand-dyers produce the Great Adirondack's color combinations, covering a wide spectrum from pastels to deep, rich tones and watercolors to semi-solids. One of her particularly striking new colorways, Starburst, combines brilliant blue, fuchsia, gold, emerald, and violet.

Above: Pouf on a rusty saw blade. According to Patti Subik, the difference between novelty yarns Pouf and Fluff is a matter of length, "Pouf is the buzzcut of Fluff."

Center: An antique plow draped with mohair boucle in the colorway Irish Cream stands idle in the riding ring. Patti is a competitive rider, and it is here that she exercises her horses.

Below: A clay ball and millifiori work with fimo clay dice are Patti's touchstones.

together. For this reason, Patti perceives her lack of a formal art background as an advantage. Not knowing the rules has left her free to break them. Even as a small child, she explains: "I couldn't draw a picture, but I was always the one who wanted the biggest box of crayons."

A self-proclaimed "fabricaholic," Patti continually strives to break down the barriers between fabric and fiber. She loves to run color and texture together at the same time. "I don't know about you, but I'm always curious about odd things that can be knit," she confides. One of her favorite tasks is to gather as many different fibers as she can and dye them all the same colorway. The fibers don't all have to be yarn. In fact, much of her novelty yarn begins life as wedding trim, which Patti's crew specially winds and prepares to be introduced to the knitting public as yarn. Her newest creation, aptly named "Surprise," is actually 11 different fibers tied together and then dyed in one colorway. The result is a delicious blend of chenille and rayon with trim and rick-rack; each hank is a spiraling fantasy of color that changes even more often than the fiber.

Because of large demands on her time, Patti takes what she considers to be the best and least-complicated approach to marketing. Although she still shows at Stitches and nearby sheep and wool festivals, much of her business is now wholesale.

Yarns from Great Adirondack are not rewound after they are dyed because of the time factor and because Patti feels no need to reskein the hanks. She chooses to present yarn simply, in the method in which it was dyed, trusting that knitters can envision the way the colors will cross when knit. For some of the same reasons, Patti hesitates to offer a lot of pattern support. Instead, she encourages knitters to explore her yarns in any way they wish.

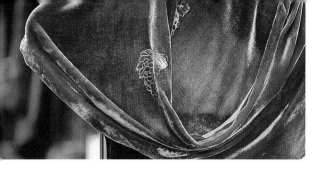

Clockwise from above: Handpainted, stamped velvet scarf; hanks of hand-dyed Chamois sell themselves on touch appeal; hand-dyed Fluff; diachroic glass buttons complement Patti's colorways; Chamois close up— this knitter-friendly yarn has a cotton core so that it will not bias.

Facing page: Painted ladies draped in velvet march through the hayfield.

Future watch When asked if she agrees that handpainted yarn has reached the height of its popularity, Patti can only throw back her head and laugh. "No, it's never going to stop!" she exclaims. "Because there's no limit to what you can do!"

Patti herself is the embodiment of that belief. Painted clothing, buttons, jewelry, and other accessories are just the beginning. She predicts that the novelty yarn market will explode in the next few years. Adventurous knitters will want more and more unusual things. Patti and Great Adirondack Yarn do not plan to disappoint.

In upstate New York, the land of Sleepy Hollow, we journey back to childhood fantasies. Handpainted ladies stalk the fields like images from a dreamscape, muses placed here to inspire.

Mixed miters designed by Ginger Luters

Lines formed by both color and texture emphasize the multi-directional miters of this comfortable vest.

MATERIALS
Yarn The Great Adirondack Yarn Company *Akala* **MC** 2 (3, 3) skeins Eggplant (4oz/114g, 200yds/182m, 100% mercerized cotton) and *Chamois* **CC** 3 (3, 4) skeins Spring Garden (2.5oz/75g, 100yds/90m, 80% rayon, 20% cotton).
Needles Size 8 (5mm) circular needle, 24"/60cm long, *or size to obtain gauge.*
Extras Five ¾"/20mm buttons.

NOTES
1 See *Techniques,* p. 228 for ssk, 3-needle bind-off, and short-row wraps. *2* Alternate between MC and CC; carrying unused yarn along side edge. *3* Follow schematic diagrams for placement of sections on all pieces. *4* Pick up all sts with right side facing.

STITCH USED
Garter ridge pat
Rows 1–2 Beginning with a RS row, with MC, work 2 rows in Garter st. *Rows 3–4* With CC, work 2 rows in St st. Rep rows 1–4 for pat.

BACK
Section 1
With MC, cast on 37 (41, 45) sts. *Row 1* (WS) K18 (20, 22), p1, k18 (20, 22). *Row 2* With CC, k17 (19, 21), sl2-k1-p2sso, k17 (19, 21)—2 sts dec'd. *Row 3* Purl. *Row 4* With MC, k to 1 st before center st, sl2-k1-p2sso, k to end—2 sts dec'd. *Row 5* K to center st, p1, k to end. *Row 6* With CC, rep row 4. *Row 7* Purl. Rep rows 4–7 until 3 sts remain. *Next RS row* Sl 2-k1-p2sso—2 sts dec'd. Fasten off last st. Section should measure 4¾ (5¼, 5¾)" square.
Section 2
Rep section 1.
Section 3
With MC, pick up and k18 (20, 22) sts along half of cast-on edge of section 1, ending at center dec point, cast on 38 (42, 46) sts, then pick up and k18 (20, 22) sts along half of cast-on edge of section 2, beg at center dec point—74 (82, 90) sts. *Row 1* (WS) K18 (20, 22), p1, k36 (40, 44), p1, k18 (20, 22). *Row 2* With CC, k17 (19, 21), sl2-k1-p2sso, k34 (38, 42), sl2-k1-p2sso, k17 (19, 21)—4 sts dec'd. *Row 3* Purl. *Row 4* With MC, k16 (18, 20), sl2-k1-p2sso, k32 (36, 40), sl2-k1-p2sso, k16 (18, 20)—4 sts dec'd. *Row 5* K16 (18, 20), p1, k32 (36, 40), p1, k16 (18, 20). *Row 6* With CC, k15 (17, 19), sl2-k1-p2sso, k30 (34, 38), sl2-k1-p2sso, k15 (17, 19). *Row 7* Purl. Continue working in Garter ridge pat, working corner sts in St st and decs as established (working 1 fewer st at beg and end of row, and 2 fewer sts between decs) every RS row until 6 sts remain. *Next row* (WS) [P2tog] 3 times. *Next row* Sl2-k1-p2sso. Fasten off last st.

Section 4
With MC, cast on 59 (61, 63) sts, pick up and k1 st (center st) in corner of section 3, then 18 (20, 22) sts along remaining half of cast-on edge of section 1—78 (82, 86) sts. *Row 1* (WS) K18 (20, 22), p1, k59 (61, 63). *Row 2* With CC, k58 (60, 62), sl2-k1-p2sso, k17 (19, 21)—2 sts dec'd. *Row 3* Purl. *Row 4* With MC, k2tog (shoulder shaping), k55 (57, 59), sl2-k1-p2sso, k16 (18, 20)—1 shoulder shaping dec plus 2 sts dec'd. *Row 5* K16 (18, 20), p1, k56 (58, 60). *Row 6* With CC, k55 (57, 59), sl2-k1-p2sso, k15 (17, 19)—2 sts dec'd. *Row 7* Purl. Continue working in Garter ridge pat, working corner st in St st and decs as established through row 15 (17, 19), and AT SAME TIME, k2tog for shoulder shaping at beg of rows 8 and 12.
Shape armhole
Row 16 (18, 20) (RS) Bind off 38 sts for armhole, continue working in pat, working center dec as established until 3 sts remain. *Next RS row* Sl2-k1-p2sso. Fasten off last st.

Section 5
With MC, pick up and k18 (20, 22) sts along remaining half of cast-on edge of section 2, 1 st (center st) in corner of section 3, then cast on 59 (61, 63) sts—78 (82, 86) sts. Continue as for section 4, reversing shaping and working shoulder shaping at beg of rows 5, 9 and 13, and armhole shaping at beg of row 17 (19, 21).

Section 6
With MC, pick up and k59 (61, 63) sts along cast-on edge of section 5, corner st of section 2, 36 (40, 44) sts along cast-on edge of section 3, corner st of section 1, then 59 (61, 63) sts along edge of section 4—156 (164, 172) sts. *Row 1* (WS) K59 (61, 63), p1, k36 (40, 44), p1, k59 (61, 63). *Row 2* With CC, k58 (60, 62), sl2-k1-p2sso, k34 (38, 42), sl2-k1-p2sso, k58 (60, 62)—4 sts dec'd. *Row 3* Purl. *Row 4* With MC, inc 1 (shoulder shaping), k57 (59, 61), sl2-k1-p2sso, k32 (36, 40), sl2-k1-p2sso, k57 (59, 61), inc 1 (shoulder shaping)—2 shoulder shaping incs plus 4 sts dec'd. *Row 5* K58 (60, 62), p1, k32 (36, 40), p1, k58 (60, 62). Continue working in Garter ridge pat, working corner sts in St st

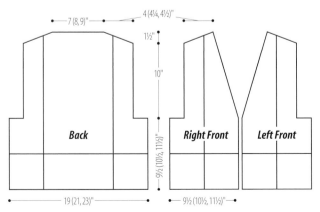

Back | *Right Front* | *Left Front*

7 (8, 9)" 4 (4¼, 4½)" 1½" 10" 9½ (10½, 11½)" 19 (21, 23)" 9½ (10½, 11½)"

Intermediate

Sizes
S (M, L)
Shown in size M.
Directions are for smallest size with larger sizes in parentheses.
If there is only 1 set of numbers, it applies to all sizes.

Finished measurements
Underarm (buttoned) 38 (42, 46)"
Length 22½ (23½, 24½)"

Gauge
15 sts and 28 rows to 4"/10cm over Garter Ridge pat using size 8 (5mm) needle.

Mixed miters

and decs as established every RS row and AT SAME TIME, inc 1 st at beg and end of row 8 for shoulder shaping, until no sts remain between corner dec sts (above section 3), ending with a WS row. Put half of sts on another needle and with RS facing, work 3-needle bind-off.

RIGHT FRONT
Section 1
Work as for back section 1.
Section 2
With MC, pick up and k18 (20, 22) sts along half of cast-on edge of section 1, ending at center dec point, cast on 19 (21, 23) sts—37 (41, 45) sts. Continue as for back section 1.
Section 3
Work as for back section 4, picking up center st in corner of section 2.
Section 4
With MC, pick up and k18 (20, 22) sts along remaining half of cast-on edge of section 2, 1 st at corner of section 1, and 59 (61, 63) sts along cast-on edge of section 3—78 (82, 86) sts. **Row 1** (WS) K59 (61, 63), p1, k18 (20, 22) sts. **Row 2** With CC, k17 (19, 21), sl2-k1-p2sso, k58 (60, 62)—2 sts dec'd. **Row 3** Purl. **Row 4** With MC, k16 (18, 20), sl2-k1-p2sso, k57 (59, 61), inc 1 (shoulder shaping)—1 shoulder shaping inc plus 2 sts dec'd. **Row 5** K58 (60, 62), p1, k16 (18, 20). Continue working in Garter ridge pat, working corner st in St st and dec as established every RS row and AT SAME TIME, inc 1 st at end of row 8 for shoulder shaping, through row 11.
Shape neck
Row 12 (RS) Work short rows at end of RS rows as follows: with MC, k12 (14, 16), sl2-k1-p2sso, k50 (52, 54), wrap next st and turn (W&T). **Row 13** K50 (52, 54), p1, k12 (14, 16). **Row 14** With CC, k11 (13, 15), sl2-k1-p2sso, k45 (47, 49), W&T. **Row 15** Purl. Continue working in Garter ridge pat, working 4 fewer sts at end of each RS row 4 (2, 0) times more, 3 fewer sts each RS row 6 (8, 9) times, 2 fewer sts each RS row 0 (0, 2) times, then 1

fewer st each RS row 0 (2, 3) times. **Next RS row** With MC, sl2-k1-p2sso, k to end, hiding wraps.

LEFT FRONT
Sections 1 and 2
Work as for right front sections 1 and 2.
Section 3
Work as for back section 5, picking up center st in corner of section 1.
Section 4
With MC, pick up and k59 (61, 63) sts along cast-on edge of section 3, corner st of section 2, k18 (20, 22) sts along remaining half of cast-on edge of section 1—78 (82, 86) sts. Continue as for right front section 4, reversing shaping and working shoulder shaping at beg of rows 4 and 8, and working short row shaping on WS rows, beg with row 13.

FINISHING
Block pieces. Sew shoulder seams.
Armhole edging
With MC, beg at underarm, pick up and k9 (10, 11) sts along underarm, 36 (37, 38) sts to shoulder seam, 36 (37, 38) sts to underarm, 9 (10, 11) sts along underarm—90 (94, 98) sts. **Row 1** (WS) K7 (8, 9), k2tog, ssk, k68 (70, 72), k2tog, ssk, k7 (8, 9)—86 (90, 94) sts. **Row 2** Knit. **Row 3** K6 (7, 8), k2tog, ssk, k66 (68, 70), k2tog, ssk, k6 (7, 8)—82 (86, 90) sts. **Row 4** Knit. Bind off knitwise. Sew side and edging seams.
Frontbands
With MC, beg at bottom right front, pick up and k162 (172, 182) sts evenly up right front, across back neck, and down left front. **Row 1** Knit. **Row 2 (buttonhole row)** K2, *bind off 2 sts, k6 (7, 8); rep from* 4 times more, k to end. **Row 3** Knit, casting on 2 sts over each set of bound-off sts. K 3 more rows. Loosely bind off.
Bottom edging
(**Note** Work joining st as follows: (WS) with yarn in front, pick up and p1 st from vest, pass last st over picked up st.) With MC, cast on 3 sts. With WS facing, work joining st in bottom right front corner of vest. **Row 1** (RS) Sl 1, k into the front and back of next st, k1—4 sts. **Rows 2, 4, 6** Knit, work joining st. **Row 3** Sl 1, k1, k into the front and back of next st, k1—5 sts. **Row 5** Sl 1, [k into the front and back of next st, k1] twice—7 sts **Row 7** Sl 1, k6. **Row 8** Bind off 4 sts, k3, work joining st—3 sts. Rep rows 1–8 around bottom edge of vest. On last row 8, bind off all sts, joining last st to left front corner of vest. Sew on buttons.

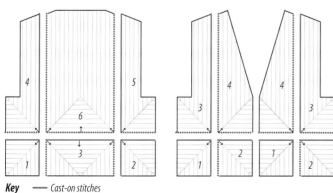

Key —— Cast-on stitches
········· Picked-up stitches

THE GREAT ADIRONDACK YARN CO. PATTI SUBIK
Cropped kimono designed by Ginger Luters

It's surprising how narrow strips concentrate the unusual textures and rich colors of many exotic yarns.

MATERIALS
Yarn The Great Adirondack Yarn Company *Surprise* **MC** 6 skeins Cancun, **A** 1 skein Grenada (each 4oz/114g, 150yds/135m, 75% rayon, 25% cotton); *Akala* **CC** 4 skeins Dark Eggplant (4oz/114g, 200yds/180m, 100% mercerized cotton); *Silk Terry* **B** 1 skein Cancun (3.5oz/100g, 75yds/68m, 75% silk, 25% Merino wool); *Pouf* **C** 1 skein Starburst (2.5oz/75g, 100yds/90m, 100% rayon); *Cyclone* **D** 1 skein Starburst (4oz/114g, 187yds/170m, 100% rayon); *Chamois* **E** 1 skein Cancun (2.5oz/75g, 100yds/90m, 80% rayon, 20% cotton); *Black/Gold Ribbon* **F** 1 skein Paintbox (100yds/90m, 90% rayon, 10% polyester).
Needles One pair size 8 (5mm) needles, *or size to obtain gauge.* Two size 8 (5mm) circular needles, 24"/60cm long.
Extras Three ⅝"/15mm buttons. One smaller plain shank button (for inside of bottom right front band). Size F/5 (3.75mm) crochet hook.

NOTES
1 See *Techniques*, p. 228 for 3-needle bind-off (ridge effect), single crochet (sc), and double crochet (dc). **2** MC (Surprise) consists of various yarns tied together in random lengths. When you reach a knot, place it on the wrong side. You can either unknot ends later and weave in , or leave as is, or when working, you can place knot on right side for more texture. **3** Follow schematic diagrams for placement order of strips.

STITCH USED
Seed St
Row 1 *K1, p1; rep from* across. *Row 2* P the knit sts and k the purl sts. Rep row 2 for pat.

FRONT BAND make 2
With CC, cast on 3 sts. Working in Seed st, inc 1 st at end every other row 16 (18, 20) times—19 (21, 23) sts. Work even in Seed st until piece measures 60 (62, 64)" from beg. Continue in pat and dec 1 st at same edge as beg incs every 3rd row 18 (20, 22) times—1 st. Fasten off, pulling yarn through last st.

BACK
Strip 1
With MC, cast on 23 sts. **Row 1** (WS) Knit. Beg working in St st (k on RS, p on WS), using mainly MC, changing yarns randomly to work small areas with other yarns and working occasional Garter stitch ridge (k on RS and WS) with CC. When working with Pouf or Silk Terry, work in Rev St st (p on RS, k on WS) so that texture is on the RS. When piece measures 19 (21, 23)" from beg, bind off.

Strip 2
With MC, cast on 18 (23, 27) sts. Work as for Strip 1 until piece measures 19 (21, 23)" from beg, end with a WS row.
Shape shoulder
(RS) Bind off 4 (5, 6) sts at beg of every RS row 3 times, bind off remaining 6 (8, 9) sts.

Strip 3
Work as for strip 2, working shoulder shaping at beg of WS rows.

Strip 4
With MC, cast on 18 sts. Work as for strip 1 until piece measures 10 (12, 14)" from beg, end with a WS row.
Shape underarm
(RS) Bind off 9 sts, work even until piece measures 19 (21, 23)" from beg. Bind off remaining 9 sts.

Strip 5
Work as for strip 4, working armhole shaping at beg of WS row.

Strip 6
With MC, cast on 3 sts. Work as for strip 4, and AT SAME TIME, inc 1 st at end of every RS row 15 times—18 sts. Continue working as for strip 4, working armhole shaping at beg of WS row.

Strip 7
With MC, cast on 3 sts. Work as for strip 4 and AT SAME TIME, inc 1 st at beg of every RS row 15 times—18 sts. Continue working as for strip 4.

Strip 8
With MC, cast on 3 sts. Work as for strip 1 and AT SAME TIME, inc 1 st each side every RS row 5 (6, 8) times, then 1 st at end every RS row 5 (8, 8) times—18 (23, 27) sts. Work even until piece measures 26 (29½, 32)" from beg, then shape shoulder as for strip 2, working shoulder shaping at beg of WS rows.

Strip 9
With MC, cast on 3 sts. Work as for strip 1 and AT SAME TIME, inc 1 st each side every RS row 5 (6, 8) times, then 1 st at beg of every RS row 5 (8, 8) times—18 (23, 27) sts. Work even until piece measures 26 (29½, 32)" from beg, then shape shoulder as for strip 2.

SLEEVES
With CC, cast on 38 sts. Work for 3" in Seed st. **Next row** (WS) Purl, inc 4 sts evenly spaced—42 sts. Change to MC and work as for strip 1 and AT SAME TIME, inc 1 st each side every 4th row 6 times, then every 6th row 13 times—80 sts. Work even until piece measures 22 (23, 24)" from beg. Bind off all sts. At top, mark 2" down on each edge.

FINISHING
Lightly block strips and sleeves to measurements.
Join strips
(**Note** For ease in picking up sts, mark length of strips

Cropped kimono

in 4ths. Then divide number of sts to be picked up by 4 to determine approx how many sts to pick up for each quarter. Follow schematic diagrams for placement order of strips.)

Join strip as follows: With RS facing, circular needle and CC, pick up and k107 (116, 125) sts along right edge of strip 9. With other circular needle and CC, pick up and k same number of sts along left edge of strip 7. With WS tog, join both pieces using 3-needle bind-off (ridge effect). Join remaining strips in order in this fashion, picking up and knitting the following number of sts per strip: To join strips 7 and 5: 45 (54, 63) sts; strips 5 and 3, 3 and 1, 1 and 2, 2 and 4: 85 (94, 103) sts; strips 4 and 6: 45 (54, 63) sts; strips 6 and 8: 107 (116, 125) sts.

Sew shoulder seams. Sew top of sleeves to armholes. Sew straight portion at top of sleeves (above markers) to bound-off armhole sts. Sew sleeve seams, making cuff seam on outside (so that seam doesn't show when cuff is turned up). With shorter tapered ends at bottom, sew front band sections to strips 8 and 9, then sew onto 1" of back neck (strip 1). Place markers along right front band for 3 buttonholes spaced 4" apart, with the first at end of inc at bottom. Place marker on left front band at end of inc at bottom.

Trim

With crochet hook and RS facing, join CC where strips 4 and 6 join at bottom. Work 1 rnd of sc around entire out-side edge of jacket, including front bands as follows: dec 2 sts evenly across back neck, work 3 sc at points at top of front bands, and 2 sc at other points, and working buttonholes at markers as ch 2, skip 1 st, continue in sc. Join rnd with a sl st. Turn, ch 3, dc in each sc across bottom to where strips 5 and 7 join, working 3 decs evenly spaced. Turn, ch 1, sc in each dc along bottom. Fasten off.

Sew on buttons to correspond to buttonholes: 3 buttons along left front band and strip 9 seam, smaller shank button at right front band and strip 8 seam.

Shoulder pleats optional

Fold pleats into position according to schematic diagram. With CC, stitch pleat into place and tack lightly to inside of shoulder seam.

"Nine quick-to-knit strips are the basis of this dramatic jacket and they are the perfect way to show off the beautiful colors and textures of these Great Adirondack yarns. The unique long front band ties can be worn in several different ways. Try leaving one end hanging straight down the back while the other one wraps around your neck. They can be crossed at the back neck and left to hang loosely down the front, or, one or both ends can be tossed dramatically to the back, or the ends tied low in front... how about tying them up high at the side, with the ends hanging down the back."

Ginger Luters

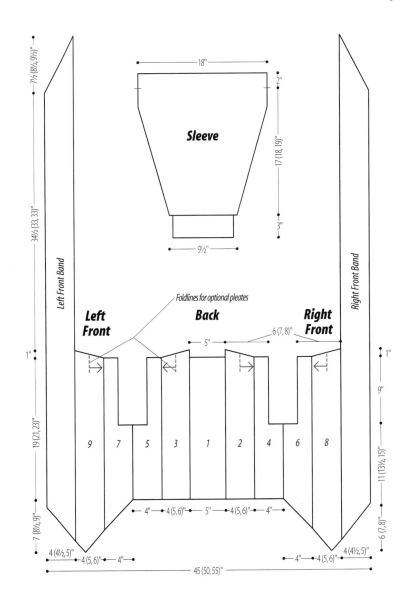

Northeast

When we arrive back in New England, autumn has already announced itself. Crisp air and a riot of foliage belie the onset of winter. A sense of haste prevails as the sun rises later and sets a little too early to finish all the chores around the farm at Cherry Tree Hill. We are out early, eager to capture all the color before daylight fades.

CHERRY TREE HILL YARN CHERYL POTTER

Barton, Vermont

MARTIN BRIDGE

Cheryl Potter

CHERRY TREE HILL YARN CHERYL POTTER
Barton, Vermont

Clockwise from top:
Exotic boucles shown in the colorway Peacock; at Cherry Tree Hill, semi-solids are called heathers—here they hang inside a covered bridge; sumac leaves, touched by frost, brighten a hank of mohair boucle.

"It really started when Kaffe Fassett's *Glorious Knits* was published and the yarn world exploded into a new realm of color and texture," Cheryl Potter explains. "At the time I earned extra money by knitting custom and one-of-a-kind garments while working on an MFA in Creative Writing at the University of Arizona."

As she went on to knit many multicolored sweaters in intarsia, she began imagining another way to achieve a painted look. "If only a single yarn could graduate in color as one knit it," she thought. "But how?" That question spurred her eventual move from the academic world to the yarn world, from dealing in words to dealing in color.

Looking back Cheryl has always been surrounded by needlework and fibers. Both her mother and grandmother were avid knitters, crocheters, and needlepointers who kept ample supplies of yarn and embroidery floss in the house. Cheryl remembers the handknit yellow dress she wore the first day of kindergarten and baby pictures of herself in angora buntings.

In first grade Cheryl picked up wooden needles and began "pretend knitting" with tissues. Her mother saw all the torn strips of paper and knew it was time for her daughter to knit for real. Cheryl's first project was a neon green and yellow striped sailor shirt. "This was in the '60s; I must have been seven at the time and thought it was so beautiful," she recalls.

Cheryl's love of knitting never waned, but her formal training was as a writer. She began writing stories about the same time she started knitting and was published by the time she edited her high school yearbook. So in 1989, when she returned to Vermont from the Southwest, she planned to work on The Novel.

But the view atop Cherry Tree Hill took over her imagination. The manuscript languished while she began dyeing yarn in those graduated colors she had longed for. At the American Craft Council shows she attended, the yarns she painted were more popular than her knitted garments. "I knew I had found my calling," she remembers. "It was to spread the word of handpainted yarn to everyone."

Green Mountain Madness A visit from Meg Swansen gave Cheryl the encouragement she needed to make hand-dyeing a way of life. At the Maryland Sheep and Wool Festival in 1994, she met other handpainters. "It was overwhelming, yet it was also reassuring to know I wasn't alone." Back in Vermont, she sold yarn at her farm-turned-bed-and-breakfast, an artist's co-op, and area yarn stores. Her dye kitchen moved from the farmhouse to the basement laundry to a renovated barn overlooking the Green Mountains. "My first colorway was called 'Green Mountain Madness' because trying to reproduce all those indescribable blues and greens could drive you crazy."

Cheryl's big break came in 1997, when *Interweave Knits* discovered Cherry Tree Hill Yarns. The response gave her the courage to close her B & B and never look back.

So many yarns in so many colors Many of Cheryl's colorways like Wild Cherry and heather solids like Leaf are inspired by her panoramic views. Cheryl finds that the newest colorway is usually the most popular. "Java,

Color: fast, fresh, and knitter-friendly

Cheryl's yarns undergo a unique dye process. "We fry our yarns in pans on the stove," she reveals. "That's our secret." Frying controls the spread of color and sets the dyes quickly so that the colors stay bright. "It's the equivalent of flash-frozen vegetables. Our colors are very fresh."

Frying yarn is a rapid technique. Couple this speed with employees who run commercial dryers and machine winders, and Cherry Tree Hill can get even the largest order out quickly. "Provided the yarn is available, we pride ourselves on a two-day turnaround. I know what it's like to be itching to knit."

Cheryl also knows that knitters appreciate a good value. For example, Cherry Tree Hill offers the versatile, moderately priced Supersock Merino; a few ounces is all it takes for children's wear, shawls, or a pair of socks. "We would rather make a little bit of money on a lot of yarn and see it out there being used."

Top: A harvest of acorn squash garnished by painted mill-end yarns at a local farm stand. Cheryl always has novelty mill ends on hand to explore new fibers and color combinations.

Left: The colorway Champlain Sunset shown in a multitude of yarns drapes fall pumpkins.

which we call 'the colors of coffee,' was the hit until Birches came along." Cherry Tree Hill introduces one or two new colorways a year and just a handful of semi-solids. "With a wide range of yarns, it's a big investment. You hope you're right and the colors will sell."

Cherry Tree Hill's broad selection of more than 50 yarns includes everything from fine cashmere to novelties like fringed eyelash to thick cotton chenille, and most are available in all colorways. "It's not easy to get pima cotton to match fake fur or silk boucle, but we try. Otherwise, we wouldn't have enough fun," Cheryl says with a laugh.

A half dozen mill-end yarns appear each season. Many already contain a machine-dyed component such as an acrylic slub or fancy binder. The crew overdyes these yarns in color families like Earthtones and Watercolors to enhance the existing color. Some yarns are designed in-house, often by mixing component yarns made of fibers that will take the dyes differently. In the silk and rayon blend, Silky Pastels, only the silk takes dye, yielding a rich wash of pastels. Ever-popular Potluck yarns appear every fall. "Potluck is literally the luck of the dye pot. We dye it in what we call 'Potluck Sixpacks' and no two sets are ever the same."

"When knitters buy our yarn, they are also looking for consistency. Our yarns are tagged and bagged with dye lot numbers, just like machine-dyed yarns. We have developed a huge amount of pattern support and we advertise in magazines. It may be impossible to mass-market handpainted yarn, but we're trying to make it knitter-friendly and readily available."

Popular paints Cheryl is encouraged by the growing acceptance of handpainted yarns. Designers are creating patterns geared specifically for immersion-dyed or space-dyed yarn, and magazine articles describe ways to incorporate hand-dyed yarns in a knitted piece. The fear is gone, she believes. "Knitters realize that painted yarn is just yarn with a lot of color on it."

Knitters are now more apt to put yarns and colors together in unexpected ways. Often, they reinvent a favorite pattern with handpaints or mix hand- and machine-dyed yarns in a garment. Another trend is the advent of complex color. "Knitters don't just want gray; they want slate gray, maybe with a touch of blue in it and a little color variation within the monochrome.

The finished garment is more sophisticated, a piece of wearable art."

But that doesn't mean the knitting has to be more complicated. More and more, knitters are letting the color and texture of hand-dyed yarns determine the outcome of the garment.

Future watch

Cherry Tree Hill has begun to import exotic fibers like Furlana, a merino/possum blend from New Zealand. Cherry Tree Hill also serves as a dye house for such companies as Cashmere America, Alpaca Fiber Co-op, and Lion Brand Yarn.

Between dye baths, Cheryl has turned back to the design work of her early years."I do enjoy designing easy-to-knit garments with handpainted yarns."

Cheryl believes that all hand-dyers start with the same basic techniques. "As fiber artists, each of us has our own color sense, fibers and textures we favor, different ways of presenting what we know. It's the knitters who excite me. After all, my finished product becomes their raw material."

Clockwise from top: Cotton Ragg, a yarn that begins life as drapery fabric, on a bed of Hubbard squash; a variety of fibers shown in Northern Lights, a colorway inspired by the Aurora Borealis on a subzero winter night at Middlebury College; hand-paint dinner for three at the farm—Glimmer, Ballerina, and more Glimmer.

End Notes Cherry Tree Hill Yarns has moved from the farm on the hill that gave it its name to a remote area of Vermont locally referred to as the Northeast Kingdom. As this book goes to press, Cherry Tree Hill is settled into new quarters in a former Ben Franklin store in the village of Barton. With increased space and staff, Cheryl can process hundreds of hanks per day. The company has gone from retail to wholesale, and she enjoys the new challenge.

CHERRY TREE HILL YARN CHERYL POTTER

Double vested designed by Barbara Venishnick

Two coordinating solids are pulled from the colorway Gypsy Rose for this striking outer layer. The black of the edging repeats in a great pair of knitted pants.

Sizes

S (M, L)

Shown in size M.

Directions are for smallest size with larger sizes in parentheses.

If there is only 1 set of numbers, it applies to all sizes.

Finished measurements

Vest: Underarm (buttoned) 57 (61, 65)"

Length 32"

Tunic: Underarm 21 (23, 25)"

Length 28½ (29, 29½)"

Gauge

21 sts and 32 rows to 4"/10cm over pat using size 4 (3.5mm) needles.

MATERIALS

Yarn Cherry Tree Hill *Silk Bouclé* (each skein 8oz/228g, 560yds/512m, 100% silk). **For Vest: A** 2 skeins Plum, **B** 2 (2, 2) skeins Rose, **C** 1 (1, 1) skein Black, **D** small amount Gray. **For Tunic** 3 (3, 4) skeins Gypsy Rose.

Needles Size 4 (3.5mm), *or size to obtain gauge.* **For Vest** 32"/80cm circular needle. **For Tunic** One pair size straight needles and 16"/40cm circular needle.

Extras Stitch holders and markers, small amount of smooth yarn in coordinating color for sewing. **For Vest** four 1¼"(32mm) buttons: two Plum, two Rose. Extra circular needle used as stitch holder.

STITCHES USED

Pat st *Worked Back and Forth* multiple of 3 sts plus 1
Row 1 (RS) K1, *p2, k1; rep from*. **Row 2** P1, *k2, p1; rep from*. **Row 3** Knit. **Row 4** Purl. Rep row 1-4 for pat worked back and forth.
Worked Circularly in Rnds multiple of 3 sts
Rnds 1 and 2 (RS) *K1, p2; rep from*. **Rnds 3 and 4** Knit. Rep rnds 1-4 for pat worked circularly in rnds.

VEST

NOTES

1 See *Techniques*, p. 228 for ssk, cable cast-on, and 3-needle bind-off. *2* Vest is knitted side to side in 2 sections. *3* Cast on all stitches using cable cast-on method.

RIGHT HALF

Button section (back)
With A, cable cast on 3 sts. **Row 1** (WS) P3. **Row 2** Cast on 2 sts, k1, p2, k1, p1—5 sts. **Row 3** Cast on 2 sts, p1, [k2, p1] twice—7 sts. **Row 4** Cast on 2 sts, k9—9 sts. **Row 5** Cast on 2 sts, p11—11 sts. Continue as established, working in pat st back and forth and casting on 2 sts at the beg of every row (working incs into pat) to 171 sts, end with a WS row. Place all sts on hold.

Buttonhole section (front)
With A, work as for button section to 19 sts, ending with a WS row. **Next row: Divide for buttonhole** (RS) Cast on 2 sts, work these 2 sts and 9 more, insert RH needle into the row below of next st (center st) and knit, leaving center st on LH needle. Drop yarn, join 2nd ball of yarn and knit center st, work across in pat. Working both sides of buttonhole with separate balls of yarn, continue in pat, casting on 2 sts at

the beg of each row until there are 26 sts on each side of buttonhole. **Next row: Join buttonhole** Cast on 2 sts, work these 2 sts and 25 more, k2tog joining buttonhole, cut 2nd ball of yarn and continue working across in pat with first ball. Continue working as established to 119 sts, end with a WS row. **Next row: Divide for buttonhole** (RS) Cast on 2 sts, work these 2 sts and 59 more, continue as for other buttonhole until there are 76 sts on each side of buttonhole. **Next row: Join buttonhole** Cast on 2 sts, work these 2 sts and 75 more, k2tog joining buttonhole, cut 2nd ball of yarn and continue working across in pat with first ball. Continue working as established to 171 sts, ending with a WS row.

Join sections
(RS) Work across 171 sts in pat, then work across 171 sts of button section—342 sts. Work 3 rows even in pat.

Shape shoulder
(RS) Work 168 sts in pat, k2tog, place marker (pm), p2, pm, ssk, work across remaining 168 sts in pat. **Next row and every WS row** Work even in pat to 1 st before marker, p1, work in pat to next marker, p1, work in pat to end. Continue in pat, working decs every 4th row 18 (20, 22) times more as follows: Work in pat to 2 sts before marker, k2tog, work in pat to next marker, ssk, work in pat to end. End with a WS row, 304 (300, 296) sts remain, 151 (149, 147) sts outside of markers.

Shape armhole
Place first and last 96 (94, 92) sts on hold for sides. With WS facing and working on center 112 sts, work 4-color cord as follows: K1 D, k1 A, k1 C, k1 B, *carrying yarn over the 3 colors left hanging in back of work, k1 D, k1 A, k1 C, k1 B; rep from* across. Cut all colors except C. Turn. With C and RS facing, work in St st for 11 rows beg with a k row. Bind off loosely.

FINISHING

Fold piece in half at the shoulder with RS tog. Join sides using 3-needle bind off. Sew ends of armhole trim tog and roll to outside of vest with purl side showing. With smooth coordinating yarn, sew to first row of C.

Body trim
With RS facing, A and circular needle, beg at bottom of the button section, *pick up and k1 st in each of the next 3 rows, skip 1 row; rep from* along bottom, then pick up and k1 st in each cast-on st around. Turn. With WS facing, work 4-color cord as for armhole, then 11 rows St st with C. Bind off loosely. Sew ends of trim tog and roll to outside of vest with purl side showing. With smooth coordinating yarn, sew to first row of C.

LEFT HALF

Using B, work as for right half, picking up sts with B for body trim. Sew 2 color B buttons to left half and 2 color A buttons to right half.

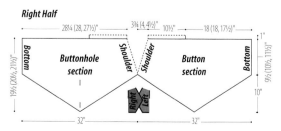

Right Half

28¼ (28, 27½)" · 3¾ (4, 4½)" · 10½" · 18 (18, 17½)"

Bottom · Buttonhole section · Shoulder · Shoulder · Button section · Bottom

19½ (20½, 21½)" · 9½ (10½, 11½)" · 1" · 10"

32" · 32"

Gypsy Rose designed by Barbara Venishnick

Use the vest's yarn and stitch, add a colorway, and change from side-to-side to diagonal construction for this versatile tunic.

TUNIC
NOTES
1 See *Techniques*, p. 228 for M1 and ssk.

BACK AND FRONT make 2
(***Note*** When inc at beg and end of rows, M1 after first st or before last st.)

Left side
Cast on 19 sts. Work in pat st back and forth and AT SAME TIME, beg with 3rd row, inc 1 st each side (working incs into pat) every RS row 18 (21, 24) times, end with a WS row—55 (61, 67). Cast on 7 sts for center—62 (68, 74) sts. Place all sts on hold.

Right side
Work as for left side through last inc, end with a WS row—55 (61, 67) sts.

Join sides
(RS) Continuing in pat, k1, M1, work to last 2 sts, k2tog, place marker (pm), work across sts on holder as follows: ***Sizes S and L*** K7; ***Size M*** K1, [p2, k1] twice; ***All sizes*** Pm, ssk, work across in pat to last st, M1, k1—117 (129, 141) sts. ***Next row*** Work even in pat to 1 st before marker, p1, work in pat to next marker, p1, work in pat to end. ***Next row*** K1, M1, work in pat to 2 sts before marker, k2tog, work in pat to next marker, ssk, work in pat to last st, M1, k1. Continue in pat, working incs and decs every RS row, and working first and last st outside of markers in St st, until piece measures 23 (24, 25)" from outside cast-on edges, end with a WS row.

Shape shoulders
(RS) K1, ssk, work across to 2 sts before marker, k2tog, work to next marker, ssk, work to last 3 sts, k2tog, k1. ***Next row*** Work even in pat to 1 st before marker, p1, work in pat to next marker, p1, work in pat to end. Continue in pat, dec 1 st each side and before first marker and after last marker every RS row, and working first and last st outside of markers in St st, until 45 sts remain. Place on hold.

SIDE GUSSETS make 2
Cast on 24 sts. ***Set up pat*** (RS) K2, [p2, k1] twice, p2, pm, k1, p2, k1, pm, [p2, k1] twice, p2, k2. ***Next row*** K the knit sts and p the purl sts. Continue in pat st back and forth as established and AT SAME TIME, work incs and decs as for Back and front (inc 1 st each side and dec 1 st before first marker and after last marker every RS row, and working first and last st outside of markers in St st), until piece measures 14½ (15, 15½)" from outside cast-on edges. Bind off all sts.

SLEEVES
Cast on 19 (19, 25) sts. Work in pat st back and forth and AT SAME TIME, beg with 3rd row, inc 1 st each side (working incs into pat) every RS row 12 times—43 (43, 49) sts. Mark each end of this row for end of bottom

shaping. Continue in pat st and inc 1 st each side every 6th row 18 (21, 20) times—79 (85, 89) sts. Work even in pat until piece measures 17" from marker, end with a WS row. Mark each side 1¾" down.

Shape cap
(RS) Bind off 3 sts at the beg of the next 20 (22, 24) rows, 5 (5, 4) sts at beg of next 2 rows—9 sts remain for shoulder strip. Work even in pat for 6 (7, 8)". Place sts on hold.

FINISHING
(***Note*** Use smooth coordinating yarn for all sewing.)
Place markers 8 (8½, 9)" down from shoulders on front and back. Place markers 1" up from side cast-on edges on front and back. Sew side gussets to front and back between markers with cast-on edge at bottom marker. Sew sleeve shoulder strips to front and back at shoulders. Sew top of sleeves to front and back between gussets. Sew portion at top of sleeves (above markers) to top of gussets. Sew sleeve seams from markers to underarm.

Neckband
Beg with a shoulder strip, sl all sts from hold (front, back and shoulder strips) to circular needle, join—108 sts. ***Rnd 1*** Sl 1, *pm, k1, [p2, k1] twice, pm, p2tog, [p2, k1] 6 times, pm, k1, [p2, k1] twice, pm, [k1, p2] 6 times, p2tog; rep from* once, working last p2tog over last st and first sl st—104 sts. ***Rnd 2*** *K1, [p2, k1] twice, sl marker, p2tog, p1, k1, [p2, k1] 5 times, sl marker, k1, [p2, k1] twice, sl marker, [k1, p2] 5 times, k1, p1, p2tog, sl marker; rep from* once—100 sts. Continue in pat st circularly in rnds, working incs and decs to maintain established bias pat every other rnd as follows: *work in pat to marker, sl marker, M1, work in pat to 2 sts before marker, k2tog, work in pat to next marker, ssk, work in pat to next marker, M1, sl marker; rep from* once. When neckband measures 2", p1 rnd for turning ridge, then k every rnd for 2". Bind off loosely. Fold neckband to WS at turning ridge and sew bound-off edge to inside.

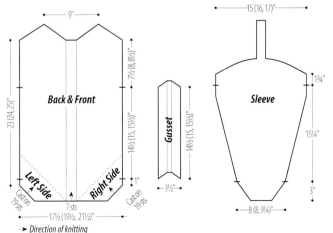

Back & Front

23 (24, 25)"

9"

7½ (8, 8½)"

14½ (15, 15½)"

Left Side

Right Side

Cast on 19 sts

1"

7 sts

17½ (19½, 21½)"

Cast on 19 sts

→ *Direction of knitting*

Gusset

14½ (15, 15½)"

3½"

15 (16, 17)"

Sleeve

1¾"

15¼"

3"

8 (8, 9¼)"

Why not pants designed by Barbara Venishnick

The same moss rib stitch is worked vertically in a wool-silk solid for these tailored pants.

Intermediate

Sizes

S (M, L)

Shown in size S.

Directions are for smallest size with larger sizes in parentheses. If there is only 1 set of numbers, it applies to all sizes.

Finished measurements

Waist 37¼ (39½, 41¾)"

Hip 42 (44½, 46½)"

Inseam 29"

Gauge

22 sts and 32 rows to 4"/10cm over pat using size 4 (3.5mm) needles.

MATERIALS

Yarn Cherry Tree Hill *Rustic Silk* 3 (3, 4) balls Black (8oz/228g, 600yds/548m, 80% raw silk, 20% wool).

Needles One pair size 4 (3.5mm) needles, *or size to obtain gauge*. Size 4 (3.5mm) circular needle, 29"/74cm long.

Extras 1 yard of 1" wide no-roll elastic, stitch holders, and markers.

NOTES

1 See *Techniques*, p. 228 for short-row wraps. *2* For a shorter or longer inseam, work fewer or more rows between increases in the first (bottom) section of each piece.

STITCHES USED

Pat st

Worked Back and Forth multiple of 3 sts plus 1

Row 1 (RS) K1, *p2, k1; rep from*. **Row 2** P1, *k2, p1; rep from*. **Row 3** Knit. **Row 4** Purl. Rep row 1–4 for pat worked back and forth.

Worked Circularly in Rnds multiple of 3 sts

Rnds 1 and 2 (RS) *K1, p2; rep from*. **Rnds 3 and 4** Knit. Rep rnds 1–4 for pat worked circularly in rnds.

RIGHT BACK

With straight needles, cast on 43 (49, 55) sts. Work in pat st back and forth and AT SAME TIME, inc 1 st at end of every 20th row (RS) 6 times, 1 st at the end of every 6th row 12 times, then 1 st at the end of every 4th row 9 times—70 (76, 82) sts. Work even until piece measures 29" from beg, end with a RS row.

Shape crotch

(WS) At the beg of each WS row, bind off 4 (5, 5) sts once, 3 (4, 4) sts once, 2 (3, 3) sts once, 0 (0, 2) sts once, 0 (0, 1) st once—61 (64, 67) sts. Work even in pat until piece measures 3¾" from beg of crotch shaping, end with a WS row. **Next row** (RS) Dec 1 st at beg of this row, then every 10th row 4 times more—56 (59, 62) sts. Work even until piece measures 9½" from beg of crotch shaping. Place all sts on hold.

LEFT BACK

Work as for right back, reversing all shaping.

RIGHT FRONT

With straight needles, cast on 37 (43, 49) sts. Work in pat st back and forth and AT SAME TIME, inc 1 st at beg of every 20th row (RS) 6 times, then 1 st at the beg of every 6th row 18 times—61 (67, 73) sts. Work even until piece measures 29" from beg, end with a WS row.

Shape crotch

(RS) At the beg of each RS row, bind off 4 (4, 5) sts once, 2 (3, 4) sts once, 0 (2, 3) sts once—55 (58, 61) sts. Work even in pat until piece measures 3¾" from beg of crotch shaping, end with a WS row. **Next row** (RS) Dec 1 st at end of this row, then every 10th row 4 times more—50 (53, 56) sts. Work even until piece measures 9½" from beg of crotch shaping. Place all sts on hold.

LEFT FRONT

Work as for right front, reversing all shaping.

JOIN BACK SECTIONS

Sew center back seam from beg of crotch shaping to top of pieces. Sl all sts onto needle—112 (118, 124) sts. **Beg short row shaping: Row 1** (RS) Work 55 (58, 61) sts in pat, k2tog at center seam, work next 52 (55, 58) sts, turn, leaving remaining sts unworked. **Row 2** Work 105 (111, 117) sts in pat, turn, leaving remaining sts unworked. Continue in this manner, working 3 less sts each row 14 times more. Place all sts on hold on circular needle.

JOIN FRONT SECTIONS

Sew center front seam from beg of crotch shaping to top of pieces.

JOIN BACK AND FRONT

Slip front onto circular needle with back sts, with left sides edges tog. Join, place marker for beg of rnd at beg of right side of back. **Rnd 1** Working pat st circularly in rnds, k2tog, work 107 (113, 119) sts in pat, k2tog (end of back); join left side seam as follows: k2tog, pass last back st back over first front st; work across 47 (50, 53) sts, k2tog at center seam, work 47 (50, 53) sts, k2tog—205 (217, 229) sts. Work even in pat circularly until waistband measures 1½" from join. P 1 rnd.

Make casing

Work back and forth in St st for 1½". Bind off loosely.

FINISHING

Sew right and left inseams from bottom to beg of crotch shaping. Sew side seams, leaving 2½" at bottom edge open for side slits. Fold casing to WS at turning ridge and sew bound-off edge to inside, leaving casing side slit open. Insert elastic through casing slit. Pin and sew elastic to desired tightness.

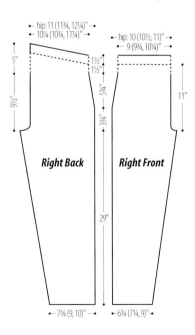

Right Back   *Right Front*

CHERRY TREE HILL YARN CHERYL POTTER
Quilted tuxedo designed by Barbara Venishnick

The jacket's quilted look is formed by knits and purls, increases and decreases. A plush but muted combination of multi-colored mohair loop and a smooth, almost-solid gray merino works up quickly.

MATERIALS
Yarn Cherry Tree Hill *Froth A* 3 skeins Gypsy Rose(8oz/ 228g, 500yds/457m, mohair with a touch of wool); *Superwash Merino B* 6 skeins Heather Grey, *C* 1 skein Heather Black, *D* Small amount Heather Plum (each 4oz/114g, 280yds/250m, 100% wool).
Needles One pair each sizes 8, 10½, and 11 (5, 6.5 and 8mm) needles, *or size to obtain gauge.* Size 8 (5mm) circular needle, 29"/74cm long.
Extras Four 1¼" buttons. Stitch holders.

NOTES
1 See *Techniques*, p. 228 for ssp, Make 1 purl (M1P), and short-row wraps. *2* In order to maintain correct stitch count when working shaping in chart pattern, each decrease must be paired with a M1P. *3* Chart is worked with 1 strand A and 1 strand B held together as 1.

STITCHES USED
Chart pat multiple of 14 sts plus 1
Row 1 (RS) *K1, p3, k7, p3; rep from*, end k1. *Row 2* *P1, M1P, k3, p2tog, p3, ssp, k3, M1P; rep from*, end p1. *Row 3* K2, *p3, k5, p3, k3; rep from*, end last rep k2. *Row 4* P2, *M1P, k3, p2tog, p1, ssp, k3, M1P, p3; rep from*, end last rep p2. *Row 5* K3, *p3, k3, p3, k5; rep from*, end last rep k3. *Row 6* P3, *M1P, k3, p3tog, k3, M1P, p5; rep from*, end last rep p3. *Row 7* K4, *p3, k1, p3, k7; rep from*, end last rep k4. *Row 8* P2, *ssp, k3, M1P, p1, M1P, k3, p2tog, p3; rep from*, end last rep p2. *Row 9* K3, *p3, k3, p3, k5; rep from*, end last rep k3. *Row 10* *P1, ssp, k3, M1P, p3, M1P, k3, p2tog; rep from*, end p1. *Row 11* K2, *p3, k5, p3, k3; rep from*, end last rep k2. *Row 12* Ssp, *k3, M1P, p5, M1P, k3, p3tog; rep from*, end last rep p2tog. Rep rows 1–12 for chart pat.

Half brioche pat odd number of sts
Rows 1 and 3 (WS) Purl. *Row 2* *K1, k1 in row below (k1b); rep from*, end k1. *Row 4* K2, *k1b, k1; rep from*, end last rep k2. Rep rows 1–4 for pat.

BACK
With size 11 (8mm) needles and 1 strand A and B, cast on 85 (92, 99) sts. Work in chart pat until piece measures 17 (18, 19)" from beg, end with a WS row.
Shape armholes
(RS) Bind off 4 (5, 5) sts at beg of next 2 rows, 3 (4, 4) sts at beg of next 2 rows, 3 sts at beg of next 2 rows, 1 (1, 2) sts at beg of next 2 rows—63 (66, 71) sts. Work even until armhole measures 10 (10½, 11)", end with a WS row.
Shape Shoulders
(RS) Bind off 6 (6, 7) sts at beg of next 4 (2, 4) rows, 7 (7, 8) sts at beg of next 2 (4, 2) rows. Place remaining 25 (26, 27) sts on hold for back neck.

POCKET LININGS make 2
With size 10½ (6.5mm) needles and 1 strand A and B, cast on 21 sts. Work in St st until piece measures 6½" from beg. Place sts on hold. Cut yarn leaving a tail long enough to sew lining to inside of jacket.

RIGHT FRONT
With size 11 (8mm) needles and 1 strand A and B, cast on 57 (57, 64) sts. Work in chart pat, beg and end as indicated on chart, until piece measures 8" from beg, ending with a WS row.
Place pocket lining
(RS) Work in pat over 32 sts, sl next 21 sts onto holder, continuing in pat work across 21 sts of pocket lining, work remaining 4 (4, 11) sts. Continue in chart until piece measures 9½ (10½, 11½)" from beg, end with a WS row.
Shape neck
(RS) Working in pat, dec 1 st at beg of this row then every other row 11 (8, 12) times more, then every 4th row 15 times. AT SAME TIME, when piece measures same as back to armhole and shoulder shaping, shape as for back at beg of WS rows.

LEFT FRONT
Work as for right front, beg and end as indicated on chart, until piece measures 4 (5, 6)" from beg, end with a WS row. **Buttonhole row** (RS) Work 32 (32, 39) sts in pat, bind off 4 sts for buttonhole, work until 13 sts on needle after buttonhole, bind off 4 sts for buttonhole, work to end. **Next row** Work in pat, casting on 4 sts over each set of bound-off sts for buttonholes. Continue in pat until piece measures 8" from beg, end with a WS row.
Place pocket lining
(RS) Work 4 (4, 11) sts in pat, sl next 21 sts onto holder, continuing in pat work across 21 sts of pocket lining, work remaining 32 sts. Continue in pat until piece measures 8½ (9½, 10½)" from beg, end with a WS row, rep buttonhole row and next row. Work in pat until piece measures 9½ (10½, 11½)" from beg, end with a WS row.
Shape neck
(RS) Shape neck as for right front at end of RS rows. When piece measures same as back to armhole and shoulder shaping, shape as for back at beg of RS rows.

SLEEVES
With size 11 (8mm) needles and 1 strand A and B, cast on 57 sts. Work in chart pat and AT SAME TIME, inc 1 st each side (working incs into chart pat) on chart row 6, then every 6th row 9 (11, 13) times more—77 (81, 85) sts. Work even in pat until piece measures 17 (18, 19)" from beg.

Quilted tuxedo

Shape cap

Work as for back armhole shaping—55 (55, 57) sts. Then dec 1 st each side every other row 7 times, then every row 3 times—35 (35, 37) sts. Bind off 2 sts at beg of next 2 rows, bind off remaining 31 (31, 33) sts.

FINISHING

Pocket edging

With WS facing, size 8 (5mm) needles and C, k21 sts from holder. Beg with a WS row, work Half brioche pat for 1", end with a RS pat row. Work 3-color cord as follows: with WS Half brioche pat facing, k1 B, k1 D, k1 C, *carrying yarn over the 2 colors left hanging in back of work, k1 B, k1D, k1 C; rep from* across. Cut B and D. Turn. With C and RS of Half brioche pat facing, work in St st for 1" beg with a k row. Bind off loosely. Fold along 3-color cord to WS of Half brioche pat, sew in place. Fold 2 layers of trim to outside of jacket (3-color cord at bottom). Sew to jacket front on each side of trim.

Sleeve cuffs

With WS facing, size 8 (5mm) needles and C, pick up and k57 sts along cast-on edge. Beg with a WS row, work in Half brioche pat for 2½", end with a RS pat row. Work 3-color cord as for pocket edging. With C and RS of Half brioche pat facing, work in St st for 2¼" beg with a k row. Bind off loosely.
Block pieces. Sew shoulder seams.

Collar

With WS of jacket facing, size 8 circular needle and C, beg at left front neck shaping and pick up and k76 sts along neck edge, k25 (26, 27) sts from back neck holder, pick up and k76 sts along right front neck edge to beg of neck shaping—177 (178, 179) sts. *Beg short row shaping:* **Row 1** Purl to last 31 sts, inc 0 (1, 0) st at center of back neck, turn leaving remaining 31 sts unworked. **Row 2** Work row 2 of Half brioche pat to last 31 sts, turn, leaving remaining 31 sts unworked. **Row 3** Purl to last 29 sts, turn. **Row 4** Work row 4 of Half brioche pat to last 29 sts, turn. Continue in Half brioche pat working to 2 less sts each side until 1 st remains unworked each side. **Next row** Purl to end. **Next row** Work row 2 of pat to end—177 (178, 179) sts. Work 3-color cord as for pocket edging, loosely stranding colors. With C, knit 1 row, then beg with a WS row, work in Half brioche pat and AT SAME TIME, bind off 2 sts at the beg of next 22 rows, then loosely bind off remaining 133 (134, 135) sts. Fold along 3-color cord to WS of Half brioche pat. Sew bound-off edge to neckline along RS of jacket.

Front facings

With RS facing and C, pick up and k61 (65, 69) sts along front edge between bottom and beg of neck shaping. **Turning Ridge** (WS) Knit. Beg with a k row, work 5 rows St st. Bind off. Fold to inside and sew in place.

Set in sleeves. Sew side and sleeve seams, including cuffs. Fold cuff facing with WS tog along 3-color cord and sew to cast-on edge. Fold cuff up over bottom of sleeve. Sew on buttons. Sew sides and bottom of pocket linings to WS of fronts.

Chart pat

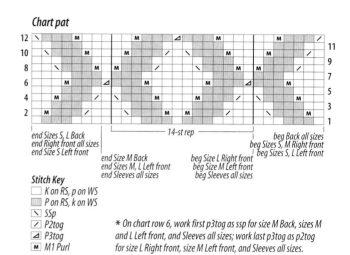

end Sizes S, L Back
end Right front all sizes
end Size S Left front

14-st rep

beg Back all sizes
beg Sizes S, M Right front
beg Sizes S, L Left front

end Size M Back
end Sizes M, L Left front
end Sleeves all sizes

beg Size L Right front
beg Size M Left front
beg Sleeves all sizes

Stitch Key
☐ K on RS, p on WS
▨ P on RS, k on WS
◣ SSp
⟋ P2tog
◢ P3tog
Ⓜ M1 Purl

*On chart row 6, work first p3tog as ssp for size M Back, sizes M and L Left front, and Sleeves all sizes; work last p3tog as p2tog for size L Right front, size M Left front, and Sleeves all sizes.

Knit in row below (k1b)
Instead of working next stitch, work into stitch directly below it, then drop stitch.

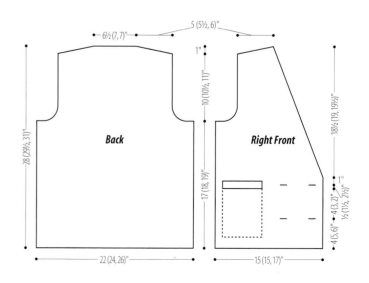

The clouds threaten rain as we travel south towards Norwich, Vermont. Sugar maples are at peak color, their leaves iridescent salmon and tomato against the darkening day. We reach Ellen's 1/2 Pint Farm without a hitch and pull up before the barn to find Ned, the family llama, guarding sheep near the pond.

ELLEN'S 1/2 PINT FARM ELLEN MINARD

Norwich, Vermont

Ellen Minard

ELLEN'S 1/2 PINT FARM ELLEN MINARD

Norwich, Vermont

Evolution Ellen Minard got the nickname "Half Pint" when she married her husband, Keith, who towers a foot above her. When they built their house and barn ten years ago, they called the place Ellen's 1/2 Pint Farm. A year later, Ellen began her dye business and the name stuck.

A native Vermonter, Ellen has been around fiber all her life. Her mother was certified as a Master Knitter by The Knitting Guild of America, and in her family, "fiber came first." Ellen recalls trading her two billy goats for sheep in order to acquire spinning fiber. As her two sheep multiplied to ten, Ellen learned from her mother how to knit and spin before discovering that her real interest was hand-dyeing. These days, Ellen's fiber animals are just pets, for she can no longer produce the quantity she needs.

Ellen began dyeing because she could never find the colors she needed for projects without having to combine several yarns. "I wanted one yarn," Ellen says. "I wanted to relax when I knit." Her answer came when she took a workshop from Deb Menz, author of *Color in Spinning* at SOAR (Spin Off Autumn Retreat) in the late '80s. Until Deb got her started painting roving, it had never occurred to Ellen that it was possible to apply so many colors to one bit of fiber. "I discovered that I love color," Ellen recalls.

A year later, she took a class from Michelle Wiplinger, a well-known colorist, and began painting fiber in earnest. As soon as she spun the yarn, her mother would knit it, developing patterns along the way. The first handpainted item Ellen sold was a pair of rainbow socks at a farmers' market in 1990. Over the next few years, it slowly dawned on Ellen that people were much more attracted to her colorways than her knitting skills, so she focused on dyeing spinning fiber and yarn.

Environment At present, Ellen still dyes yarn in her kitchen. But now, with kids grown and gone, she plans to build a dye space "down cellar" or add a room to the barn. Because she dries most of her yarn outside, she has to work around the weather, which can be harsh at times. Some months find her dyeing frantically, while others she dyes nothing at all.

She loves the peacefulness of country life and finds the long view of the valley inspiring. "Most of my inspiration comes from nature. I'll just walk around and see colors in the sky or in the trees or flowers—I love the combinations." To gather her thoughts, she spends time with her sheep and an alpaca named Chile. "I find I sometimes escape to the barn if I need some quiet time."

Clockwise from top: Hand-dyed silk caps; prepared mohair top ready for spinning; painted merino top against an autumn sky.

colors," she explains. "Usually someone will like it, or I can always over-dye it."

Yarns Ellen's 1/2 Pint Farm sells five yarns in fourteen colorways, as well as mill ends and kits. In addition, Ellen can dye solids to match any variegated in her colorways and welcomes custom orders from knitters and spinners. She works in animal fibers only—alpaca, wool, and silk.

Ellen sells her yarn at nearly a dozen retail shows per year. She has set up a small shop at her house, open by appointment only (because she and Keith both have "real jobs"), and lately, she has employed her sister to help her keep up with the dyeing and knitting.

Her best-selling yarn has always been the brushed mohair, but her fine-gauge 100% alpaca is gaining in popularity. Ellen's favorite colorways include Berry Patch, a tasty combo of raspberry and maroon with teal, Stormy Skies, made of dark gray, blues, and a little bit of purple, and Florida Skyline, her first attempt at pastels.

At first, Ellen worked with only her favorite colors. After awhile, her husband reminded her that not everybody enjoyed the rainbow as much as she did, and she might have to dye colors that other people liked, such as brown. "I'll try it," Ellen remembers telling him grudgingly. The result was a colorway called New England Autumn. It sold out at the very next show. These days inspiration comes from other places, the yellows of an Alaskan sunrise, the pastels of a Miami skyline.

Technique Ellen paints prepared roving, silk caps, and loose fiber, as well as yarn. To keep colors separate and vibrant, she space-dyes yarn and then wraps it in plastic for steaming. She paints with stencil brushes, sponges, or squirt bottles, depending on the desired spread of color. In order to achieve tonal gradations, she sometimes blends color by squishing fiber with her gloved hands. "If I'm trying to place the color in a certain area, especially on silk caps, I am more apt to use stencil brushes," she explains.

"I like vibrant colors," says Ellen, who does much of her experimenting on mill-end yarns. Sometimes she throws together colors that normally don't go with each other, just to see the results. "I'm not afraid to play with

Ellen is encouraged when she sees knitters using more than one of her colorways in a garment. "They go together because they have been dyed together," she observes. In addition to the color, Ellen offers quality yarns with a pleasing hand. "If you're going to spend a lot of time, you need to enjoy knitting with it," Ellen says. "It's funny when

Top: A sweaterhank of rainbow wool graces the barn door. It is here in the quiet of the barn that Ellen retreats to gather her thoughts.

Bottom: Ned, the llama guards the sheep and alpaca as they drink from the pond.

Clockwise from top: Painted rib shown in Northern Lights with hand-dyed red; children's garments knit in Ellen's bright colorways; a handpainted chair.

you walk into a store, they say 'Don't touch.' Well, when you walk into my booth, I say 'Please touch!'"

Ellen believes that the brilliant colors keep people coming back. "People say the colors just jump out at them." She rewinds her yarn to help knitters get a better sense of the color spread. She has no dyelots, but dyes large sweater hanks and small skeins for accent.

Future watch Ellen hopes her business will grow so she can cut back on her job as a dental hygienist. She plans a lively mail-order business and a shop with regular hours. Ellen likes to teach her techniques for painting roving to fiber enthusiasts. Soon, she and her sister plan to apply their vibrant color range to cottons.

Although Ellen does not think hand-painted yarn will ever dominate the market, she feels that its popularity will continue to grow. "If I had to say one word it would be 'Enjoy'," Ellen says. "Hand-painted yarn is cheerful. Don't worry about all the colors—colors are good for the spirit."

ELLEN'S 1/2 PINT FARM ELLEN MINARD
Rainbow trio designed by Celeste Pinheiro

Doubled yarn and a reversible rib stitch blend the rainbow colors of this scarf and vest. On a crisp fall day, add the simplest of hats.

Easy

Sizes

Child sizes 2 (4, 6)

Shown in size 2.

Directions are for smallest size with larger sizes in parentheses. If there is only 1 set of numbers, it applies to all sizes.

Finished measurements

Vest

Underarm (buttoned) 31 (34, 37)"

Length 13½ (15, 16½)"

Hat

Circumference 20"

Scarf

7¾" wide by 36" long

Gauge

14 sts and 21 rows to 4"/10cm over St st (k on RS, p on WS) using size 10 (6mm) needles with 2 strands of yarn held tog.

16 sts and 23 rows to 4"/10cm in Rib pat using size 10 (6mm) needles with 2 strands of yarn held tog.

MATERIALS
Yarn Ellen's 1/2 Farm *Falkland Wool* 1 skein Rainbow (16oz/457g, 1350yds/1234m, 100% wool).
Needles One pair size 10 (6mm) needles, *or size to obtain gauge*.
Extras Three 1"/2.5mm buttons or clasps. Stitch markers and holders, crochet hook size I/9 (5.5mm).

NOTES
1 See *Techniques*, p. 228 for 3-needle bind-off (ridge effect), single crochet (sc), and reverse single crochet (rev sc). **2** Vest is worked in one piece to underarms, then divided for fronts and back. **3** Work with 2 strands of yarn held together as one throughout.

STITCH USED
Rib pat multiple of 4 sts plus 3
Row 1 (WS) K1, *p1, k3; rep from*, end last rep p1, k1.
2 *K3, p1; rep from*, end last rep k3. Rep rows 1–2 for pat.

VEST
BODY
With 2 strands of yarn, cast on 123 (135, 147) sts. Work in Rib pat until piece measures 7½ (8½, 10)" from beg, end with a WS row.
Divide for fronts and back
Next row (RS) Continuing in pat, work 26 (28, 30) sts for right front and put those sts on hold, bind off 10 (12, 14) sts (underarm), work until there are 51 (55, 59) sts for back, bind off 10 (12, 14) sts (underarm), work to end for left front and put those sts on hold.

BACK
With WS facing, join 2 strands of yarn at armhole edge and continuing in pat, bind off 1 st each side every other row 5 times—41 (45, 49) sts. Work even until armhole measures 5½ (6, 6)", end with a WS row. Mark center 17 (21, 25) sts for neck.
Shape neck
(RS) Continuing in pat, work to marker, join 2nd ball of yarn (2 strands) and bind off marked sts, work to end. Working both sides at same time, dec 1 st at each neck edge once—11 sts each shoulder. Work even in pat until armhole measures 6 (6½, 6½)". Place sts on hold.

LEFT FRONT
With WS facing, join 2 strands of yarn at front edge. Continue in pat and bind off 1 st at armhole edge every other row 5 times—21 (23, 25) sts. Work even until armhole measures 5 (5½, 5½)", end with a RS row.
Shape neck
Next row (WS) Bind off 6 (8, 10) sts, continuing in pat, work to end—15 sts. Dec 1 st at neck edge every other row 4 times—11 sts. Work even until armhole measures same as Back. Place sts on hold.

RIGHT FRONT
With WS facing, join 2 strands of yarn at armhole edge and work as for left front, reversing shaping.

FINISHING
With WS tog, work 3-needle bind-off (ridge effect) to join shoulder seams. With RS facing and 2 strands of yarn, beg at lower right front, work 1 row sc up front, around neck, and down left front. *Do not turn*. Working left to right, ch 1, work rev sc in each sc, ending at lower right front. Fasten off. Beg at shoulder seam on armhole, work 1 rnd sc, 1 rnd rev sc as for front. Working with 2 strands held as one, work 3 braids, 8½" long each. Fold in half and tie ends tog with an overhand knot. Attach to right front edging as for fringe: the first approx ¾" from beg of neck shaping, and the other 2 spaced 2" apart (attached with horizontal bar of braid on RS).

HAT
With 2 strands held tog, cast on 72 sts. Work in St st for 5½", end with a WS row. *Next (dec) row* (RS) K9, k2tog, place marker (pm), *k8, k2tog, pm; rep from*, end k1. *Next row* Knit. *Next (dec) row* *K to 2 sts before marker, k2tog; rep from*, end k1. Rep last 2 rows 3 times, then rep last dec row until 9 sts remain. Cut yarn, pull through sts.

FINISHING
Sew seam, reversing at bottom edge for roll.
Tassles make 6
With crochet hook and 2 strands held tog, ch 15 sts, work 2 sc in 2nd ch from hook and in each ch across. Fasten off leaving a tail for sewing. Sew 6 tassles to top of hat.

SCARF
With 2 strands held tog, cast on 31 sts. Work in Rib pat until piece measures 36". Bind off.
Fringe
Cut 8 strands 11" long per fringe. With WS facing, attach 8 fringes on each end. Trim fringe even.

Attach fringe

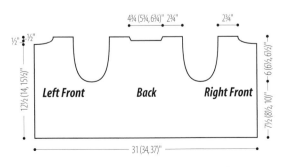

ELLEN'S 1/2 PINT FARM ELLEN MINARD
Big basketweave designed by Celeste Pinheiro

This basketweave mix of knits and purls is cozy and compelling. And with doubled yarns, it's a fool-proof blender of color.

MATERIALS
Yarn Ellen's 1/2 Pint Farm *Falkland Wool MC* 1 skein Stormy Skies **CC** Small amount Red (each 16oz/457g, 1350yds/1234m, 100% wool).
Needles One pair each sizes 8 and 10 (5 and 6mm) needles, *or size to obtain gauge.*

NOTES
1 Work with 2 strands of yarn held together as one throughout.

STITCHES USED
Basketweave pat multiple of 18 sts plus 1
Row 1 (RS) Knit. *Row 2* P2, *[k2, p2, k2, p12] rep from* across; end last rep p2 (11, 2). *Row 3* [K2, p2] 2 (0, 2) times; k2 (1, 2), *p8, [k2, p2] twice, k2; rep from* across. *Row 4* P2, *[k2, p2] twice, k8, p2; rep from* 3 (4, 4) times; **Small and Large Sizes Only** [k2, p2] twice; **Med Size Only** end last rep p1. Row 5 [K2, p2] 2 (0, 2) times; k12 (11, 12), *p2, k2, p2, k12; rep from* across, end last rep k2. *Rows 6–9* Rep rows 2–5. *Row 10* Purl. *Row 11* K11 (2, 11), *p2, k2, p2, k12; rep from* across, end last rep k11. *Row 12* P1, *k8, [p2, k2] twice, p2; rep from* across; **Small and Large Sizes Only** k8, p1. *Row 13 Small and Large Sizes Only* P1, k8; *All Sizes* [k2, p2] twice, k2, p8; rep from* 3 (4, 4) times, k1. *Row 14* P11, *k2, p2, k2, p12; rep from* across, end last rep p11 (2, 11). *Rows 15–18* Rep rows 11–14. Rep rows 1–18 for pat.
K2, p2 rib
Row 1 (WS) P2, *k2, p2; rep from* across. *Row 2* K2, *p2, k2; rep from* across. Rep Rows 1–2 for pat.

BACK
With smaller needles and 2 strands of MC, cast on 66 (75, 84) sts. **Begin Basketweave pat** (RS) Work in Basketweave pat, working first and last st in St st for selvages, until piece measures 8½ (8½, 9½)" from beg, end with a WS row.
Shape Armhole
(RS) Continuing in pat, bind off 9 sts at beg of next 2 rows—48 (57, 66) sts. Working first and last st in St st for selvages, work even until armhole measures 5½ (6½, 7½)", end with a WS row. Mark center 24 (27, 30) sts for neck.
Shape neck
Next row (RS) Continuing in pat, work to marker, join 2nd ball of yarn (2 strands) and bind off marked neck sts, work to end in pat. Working both sides at the same time, bind off at each neck edge 1 st once—11 (14, 17) sts each shoulder. Work even in pat until armhole measures 6 (7, 8)". Bind off.

FRONT
Work as for back until armhole measures 4½ (5½, 6)", end with a WS row. Mark center 12 (13, 14) sts for neck.

Shape neck
Next row (RS) Continuing in pat, work to marker, join 2nd ball of yarn (2 strands) and bind off marked neck sts, work to end in pat. Working both sides at the same time, bind off at each neck edge 3 sts 1 (2, 2) times, 2 sts 2 (1, 1) times, 1 st 0 (0, 1) time—11 (14, 17) sts each shoulder. Work until piece measures same length as back. Bind off.

SLEEVES
With smaller needles and 2 strands of CC, cast on 30 (30, 34) sts. K 1 row. Cut CC. **Next row** With MC, knit. Work 3 rows of k2, p2 rib. **Next row** (RS) Change to larger needles and work in St st, AT SAME TIME, inc 1 st each side this row then every 4th row 0 (6, 10) times, then every 6th row 6 (4, 2) times—44 (52, 60) sts. Work even until piece measures 12 (13, 14)" from beg. Bind off. Mark each side 2" down from top.

FINISHING
Block pieces. Sew right shoulder seam.
Neckband
With RS facing, smaller needles and 2 strands MC, pick up and k60 (64, 68) sts evenly around neck edge. Work 7 rows of k2, p2 rib. Cut MC. **Next row** With CC, k 2 rows. Bind off. Sew left shoulder and neckband seam. Sew top of sleeves to armholes. Sew straight portion at top of sleeves (above markers) to bound-off armhole sts. Sew side and sleeve seams.

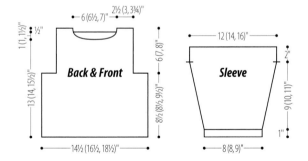

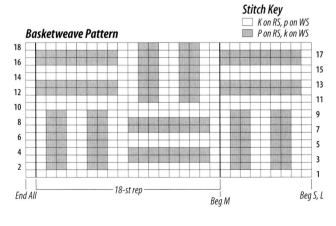

Stitch Key
☐ K on RS, p on WS
▨ P on RS, k on WS

Basketweave Pattern

Painted rib designed by Celeste Pinheiro

Handpainted yarn is only half the story when corrugated rib takes over. Bright red provides high contrast to the narrow columns of the colorway.

MATERIALS

Yarn
Ellen's Half Pint Farm *Falkland Wool A* 1 ball Northern Lights, *B* 1 ball Red (each 16oz/457g, 1350yds/1234m, 100% wool).

Needles
One pair size 10 (6mm) needles, *or size to obtain gauge.*

Extras
Stitch holders.

NOTES
1 See *Techniques*, p. 228 for ssk. *2* Work with 2 strands of yarn held together as one throughout.

STITCH USED
Corrugated rib multiple of 4 sts plus 2
Row 1 (RS) K2 B, *k2 A, k2 B; rep from* across. *2* (WS) K2 B, *p2 A, k2 B; rep from* across. Rep rows 1–2 for pat.

BACK
With 2 strands of A, cast on 62 (66, 74) sts. K 1 row. *Begin Corrugated rib* (RS) Work in Corrugated rib until piece measures 7 (7½, 8½)" from beg, end with a WS row.

Shape raglan
Next row (RS) Continuing in pat, work 3 sts, ssk, work to last 5 sts, k2tog, work to end. Continue in pat and dec 1 st each side as established every RS row 15 (15, 19) more times, end with a WS row. Work last WS row as follows: work to last 2 sts, k2tog—29 (33, 33) sts. Place sts on hold.

FRONT
Work as for back, working last WS row as follows: ssk, work to last 2 sts, k2tog—28 (32, 32) sts.

LEFT SLEEVE
With 2 strands of A, cast on 34 (34, 38) sts. K 1 row. *Next row* (RS) Begin working corrugated rib as for back, AT SAME TIME, inc 1 st each side this row, then every 6th row 5 (5, 7) times more—46 (46, 54) sts. Work until piece measures 8½ (9½, 10½)" from beg, end with a WS row.

Shape raglan
Work as for back, working ssk at beg of last WS row—13 sts, place on hold.

RIGHT SLEEVE
Work as for left sleeve, working ssk at beg and k2tog at end of last WS row—12 sts.

FINISHING
Sew right sleeve to front and back along raglan edge and left sleeve to front only. With RS facing and continuing in rib as established, work 13 sts from left sleeve

holder, 28 (32, 32) sts from front holder, 12 sts from right sleeve holder, 29 (33, 33) sts from back holder—82 (90, 90) sts. Work 5 more rows in rib. *Next row* (RS) With A, k 2 rows. Bind off in knit. Sew left sleeve to back along raglan edge and neck band. Sew side seams.

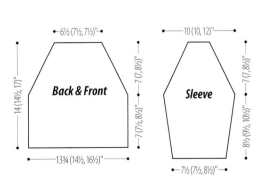

Back & Front
← 6½ (7½, 7½)" →
14 (14½, 17)"
7 (7½, 8½)"
7 (7½, 8½)"
← 13¾ (14½, 16½)" →

Sleeve
← 10 (10, 12)" →
7 (7, 8½)"
8½ (9½, 10½)"
← 7½ (7½, 8½)" →

Intermediate

Sizes
2 (4, 6)
Shown in size 4.
Directions are for smallest size with larger sizes in parentheses.
If there is only 1 set of numbers, it applies to all sizes.

Finished measurements
Underarm 27½ (29, 33)"
Length 14 (14½, 17)"

Gauge
18 sts and 19 rows to 4"/10cm over corrugated rib using size 10 (6mm) needles with 2 strands of yarn held together.

OAK GROVE YARNS LINDA MACMILLAN

Linda MacMillan

Pale sun streaks warm us on the drive to southern Vermont. Bright maple leaves still burn on the trees. The season is Indian Summer, that delicious time of year between summer's end and true fall. We pull off the Putney exit and head toward Linda MacMillan's Oak Grove Yarns.

OAK GROVE YARNS LINDA MACMILLAN

Putney, Vermont

On her own Linda MacMillan's adventure with hand-dyed yarn began nearly 15 years ago. After her daughter, Lisa, went to college, Linda realized she could make a new life of her own choosing. Originally, she wanted to found a fiber collective with other spinners, weavers, and knitters. This was in 1987, at a time when no such venues existed in Vermont. Although others were interested, no one wanted the responsibility of a business. Instead, Linda quit her job and opened a shop.

She called her shop Oak Grove, after her farm, and filled it with products from local sheep farms. She raised Merino sheep, Angora goats, and Angora rabbits and had the fiber spun into yarn nearby at Green Mountain Spinnery. An abundance of naturally colored yarn prompted Linda to try her hand at dyeing. "I discovered that dyeing turned me on," she says.

Linda's mother was a watercolor artist, and her father was a lawyer. "That combination has served me well," Linda says. "There was something creative in my genes and something business-minded, too." Although she knew color would play a significant part in her life, knitting has always come first. She began designing sweaters in her early twenties, but eventually found herself frustrated with the available colors. When she began to develop her technique of painting yarn in the dyepot, people told her that was not possible, but she went ahead. "When I started dyeing, there was Melinda Bickford, Margie Mills, and Christella from Fiesta," Linda recalls.

Painting among the oaks For years, Linda painted yarn in the back room of her shop. When she closed her store in 1995, to do trade shows, she renovated a goat barn on her farm for studio space. There she paints colorways inspired by her New England surroundings. The time of year affects her color choices; they are usually brighter in the summer light and muted during the dusk of winter. "I'm influenced by my mood, as well," Linda notes. "If I'm happy, or miserable, it affects my outlook and therefore my dye process."

Tranquility is important to Linda. Her farm is well off the road, where she surrounds herself with space and privacy. She lives in a "hippie-built house" half hidden by an oak grove, which keeps her large common room warm in winter and cool in summer. "It's like a Japanese tea house," Linda says of her distinctive dwelling, which has decks on the east, south, and west sides, where the view is gorgeous.

Color flow Linda dyes yarn using a unique color-flow technique that she has fine-tuned over the years. She strives to create painted yarns without rigid color repeats, while maintaining consistency from skein to skein. Linda envisions colorways that sometimes take her two to three months to develop. She adjusts color and technique, depending on how she wishes the dyes to segue. "I work in a pot with liquid dyes, and basically add color as is appropriate," she explains. "That's why every dye pot is different." She generally does three-pound dyelots, enough for a project. Saturation is important to Linda's process. "I use a lot of dye and I don't do pastels. I have to keep putting dye in until I'm satisfied."

Linda favors neither primary nor clear colors. Instead, she works with the inner circle of the color wheel, where she finds complements for all of her shades. "I like my colors complicated, with a lot going on," she says. Linda draws from a palette of between 20 and 30 basic colors. Her three reds all use the red/gold blend, for example. The wine color she creates shows up in another related color group. In this way, more than one color flow can be coordinated for use in the same project. Linda also dyes solids that complement her colorways.

Top: Fall Leaves, a colorway inspired by Linda's surroundings among the oaks in Putney, Vermont, shown in a kid mohair and merino blend. Linda has much of her yarn spun at Green Mountain Spinnery, a local mill.

Right: A selection of yarns in Tumbleweed colorway are dyed using Linda's unique color-flow technique, in which she creates painted yarns that are reproducible without rigid color repeats.

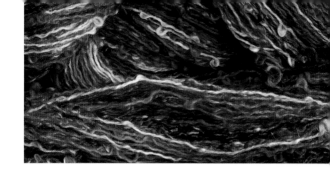

Keeping it simple Although Linda holds a master's degree in marketing, she tries not to use it. After closing her store, she attended more shows, and now sells yarn via mail order and word of mouth. If her business grows so large that she needs help, it will be time for a re-evaluation. She wishes to dye yarn, not be an employer.

Most of Linda's designs include simple motifs—often Fair Isle patterns—and are usually knit from cuff to cuff to avoid horizontal striping. "I have built my business on the beginning knitter," she says, and for this reason, she offers uncomplicated designs that the yarn can carry off effortlessly. Linda kits all of her designs in a freeform manner. "My kit is yarn, the pattern, and a plastic bag," she explains. "You pick the yarn, I'll put it in plastic, and we'll call it a kit."

Yarns Linda sells a handful of yarns—kid mohair (her best seller); a boucle of mohair, silk, and wool; pure silk, and an angora/merino blend—all custom-spun. She prefers bulkier yarns, explaining, "I don't believe in knitting on anything smaller than a size 7 needle." Linda loves to tweak and reinvent her color flows and for this reason, she dyes 10 to 12 ever-evolving colorways. "I bring them back and send them packing," she says. Her

most popular colorways are Tumbleweed, Antique Rose, and Golden Roses.

Because her yarns are custom-spun to her specifications, and she works with her own colors and patterns, Linda is involved in many creative processes. "My vision comes first," she says. "I see it and then I work to that vision." She designs her yarns and patterns (about 25 now) to be sold as kits, such as her Golden Roses cardigan, which has a distinctive color flow of black, gold, and wine with a reddish gold worked in.

Future watch Although she has been selling yarn for 15 years, Linda doesn't predict fashion trends. She believes that knitters favor what looks good on them. And she also thinks handpainted yarns cannot have a mass appeal because they are so unique and inconsistent. "It is difficult for the shops to deal with that," she explains. "Knitters who use handpainted yarn tend to be more adventuresome."

However, she believes the appeal for painted yarns will hold up. Once a knitter becomes familiar with the subtle effects hand-dyed yarns can produce, there is no turning back. This strong base of appreciation will support the handpaint market, Linda believes. "The most important thing that I can say to knitters is, 'Have a good time,'" Linda says with a smile. "That is, after all, the whole point."

Linda is at a restless point in her career. "Every five years I get bored and re-create my business," she confesses. "I have cycled." Ever seeking new creative territory, Linda is on an exciting new path with color—new palette, new techniques, new medium. Currently, she creates lampwork beads and jewelry to complement her yarns: "All that I've learned about color with the yarn is going to be translated into the beads."

Clockwise from top: Golden Roses colorway; luxury boucle blends enhance Linda's complex colors; smooth and textured yarns in the same colorway.

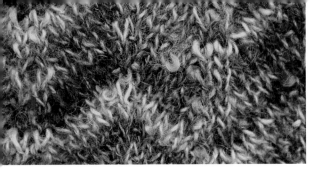

OAK GROVE YARNS LINDA MACMILLAN

Winter wave designed by Melissa Lumley

The colors move with the waves on this easy-to-knit, easy-to-wear classic.

MATERIALS
Yarn Oak Grove Yarns *Glimmer Kid Mohair* 9 (11, 13) balls Tumbleweed (each 1¾oz/50g, 100yds/92m, 80% kid mohair, 15% wool, 5% nylon).
Needles One pair size 8 (5mm) needles, *or size to obtain gauge.* Size 7 (4½mm) circular needle, 16"/40cm long.
Extras Stitch markers and holders.

NOTES
1 See *Techniques,* p. 228 for ssk and 3-needle bind-off.

STITCH USED
Waves pat multiple of 14 sts plus 2
Row 1 (RS) K1, *k into front and back of next st, k4, k2tog, ssk, k4, k into front and back of next st; rep from* to last st, k1. *Row 2* Purl. Rep rows 1–2 for pat.

BACK
With larger needles, loosely cast on 86 (100, 114) sts. Work in Waves pat until piece measures 15" from beg, end with a WS row.
Shape armholes
Next row (RS) Bind off 6 sts, k1 (2 sts on RH needle), continue across in established pat. *Next row* Bind off 6 sts, p across—74 (88, 102) sts. Continue working even in pat, working the first and last 2 sts in St st until armhole measures 10 (11, 11)", ending with a WS row. Place all sts on hold.

FRONT
Work as for back until armhole measures 6½ (7½, 7½)", end with a WS row.
Shape neck
(RS) Work 30 (37, 44) sts, sl next 14 sts onto holder for front neck, join a second ball of yarn and work to end. Working both sides at the same time, dec 1 st at each neck edge every row 7 times—23 (30, 37) sts each shoulder. Work even until armhole measures same as back, end with a WS row. Place all sts on hold.
SLEEVES
(**Note** Work the sleeve increases into the pattern when there are 8 sts outside of markers. Remove markers and on RS row k1, pm, ssk, k4, k into front and back of next st, work Waves pat from* across, end last rep with k into front and back of next st, k4, k2tog, pm, k1. Continue shaping and working in pat and when there are 8 sts outside of

markers again, remove markers and on RS row, k1, pm, work Waves pat from* across to last st, pm, k1. Then continue working new sts into pat in groups of 7 as established.)
With larger needles, cast on 46 (50, 50) sts. **Begin Waves pat: Row 1** (RS) K2 (4, 4), place marker (pm), work row 1 of Waves pat from* across to last 2 (4, 4) sts, pm, k to end. *Row 2* Purl. Continue in pat, working sts outside of markers in St st (k on RS, p on WS) and AT SAME TIME, inc 1 st each end on 5th row, then every 4th row 21 (23, 23) times more (working incs into pat in groups of 7)—90 (98, 98) sts. Work even until piece measures 18¾ (19¾, 19¾)" from beg, end with a WS row. Mark each end of row for underarm. Work in St st for 1¼". Loosely bind off all sts.

FINISHING
With RS tog, join shoulders using 3-needle bind-off, leaving 28 sts at center back on hold.
Neckband
With RS facing and circular needle, pick up and k28 sts from back neck holder, 14 sts along left neck edge, 14 sts from front neck holder, and 14 sts along right neck edge—70 sts. Pm for beg of rnd. K 10 rnds. Bind off loosely. Sew straight portion at top of sleeves (above markers) to bound-off armhole sts. Sew side and sleeve seams.

Wet block sweater as follows: get sweater completely wet, then gently squeeze out water by rolling in a towel. Block and pin to measurements, pinning out where necessary, especially at wave points. Do not remove pins until completely dry.

Easy+

Sizes
S (M, L)
Shown in size S.
Directions are for smallest size with larger sizes in parentheses. If there is only 1 set of numbers, it applies to all sizes.

Finished measurements
Underarm 37 (43, 49)"
Length 25 (26, 26)"

Gauge
14 sts (1 pat rep) and 14 rows to 4"/10cm over Waves pat using larger needles.

When shaping the sleeves, remember to keep the stitch pattern increases (knit in the front and back of the stitch) and decreases (k2tog or ssk) paired. As the sleeve widens, don't work the new stitches into the Wave pattern until there are enough stitches to work both the increase and the adjacent decrease.

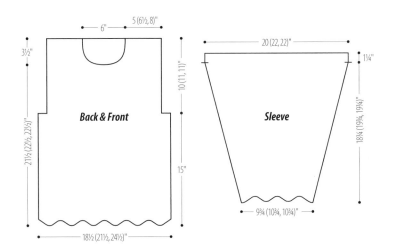

Foliage blazes on the hillsides
as we travel the broken
pavement of Route 2 across
Vermont and into Maine.
Passing through mill towns we
angle north toward the
lesser-known coastal villages.
Steuben is not on the map and
neither is Strawberry Point.
"You can't get there from
here," comes to mind as we
bump along a sandy track.
Soon, we are rewarded with
a bright, hand-lettered sign
that says "Tess' Yarns."
The drive ends at a weathered
Cape Cod overlooking Pigeon
Hill Bay.

Melinda Bickford

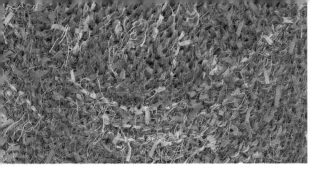

TESS' DESIGNER YARNS MELINDA BICKFORD
Steuben, Maine

Friendly dogs accompany Melinda Bickford up from a gravel beach strewn with driftwood and sea weed. Founder of the company named after her daughter Tess, Melinda has lived along the edge of this saltwater bay for nearly 25 years.

From sheep to Stitches Melinda is no newcomer to the world of hand-dyed fiber. In 1980, she bought Romney sheep and began spinning and dyeing their wool with cochineal and indigo. But she found natural dyes increasingly difficult to obtain and learned that the salt air rendered her colors unstable. After Tess was born, Melinda's handspinning tapered off. It seemed to her that people were after her vibrant colors more than her handspun yarn, so she sold her ewes to buy fleeces in 1987 and turned to commercial dyes.

Melinda learned dyeing from a Mexican dyer. "I liked the whole process—the smell of the sheep, the feel of the fleece," she remembers. She calls her process hand dyeing rather than hand-painting. "But I don't consider that an important distinction," she adds. Her technique is not limited by label. She learned by experimentation. "Sometimes my mistakes were wonderful," she recalls.

From selling baskets of wool at sheep shows, Melinda turned to marketing hand-dyed yarns in upscale shops along the Maine coast. When it came time to name her company, Melinda chose to use her daughter's name, and her logo depicts Tess as a toddler surrounded by a sea of yarn. "Tess was my de facto designer," Melinda chuckles. "Whenever I had to stop dyeing to tend to her, the yarn would darken in the pot just that much more."

Cooking up colors Melinda feels a special attachment to this stretch of coastline she calls home. The house with its weathered, shingled roof, hand-hewn beams, and pumpkin pine floors has perched above Pigeon Bay for 250 years. Her father was born in this house, and her family has lived here since they came over from the island in 1902. When Melinda moved in, she installed indoor plumbing and began dyeing yarn in the kitchen. "Eventually the yarn overtook us and drove us out," she says with a laugh. That was four years ago.

Clockwise from top:
Dip dyed boucle in circle pattern stitch; brilliant shades of handdyed ribbon on the rocks overlooking the bay; hanks rest on the rail of a beached boat; the family cat, Harry, lounges beneath hanks drying in the salt air.

Now she uses the entire house for her dye studio and retail space.

A cross country trip in her early days as a hand dyer may have pushed Melinda's palette into the brilliant range. Or maybe her colors intensified as a reaction to the long Maine winters, Melinda isn't quite sure. "I just do the yarn until it looks right," she says matter-of-factly. "When it looks right, it's done." She finds that she tends to dye darker colors for the eastern cities and brighter ones for the West Coast, as well as lighter colors in spring and darker ones in fall. Other colors, she just cannot explain; one customer attributes them

huge amount of rinse water. Living on the rocky seacoast, Melinda does not have "endless amounts" of fresh water. Her approach is in harmony with both her environment and her lifestyle. "My process is absolutely simplistic," Melinda says. "A pot on the stove, sometimes two pots—this is as technical as I want to get."

Melinda attributes the rich incandescence of her yarns to her 20 years of experience with color application. Although many of her colors may appear monochromatic, they are not dyed as "true solids." Instead, she uses a layering process, so that there is always an undercurrent of another color present in the yarn. When mixing colors within the skein, she strives for complementary colors that flow into one another without harsh changes. Melinda sells yarn directly from the dye pot, explaining, "Reskeining is not part of the dye process for me." She couples her sometimes intense colors with exotic fiber blends that are incredibly soft to the touch,

Clockwise from top:
Wool boucle dyed in a shade Melinda jokingly calls "hurts-to-look-at green;" a cluster of exotic blends hug the rocks like barnacles at low tide; catch of the day—a lobster and a mohair shawl.

to the "color witch" that she feels must haunt the ancient house.

"I dye the way I cook," Melinda tells us. "Add a little here and there, work with what I have on hand." She combines immersion dyeing with dip dyeing and does a little painting on the side, manipulating yarns in the pot in order to produce her desired effect. Melinda avoids muddy colors and goes for longish stretches of clear shades sequenced within the same hank.

Melinda is best known for her wide array of distinctive solids. "We all have our own palette and mine's always changing," she says. When she finds a new combination she likes, she experiments with it in a variety of yarns. She carries a standard palette of 35 to 40 colors and combinations, from which she continually adds and deletes.

Because she likes to dye yarns quickly for an instant appraisal of certain shades, Melinda prefers to stick to animal fiber as a medium. "I like to fine-tune the color," she explains. "Sometimes all I need to do is swoosh the yarn in and out of a dye bath." One reason she avoids plant fibers is because cotton requires a much longer stay in the dye bath. In addition, plant fibers require a

such as angora and silk. She believes that her yarns should feel as luxurious as they look.

Balancing business with family Melinda markets yarn at trade shows, through mail order, and by word of mouth. She resists wholesale for several reasons. "Retail is more fun because of the direct contact with the knitter," she says. In addition, she doesn't want to become more production-oriented. She has always put her family life ahead of yarn. Although she loves her business, there is nothing she would rather be doing than raising her daughter. "Dyeing yarn and family life are just different chapters in the book of my life," she explains. "Right now I'm involved in the child-raising chapters."

When purchasing hand-dyed yarn, knitters should consider the source, Melinda believes. "I think it is better to buy from experienced hand dyers," she advises. "They do a better job." She has discovered complexities that she was unaware of in the beginning and techniques that could only be learned over time. Now, she is able to produce softer yarns with truer, lasting colors. Although she does not want to discourage new dyers, she

says, "It's like anything—the more you do, the better you become."

The brilliant colors of Melinda's yarns simply make her feel good. It is a feeling she tries to give her customers, some have become more like friends and family. As her fibers became less "sheepy" and more refined, her clientele has become more educated about knitting and design. "I am impressed," she says. "Now everyone's a better knitter than I am."

From novelty to mainstream
Melinda has seen trends come and go. When once her yarns were perceived as a novelty, now they are widely accepted by the knitting public. Her yarns are made of exotic fibers such as mohair, angora, and silk blends in both plain and textured yarns. Years ago, she had little competition. Now although there are many hand dyers in the market, she feels "competition in a good way. Because there is so much to choose from, more and more knitters are being drawn into the world of hand-dyed yarns."

Clockwise from top:
Ikat design in Stacked Stole;
Melinda's sign recalls the saying, "You can't get there from here"; Tess, Melinda Bickford's daughter and the company's namesake, models a Lily Chin design knit from microfiber ribbon; looking out from Strawberry Point.

Melinda is amazed at how much pattern support has been developed for hand-dyed yarns. She and Tess do their part by sponsoring design competitions and working with new designers, as well as their tried-and-true favorites, including Ginger Luters and Lily Chin.

Future watch As she finds more time to spend on her yarn, Melinda expects her business to grow. Plans include breaking into the wholesale market, as she sets up her Web site. Both knitters and dyers are more willing to experiment, which helps the expansion of the market. After all this time, Melinda never tires of experimentation, developing new colors and coordinating yarns. "I'm happy to still be doing it," she says, looking to the next chapter.

The Maine coast is a timeless place. Screeching seagulls follow lobster boats back to port. Across the shallow bay, tidal pools teem with new life. The tide recedes, leaving behind seaweed and bits of colored glass worn by sand and time.

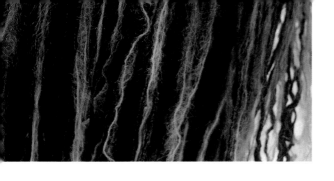

Both of these stoles are worked from the same skein of hand-dyed yarn! Take charge of your stripes; learn to work with the color repeat already built into the yarn.

MATERIALS

Yarn Tess' Designer Yarns *Brushed Mohair MC* 1 skein Lime Splash (makes both) (15oz/428g, 920yds/840m, 78% mohair, 13% wool, 9% nylon), *Cultivated Silk & Wool CC* 3 skein Black (per shawl) (3½oz/100g, 200yds/182m, 50% silk, 50% wool).
Needles Size 10½ (6.5mm) circular needle, *or size to obtain gauge:* 16"/40cm long for Diagonal Stripe version, 29"/74cm long for Vertical Stripe version. Two size 10½ (6.5mm) double-pointed needles (dpn).
Extras Crochet hook size K/10½ (6.5mm) for both versions, crochet hook size H/8 (5mm) for Diagonal Stripe version, stitch marker.

NOTES

1 See *Techniques*, p. 228 for chain cast-on, I-cord, attached I-cord, chain (ch), and grafting. *2* Both versions are worked circularly, then cut open. The Vertical Stripe version is unraveled at the cut to create fringe; the Diagonal Stripe version has an I-cord trim to cover the cut ends.

VERTICAL STRIPE VERSION

With MC, choose the color for fringe. Cut yarn at the start of the first section of this color, unwind 3 full color repeats (almost 6 yds), and mark center of next color section (fringe color).

With larger crochet hook and CC, loosely ch 260 for chain cast-on. ***Rnd 1*** With circular needle and MC, beg with the center of first color section, and beg with first ch, pick up and k into loop at back of each ch, until marker is reached—approx 244 sts. Unravel remaining ch sts and fasten by pulling ball of CC through last ch loop. Place marker for beg of rnd and join, being careful not to twist sts. ***Rnd 2*** With CC, knit. ***Rnd 3*** With MC, knit, making sure that colors are aligned on top of same colors from rnd 1. Rep rnds 2–3 until piece measures approx 22" from beg, end with a MC row. Fasten off MC. With CC, bind off loosely.

Finishing

Carefully cut a vertical line between the first and the last sts from the cast-on edge to the bound-off edge. Carefully unravel 5-10 sts all the way down on both ends for fringe, depending on desired fringe length. Be careful not to unravel cast-on and bound-off edges. Steam block edges to prevent curling. With sewing machine, stitch up center of outside st on both edges, including cast-on and bound-off edges, to prevent unraveling.

Trim

With dpn and CC, cast on 3 sts, then with RS facing, *work attached I-cord along bound-off edge to corner, then bind off 3 sts. Fasten off. Turn shawl upside down and rep trim along cast-on edge.

DIAGONAL STRIPE VERSION

With MC, cut the yarn at the beg of the next color section for beg of yarn. Unwind 1 full color repeat (almost 2 yds) and mark center of next color section. This is the same color as beg.

With larger crochet hook and CC, loosely ch 90 for chain cast-on. ***Rnd 1*** With circular needle and MC, beg with the center of first color section and with first ch made, pick up and k into loop at back of each ch until marker is reached, then pick up and k 3–5 more sts (fewer sts cause the stripes to be less angled, more sts cause the stripes to be at a greater angle)—approx 83–85 sts. Unravel remaining chain sts and fasten by pulling ball of CC through last ch loop. Place marker for beg of rnd and join, being careful not to twist. ***Rnd 2*** With CC, k1, k1

Intermediate

Finished measurements
Approx 22" x 72"

Gauge
14 sts and 22 rows to 4"/10cm
over St st alternating 1 row MC, 1 row CC, using size 10½ (6.5mm) needle.

through back loop (tbl), k to last st, k1 tbl. **_Rnd 3_** With MC, k1, k1 tbl, k to last st, making sure that colors are aligned on top of same colors from rnd 1 and moved slightly to the right, k1 tbl. Rep rnds 2–3 until piece measures approx 72" from beg, end with a MC row. Fasten off MC. With CC, bind off as follows: K1, k1 tbl, pass 2nd st on RH needle over first st, *k1, pass 2nd st on RH needle over first st; rep from* to last st, k1 tbl, pass 2nd st on RH needle over first st. Cut yarn and pull through loop on RH needle.

Finishing

With smaller crochet hook and CC, work a crocheted steek by working a slip st vertically through each twisted st on each side of the first st (see *illustration*). Carefully cut a vertical line up the first sts between the steeks from the cast-on edge to the bound-off edge. Steam block edges to prevent curling.

Trim

With dpn and CC, cast on 3 sts, then with RS facing, *work attached I-cord along bound-off edge to corner. At corner, work 2 rows unattached I-cord. Continue attached I-cord along cut edge, picking up sts in each of next 2 rows, then skipping the 3rd row, to corner. Work 2 rows of unattached I-cord at corner. Rep from* along cast-on edge and side, ending with 2 rows unattached I-cord at corner. Graft 3 sts to 3 cast-on sts.

Crocheted steek

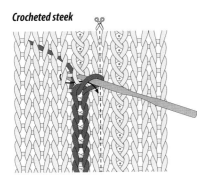

Dye pattern

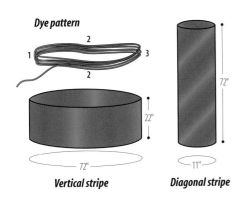

Vertical stripe   **Diagonal stripe**

This stacking technique works with multi-colored yarns with a long and consistent color repeat as shown in the skein above.

Pi in the sky designed by Lily Chin

This jacket is a circle with sleeves. It's unusual construction—pie-shaped wedges knit sideways for the center circle, then rounds of increasing length—works well with the long color repeat of a dip-dyed yarn.

MATERIALS

Yarn Tess' Designer Yarns *Silk & Ivory **A*** 2 (3, 3) skeins Periwinkle (5¼oz/150g, 665yds/608m, 50% silk/50% wool) *Spritzer **B*** 14 (16, 19) skeins Sunset Boulevard (1¾oz/50g, 95yds/86m,100% nylon).

Needles Size 10 (6mm) circular needle, 16"/40cm and 36"/90cm long, *or size to obtain gauge.* Size 10 (6mm) double-pointed needles (dpn).

Extras Stitch markers and holders.

NOTES

1 See *Techniques,* p. 228 for grafting. *2* Use 1 strand A and 1 strand B held together as 1 throughout except for trim. *3* Back is a center circle composed of 6 triangular sections worked back-and-forth. Each triangle is picked up from the side edge of the previous one, forming a circle. Stitches are then picked up all around and worked circularly around perimeter for front and collar. Sleeves are picked up and worked downwards from the top using short rows. *4* Slip all sts purlwise.

BACK

With 16" circular needle, 1 strand A and B, cast on 32 (36, 40) sts. ***Row 1*** (WS) Sl 1 with yarn in front (wyif), k to last st, sl 1 wyif. ***Row 2*** K to last 3 sts, k2tog, k1—1 st dec'd. Rep rows 1–2 until 3 sts remain, end with a WS row. ***Next row*** (RS) K1, k2tog—2 sts. ***Next row*** Sl both sts. ***Next row*** K2tog, *do not turn.* Picking up sts in sl st chains along left side (dec side) of triangle just made, pick up and k31 (35, 39) sts—32 (36, 40) sts. Rep from* until 6 triangles completed. Cut yarn leaving a 24" tail. Use tail to sew cast-on row to side of last triangle, sewing 1 st to each sl st chain.

FRONT/COLLAR

With RS facing, 36" circular needle and using 1 strand A and B, beg at any triangle join and picking up sts in sl st chains, pick up and k31 (35, 39) sts along edge of each of next 3 triangles for bottom edge, pick up and k1 in each of next 4 (6, 8) chains along next triangle, mark 4 (6, 8)th st, cast on 26 (28, 30) sts, skip remaining 27 (29, 31) chains of this triangle for right armhole, pick up and k31 (35, 39) sts along edge of next triangle for back neck, cast on 26 (28, 30) sts, skip next 27 (29, 31) chains of next triangle for left armhole, pick up and k1 in each of remaining 4 (6, 8) ch of this triangle—184 (208, 232) sts. Place marker for beg of rnd. Beg working in rnds. ***Rnd 1*** [K22 (25, 28), inc into next st] 8 times—192 (216, 240) sts. ***Rnd 2 and every even rnd*** Purl. ***Rnd 3*** K1, inc in next st, [k23 (26, 29), inc in next st] 7 times, k22 (25, 28)—200 (224, 248) sts. ***Rnd 5*** K4, inc in next st, [k24 (27, 30), inc in next st] 7 times, k20 (23, 26)—208 (232, 256) sts. ***Rnd 7*** K7, inc into next st, [k25 (28, 31), inc in next st]

7 times, k18 (21, 24)—216 (240, 264) sts. ***Rnd 9*** K10, inc in next st, [k26 (29, 32), inc in next st] 7 times, k16 (19, 22)—224 (248, 272) sts. ***Rnd 11*** K13, inc in next st, [k27 (30, 33), inc in next st] 7 times, k14 (17, 20)—232 (256, 280) sts. Continue inc every other rnd this manner, working 3 more sts before first inc, then 1 more st between each of the next 7 incs 7 (8, 10) times more—288 (320, 360) sts. ***Rnd 27 (29, 33)*** K1, inc in next st, [k35 (39, 44), inc in next st] 7 times, k34 (38, 43)—296 (328, 368) sts. ***Rnd 29 (31, 35)*** K4, inc in next st, [k36 (40, 45), inc in next st] 7 times, k32 (36, 41)—304 (336, 376) sts. Continue inc every other rnd this manner, working 3 more sts before first inc, then 1 more st between each of the next 7 incs 12 (14, 15) times more, ending with a purl row—400 (448, 496) sts.

Trim

(RS) With 2 strands of A and using cable cast-on, cast on 3 sts onto LH needle. Work attached I-cord as follows: *k2, k2tog tbl, sl 3 sts from RH needle back to LH needle, rep from* around until 3 sts remain. Graft 3 edging sts to cast-on sts.

RIGHT SLEEVE
Shape cap

With 1 strand A and 1 strand B held tog, place slip knot on 16" circular needle for first selvage st. With RS facing and beg at bottom of right armhole, pick up and k1 in the same ch as marked st, pick up and k1 st in each of the skipped 27 (29, 31) chains along triangle edge, pick up and k1 in space after cast-on sts, then pick up and k1 in last cast-on st of armhole—31 (33, 35) sts. Turn. Beg short rows as follows: ***Row 1*** Sl 1 wyif, k3, turn. ***Row 2*** (RS) Sl 1 wyif, k3, pick up and k next st along cast-on edge, turn. ***Row 3*** Sl 1, k5, turn. ***Row 4*** Sl 1 wyif, k5, pick up and k next st along cast-on edge, turn. ***Row 5*** Sl 1 wyif, k7, turn. Rep last 2 rows, picking up k1 st along cast-on edge on RS rows, and working 1 more st with each short row on WS rows until 30 (30, 34) sts have been worked, including first slipped st, turn. ***Next row*** (RS) Sl 1 wyif, k29 (29, 33), pick up and k next 2 sts along cast-on edge, turn. ***Next row*** Sl 1 wyif, k33 (33, 37), turn. Rep last 2 rows picking up and k2 sts along cast-on edge on RS rows and working 2 more sts on each short row on WS rows until 54 (58, 62) sts have been worked, including first slipped st, turn. ***Next row*** (RS) Sl 1 wyif, k53 (57, 61), pick up and k1 in space before armhole cast-on sts, cast on 1 st at end for selvage, turn. ***Next row*** Sl 1 wyif, k57 (61,65). Work back and forth in garter st for 8 (6, 6) rows. ***Next (dec) row*** K2, k2tog, k to last 4 sts, k2tog, k2—56 (60, 64) sts. Continue in garter st and rep dec row every 6th row 12 (12, 4) times more, then every

Pi in the sky

4th row 0 (1, 10) times—32 (34, 36) sts. Work even until sleeve measures 16 (15, 14)" from underarm.

Trim

Work as for body trim, grafting last 3 I-cord sts to 3 cast-on I-cord sts after sewing sleeve seam.

LEFT SLEEVE

Shape cap

With 1 strand A and B held tog, place slip knot on 16" circular needle for first selvage st. With RS facing and beg at bottom of left armhole, pick up and k1 in space after last armhole cast-on sts, pick up and k26 (28, 30) sts along cast-on edge, pick up and k1 in space before armhole cast-on sts, pick up and k1 st in each of the next 2 skipped chains—31 (33, 35) sts. Turn. Work short rows as for right sleeve, picking up sts in skipped chains, until 54 (58, 62) sts, including first slipped st, have been worked, turn. **Next row** (RS) Sl 1 wyif, k53 (57, 61), pick up and k1 in marked st, cast on 1 st at end for selvage, turn. **Next row** Sl 1 wyif, k57 (61, 65). Continue as for right sleeve.

FINISHING

Sew sleeve seams.

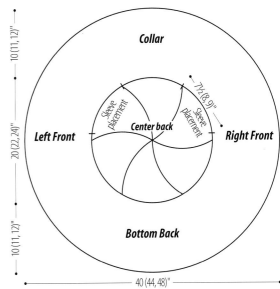

Southeast

The Blue Ridge mountains shimmer in the heat of the day as we wend our way through West Virginia. We're looking for the foothills farm owned by Merike Saarniit. Although we think we're lost, we find the gate mentioned in our directions. After a quarter mile, we spy a log house set into a pine grove—the farm and the new company Merike has started were named in memory of her first sheep, Liisu.

LOOSE YARNS MERIKE SAARNIIT

Meadows of Dan, Virginia

Merike Saarniit

LIISU YARNS MERIKE SAARNIIT
Meadows of Dan, Virginia

From fiber to art Merike Saarniit was raised in an Estonian household in upstate New York, where she learned to knit before she went to kindergarten. When she was still very young, she knew color would come to play a large part in her life. She remembers trying to figure out how people came up with names for color. "How can you end up with a name like red?" she asks. "And which red?" In college, she majored in studio art and married her anthropology professor, who was doing his doctoral studies on the Basque shepherds. Everywhere they went, from Spain to Nevada, she ended up knee-deep in fiber.

During her junior year, the college bought a loom and her medium for expression changed. She moved away from the harsh chemicals in the paints and glazes of studio art toward the enticing color, texture, and design found in the structure of weaving. "It's like knitting," Merike explains. "If you know how it really works, you can do anything."

Above: Button band detail from Fiddler's Jacket by Anna Zilboorg. The garment name reflects the fact that the brazilwood that produces the violin colors the yarn.

Center: Brazilwood-dyed yarns in a range of natural semi-solids.

Below: A mitered hat knit from the same plant-dyed yarn.

Merike was 35 when she got her own loom. She acquired two sheep, sheared them, and learned to spin their fleeces. It was only after her son did a plant-dye project for a science fair that she considered natural dyeing, and she still has the dye chart he made. Meanwhile, her flock grew, and her second husband, Dane Melvin, turned to farming and the manufacture of hay feeders full-time.

Ten years ago, she founded Carolina Homespun with two partners. She started to sell fibers and fleeces, beginning with a kit called "An Invitation to Spin." "I never wanted to carry anything I didn't know how to do or didn't understand," Merike tells us. After a year or so, she bought out her partners and started to dye custom-blended fibers.

In 1997, she began to dye yarn with commercial dyes for Anna Zilboorg's *Magnificent Mittens*.

Now, she uses both Anna's recipes and her own. She has never had color cards, for she sees them as self-limiting. Instead, Merike invites her customers to select colors for her to try. "Most of my colors come from the custom-dye arena," Merike explains, "and then I push them."

Although she was a proficient knitter and dyer before meeting Anna, she credits Anna as her mentor and supporter. Merike still dyes yarns for the mitten book. She collaborated with Anna on *Socks for Sandals and Clogs* (1999), and Anna designs patterns for Liisu Yarns.

Three kitchens and a sauna Merike paints yarn in an indoor/outdoor dye kitchen that existed when she and Dane bought the farm. She has a regular kitchen upstairs and a kind of walk-out basement kitchen at the ground level. Outside, there's a wood-burning furnace that heats water, and a sauna. She also uses a free-standing wringer and washers.

Seasonal changes have a definite effect on the way she processes yarn. When the weather is wet, she dries fiber in the sauna, and she does no carding in the winter because of the damp.

can't get from chemical ones. "There are no mistakes with natural dyes, however," she notes.

With natural dyes, it is more difficult to ensure colorfastness, and thorough rinsing is a must, Merike points out. Her concern with natural dyes is the need to use heavy metals such as copper, aluminum, and tin. Over the years, she has developed a process that requires more dyestuffs, but uses only a fraction of the amount of metal mordants used in recipes from 100 years ago.

Top: Hand-dyed Anna's Yarn, a mohair/merino blend. **Left:** Brazilwood gives Merike's yarn a range of 27 different reds.

She rewinds her yarns only if she feels the need to enhance the color play. Other times she "snaps" yarn to straighten it, or divides it into smaller amounts for mitten, sock, or sweater kits.

From retail to wholesale With Carolina Homespun, Merike owned a retail shop and sold knitting and spinning equipment as well as yarn, dyes, and kits. Now, with Liisu, she plans to sell only hand-dyed yarns, fibers and kits wholesale. Since selling Carolina Homespun in 2000, Merike knows she must leave some things behind. She is exploring hand-dyed yarns now more than ever, albeit out of the public eye.

According to Merike, handpainted yarns need not intimidate. "I have seen good knitters ooh and ahh over my yarns and then say 'Oh, but I wouldn't know what to do with it.' " Although Merike has wonderful pattern support from Anna Zilboorg, she believes that knitters should feel free to adapt any pattern to hand-dyed yarns. "Nature inspires our colors, so knitters should let our yarns inspire their knitting."

Yarns for everyone Merike dyes three lines of yarns: Dancing Yarns, commercially dyed color blends; Anna's Yarn, immersion-dyed semi-solids; and Natch, the new naturally dyed yarns. Anna's Yarn, a durable and lustrous 55% mohair/45% merino blend, is her best-selling line, but no particular color has the greatest appeal. "They are all appealing," Merike notes. She has learned that no matter how beautiful the colors, knitters seek high-quality yarn.

Merike sees yarns getting finer and finer. "But yarn is like hem lengths," she says. "They're all in style!" She loves

Merike's color choices are inspired by her natural surroundings. She finds disparate colors pleasing in nature. The uninhibited movement of natural hues in her color combinations inspired Merike's apprentice, Kelly, to name one line of yarns Dancing Fibers.

Technique Merike dyes fleeces and combed top as well as yarn. She sticks to animal fiber for the most part and loves blends such as wool and mohair, silk and alpaca. In addition to immersion-dyed solids destined for mittens and socks, Merike paints yarns using techniques from her years of studio art. The development of her painted line goes hand in hand with her experimentation with naturally dyed variegated fibers. For example, she has found that with brazilwood, she can achieve a range of colors, from the palest pinks and apricots to lipstick red. In one day, she produced twenty-seven different shades with just this one natural dye.

"I am not a snob about natural dyes," says Merike, who readily mixes naturally dyed fibers with chemically dyed ones. "Color is my focus. It doesn't matter where it comes from." She believes that there are colors you can't get from natural dyes just as there are colors you

that she can dye thick or thin yarns, chunky or plain for the same market.

Future watch Merike believes the only way painted yarn will achieve greater appeal is through education. Her goal is to help shops market one-of-a-kind yarns to their customers.

Merike teaches knitting, spinning, and dyeing classes at a variety of venues. She loves teaching and feels the future of hand-processed yarns depends on it. "Any of your students could have a major impact on your market," Merike cautions. "You've got to teach with that in mind."

Clockwise from above:
Pattern stitch detail from Fiddler's Jacket; various boucles dyed with brazilwood; brazilwood is a common wood for violins, and Merike uses the sawdust sweepings from the shops of stringed-instrument makers as a dyestuff; subtle shades of plant-dyed fleece.

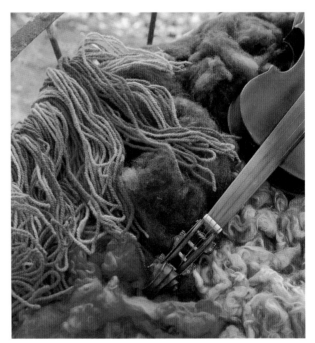

Fiddler's jacket designed by Anna Zilboorg

A symphony of reds captures our attention. The textured grain directs us across a handsome jacket that features side-to-side construction, an unusual stitch, and a splendid buttonhole.

Intermediate+

Sizes

S (M, L, XL)

Shown in size M.

Directions are for smallest size with larger sizes in parentheses. If there is only 1 set of numbers, it applies to all sizes.

Finished measurements

Underarm 40 (44, 48, 53)"

Length 21¾ (22½, 23¼, 24)"

Gauge

16 sts and 22 rows to 4"/10cm over pat with 2 strands MC held together using larger needle.

MATERIALS

Yarn Liisu Yarns *Anna's Yarn* **MC** 5 (5, 6, 6) skeins Variegated Brazilwood, **CC** 1 skein Solid Brazilwood (each 8oz/225g, 440yds/396m, 55% kid mohair, 45% wool).
Needles Size 9 (5.5mm) circular needle, 24" (60cm) long, *or size to obtain gauge.* One pair size 3 (3.25mm) needles. Size 3 (3.25mm) double-pointed needles (dpn).
Extras Five ¾"/20mm buttons. Large crochet hook.

NOTES

1 See *Techniques,* p. 228 for chain cast-on, cable cast-on, M1, attached I-cord, short-row wraps, and grafting. *2* Jacket is worked in two pieces side-to-side, from center back to center front. Sleeves are worked side-to-side, shaping with short rows. *3* MC is worked with 2 strands held together as 1 throughout.

STITCH USED

Pattern multiple of 3 sts plus 2
Rows 1–2 Knit. *Row 3* (RS) K1, *k1 wrapping the yarn twice around needle (k1 W2); rep from* to last st, k1. *Row 4* K1, *sl 3 sts one at a time purlwise dropping extra wraps; sl these 3 sts back to LH needle; (k1, p1, k1) through all 3 sts tog; rep from* to last st, k1. *Rows 5–6* Knit. Rep rows 1–6 for pat.

RIGHT BACK

With size 9 (5.5mm) circular needle and 2 strands MC, cast on 86 (89, 92, 95) sts. Work rows 1–6 of pat 6 (7, 8, 9) times, then work row 1 once more.
Shape armhole
(WS) Continuing in pat, bind off 23 (26, 29, 32) sts, then dec 1 st at beg of every WS row 7 times, ending with a WS row—56 sts. Work 4 rows even, then inc 1 st at end of every RS row 7 times, end with a RS row. Work 2 rows even. At beg of next row (pat row 6), cast on 23 (26, 29, 32) sts using cable cast-on, work to end—86 (89, 92, 95) sts.

RIGHT FRONT

Work 19 (25, 31, 37) rows even, end with pat row 1.
Shape neck
(WS) Continuing in pat, bind off 6 sts, then dec 1 st at beg of every WS row 5 times—75 (78, 81, 84) sts. Work 2 rows even, end with pat row 2. Place all sts on hold.

LEFT BACK

With size 9 (5.5mm) circular needle, 2 strands MC and RS facing, pick up and k86 (89, 92, 95) sts along cast-on edge of right back. Work rows 2–6 of pat once, then work rows 1–6 five (six, seven, eight) times, then rows 1–2 once more.

Shape armhole

(RS) Continuing in pat, bind off 23 (26, 29, 32) sts, then dec 1 st at beg of every RS row 7 times, ending with a RS row—56 sts. Work 4 rows even, then inc 1 st at end of every WS row 7 times, end with a WS row. Work 2 rows even. At beg of next row (pat row 1), cast on 23 (26, 29, 32) sts, work to end—86 (89, 92, 95) sts. Continue as for right front, beg neck shaping at beg of pat row 3, working decs at beg of RS rows and end with 1 row even (pat row 2).

SLEEVES

(**Notes 1** Sleeves are worked from side-to-side. To increase sts for first half of sleeve shaping, sts are gradually picked up from chain using chain cast-on method. To decrease sts for second half of sleeve shaping, short rows are used, leaving all sts on needle. *2* Sl first st purlwise with yarn in front on indicated chart rows. Do not sl first st at edge when it is worked straight.)
With crochet hook and 2 strands MC, loosely ch approx 100 for chain cast-on, cut yarn and pull through last loop.
Begin Chart: Row 1 (RS) With circular needle and 2 strands MC, beg with the 22nd ch from beg, pick up and k8 sts, turn. *Row 2* Sl 1, k7, turn. *Row 3* Sl 1, k7, beg in next ch, pick up and k10, turn—18 sts. *Row 4* Sl 1, k17, beg in next ch, pick up and k1, turn—19 sts. *Row 5* Sl 1, k1, [k1 W2] 17 times, beg in next ch, pick up and [k1 W2] 7 times, then pick up and k3, turn—29 sts. *Row 6* Sl 1, k2, *sl 3 sts one at a time purlwise dropping extra wraps; sl these 3 sts back to LH needle; (k1, p1, k1) through all 3 sts tog; rep from* across to last 2 sts, k2, pick up and k1 in next ch—30 sts. Continue following chart through row 32, inc by picking up sts in ch. Unravel remaining ch sts, pull yarn through last chain. Work rows 33–38 three (four, five, six) times, then work row 39. *Begin short-row shaping: Row 40* K to last 2 sts, wrap next st and turn (W&T), leaving remaining sts unworked. *Row 41* Sl 1, k1, [k1 W2] to last st, k1. *Row 42* K1, *sl 3 sts one at a time purlwise dropping extra wraps; sl these 3 sts back to LH needle; (k1, p1, k1) through all 3 sts tog; rep from* across to last 4 sts, W & T. Continue following chart through row 70, shape by working short rows. Do not turn at end of row 70; k21 to end of sleeve cap hiding wraps, turn. Bind off 21 sleeve cap sts—68 sts remain.
Join underarm seam
With RS of sleeve tog and beg at row 1 (tail marks beg), *pick up the inside edge of next cast-on chain and place on LH needle, then k2tog; rep from* once. Pass first st over 2nd st. Continue to pick up, k2tog and pass first st over 2nd st across, ending at wrist. Do not remove chain from chain cast-on.

FINISHING

Sew shoulder seams. Place 5 markers along right front for buttonholes, with the first 1" below neckline, the last 3" above bottom, and 2 others spaced evenly between.

Neckband

With 1 strand CC, size 3 (3.25mm) needle and RS facing, pick up and k24 sts along right front neck, 32 sts along back neck, and 24 sts along left front neck—80 sts. Work in St st for 2" end with a WS row. *Turning ridge* (RS) Purl. *Make facing* Beg with a p row, work 2" in St st, ending with a WS row.

Join and bind off band

With WS of jacket facing and band folded at turning ridge, *pick up the first CC loop of pick-up row and place on LH needle, loosely k2tog; rep from* once. Pass first st over 2nd st. Continue to pick up, k2tog and pass first st over 2nd st across.

Right front band

With 1 strand CC, size 3 (3.25mm) needle, and RS facing, [k2, M1] along right front, end k1 (0, 1, 0), then pick up and k12 sts along neckband through both thicknesses—124 (129, 133, 138) sts. Work 5 rows St st. *Next (buttonhole) row* (RS) Knit, and work a buttonhole centered at each marker as follows: With contrasting scrap yarn, k3 and sl sts back onto LH needle, place marker (pm) on RH needle and continuing with CC, reknit 3 sts (*illustration 1*), work to next buttonhole marker. Work 7 more rows St st (sl marker every row). *Turning ridge* (RS) Purl. *Make facing* Beg with a p row, work 7 rows St st (sl marker every row). *Next (buttonhole graft) row* (RS) K to first marker (remove marker). *Cut yarn leaving a 6" tail and thread through yarn needle. Insert dpn through each of the 4 lower loops of buttonhole that scrap yarn goes through (*illustra-*

tion 2). Fold bottom of work up at turning ridge. With yarn needle, graft buttonhole sts as follows (*illustration 3*): *1* Insert yarn needle purlwise through first st on LH needle and pull yarn through, leaving st on needle. *2* Insert yarn needle purlwise through first st on dpn removing st from dpn, then knitwise through next st on dpn leaving st on dpn. *3* Insert yarn needle knitwise through first st on LH needle removing st from LH needle, then purlwise through next st on LH needle, leaving st on needle. Rep steps 2 and 3 until all sts have been removed from dpn, end with step 3, inserting yarn needle knitwise through first st and removing from LH needle. Remove tail from yarn needle and drop. With ball of CC, k to next marker. Rep from* across, k to end after last buttonhole has been grafted.

Next row (WS) *P to buttonhole, place 3 CC loops that scrap yarn goes through onto dpn and p them, then remove scrap yarn; rep from* across, p to end. At each buttonhole, tie 2 tails tog in a square knot and cut, leaving 1" tails. Work 4 more rows St st. Join and bind off as for neckband.

Left front band

Beg at neckband, work as for right front band, omitting buttonholes.

Cuff edging

With 1 strand of CC and dpn, cast on 4 sts. With RS facing and beg at seam, work attached I-cord around cuff, picking up 1 st in every row. Graft end to cast-on edge. Sew sleeve into armhole.

Bottom edging

With 1 strand of CC and dpn, cast on 4 sts. With RS facing and beg at bottom of left front, work attached I-cord around entire bottom, including front bands, picking up 1 st in every row. Bind off.

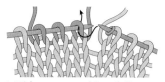

1. With scrap yarn, k3 and slip sts back onto left-hand needle, place marker on right hand needle, and continuing with contrast color, knit to next buttonhole marker.

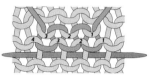

2. Insert dpn through each of the 4 lower loops that scrap yarn goes through.

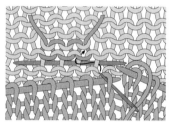

3. With yarn needle, graft sts from left-hand needle to buttonhole sts from dpn.

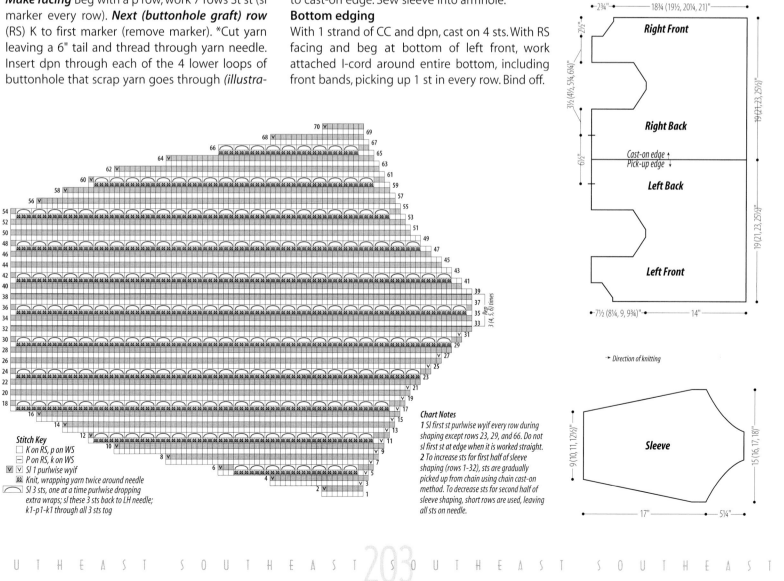

Chart Notes
1 Sl first st purlwise wyif every row during shaping except rows 23, 29, and 66. Do not sl first st at edge when it is worked straight.
2 To increase sts for first half of sleeve shaping (rows 1-32), sts are gradually picked up from chain using chain cast-on method. To decrease sts for second half of sleeve shaping, short rows are used, leaving all sts on needle.

Stitch Key
☐ K on RS, p on WS
⊟ P on RS, k on WS
☑ Sl 1 purlwise wyif
⧈ Knit, wrapping yarn twice around needle
⌒ Sl 3 sts, one at a time purlwise dropping extra wraps; sl these 3 sts back to LH needle; k1-p1-k1 through all 3 sts tog

PRISM YARNS LAURA BRYANT

St. Petersburg, Florida

We fly into Ft. Lauderdale from snow country. It isn't the sparkling coastline that excites us so much as the emerald Bermuda grass and brilliant shrubs shimmering in the breeze. Shucking our down coats, we head west along "Alligator Alley", then north to St. Petersburg, to the home of Laura Bryant and Prism Yarns.

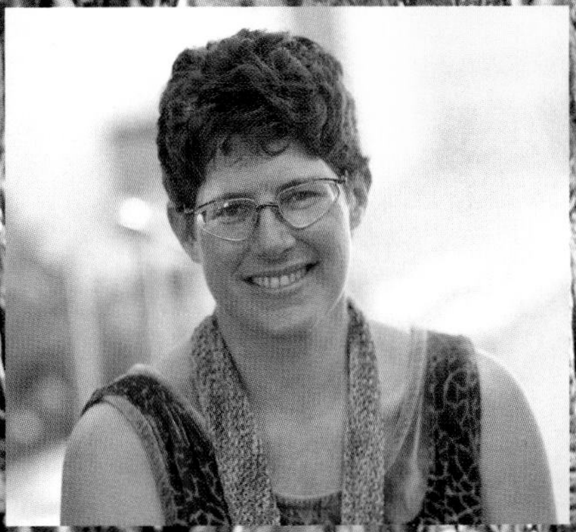

Laura Bryant

PRISM YARNS LAURA BRYANT
St. Petersburg, Florida

The Bryants' waterfront home, painted in cool peach and green, is a showcase of decorative artwork. As we enter, we see Laura's sponge-painted sunset on the cathedral ceiling in the foyer. Drawings, pottery, and a collection of handpainted furniture punctuated with antiques and modern pieces add beauty throughout the house. Several of Laura's award-winning weavings adorn the walls.

The lure of fiber and color As a college art major, Laura studied drawing, painting, and ceramics. Although she initially resisted textiles, "When I took my first weaving class, it was all over," she recalls. World-renowned fiber artist Sherri Smith became Laura's weaving mentor, while colorist Vincent Castagnacci "taught me how to see—how to analyze something with my eyes." Before then, Laura had no confidence with color. "My early weavings were white," she admits. "I didn't know color was going to be *it* until I took a color course. It changed my life."

Clockwise from above: Mosaic maze pattern stitch knit from Bon Bon and Superdazzle by Laura Bryant; brilliant mitered squares knit from Prism's "Family of Stuff," a series of yarns which are composed of custom-dyed novelties tied end-to-end in analogous color and gauge groups; novelty yarns nest in a palm in Laura's backyard.

Weaving took over. Her pieces won awards. She sold her artwork—until the bottom dropped out of the art market in 1982. In an effort to keep a share of the dwindling market, she reluctantly produced coarser and cheaper pieces. "It was destructive," Laura says of those hard times.

It wasn't until she became a sales rep for a yarn company that Laura had a 'V-8 moment.' "I realized that I already knew how to paint yarn." In 1984, Prism was born. Laura dyed yarns from British Mohair and began to design sweaters. A trade show exhibit in 1986 garnered orders that prompted the need for studio space. A garage at her husband's machine shop became Prism Yarns' new home.

From pizza to Prism A few years later, the Bryants' dream of moving to Florida to pursue their shared love of competitive sailing became a reality. They purchased a building that had previously housed a pizza factory and transformed it into the Prism Yarns warehouse. Today, Laura's production studio, staffed by five employees, houses an office, winding room, warehouse, and dye kitchen. Laura has a "personal studio inside the studio," where she sets aside two afternoons each week for her own art, often involving weaving. She shows us a woven basket project that has recently caught her interest. Stacks of art periodicals, advertisements, and fashion magazines that inspire color and texture choices are within easy reach.

Laura sees little change in her brilliant palette since her move south from New York. "Yes, I lived in Buffalo," she declares, "but I saw color everywhere." Now living amid subtropical greenery, Laura notes that not everything is brightly colored. "You have to remember that Florida is a desert, where it only rains during three months of the year." One of her best-selling new colorways, Smoke, was inspired by the subdued colors of the Gulf coast twilight—brown, plum, blue, and taupe.

Creating custom yarns To achieve her trademark palette, Laura dip-dyes yarn in a method in which the dye bath is exhausted (the yarn has absorbed all the dye). She finds this process environmentally friendly and economical (and it does not require steam, which adds heat and humidity to a climate frequently abundant in both). Dip-dyeing gives Laura complete control over the development of the long, clear color stretches she prefers. "Dyeing isn't a science, it is an

a composition of wool, mohair, cotton, rayon, silk, and nylon starring eyelash and metallic yarns. Next, Laura developed Cool Stuff, sans wool and mohair, for those in warmer climates. All are worsted weight and designed to be interchangeable. The newest family members are Impressions, a bulky blend, and Light Stuff, a combo of finer strands.

Prism Yarns also offer novelties such as Bon Bon, a flat rayon ribbon, and Super Dazzle, a glittery nylon blend. A popular line of nearly 50 hand-dyed semi-solids called "sandwashed" have a tone-on-tone effect reminiscent of suede.

Most of Prism's finished products are small one- to two-ounce hanks, re-skeined with labels and dye lots. Although winding these small skeins is labor-intensive, Laura likes them for accent and trim, and notes that creative knitters prefer this size for mixing with other yarns.

Strutting her stuff From the beginning, Laura has marketed Prism yarns wholesale only. Over the years she has built a strong core of loyal distributors who have fostered her nation-wide reputation for brilliant and outrageous yarns. Each season Laura introduces new variations of Stuff, her fashion-oriented line that appeals to urban tastes and trends. Stuff is currently available in about 50 colorways; some are discontinued when new ones are added, but the best of the trends are retained. Laura feels that appealing colorways are timeless, and that no one wishes to stray far from a palette that works, regardless of trends.

In concert with designing yarns and colorways, Laura produces up to four pattern books a year filled with garments designed specifically for her yarns. "Pattern support is very important, because the skeined yarn doesn't reveal the ultimate look of the knitted piece," Laura notes, "and Prism Yarn doesn't really fit in regular patterns."

Since many knitters are unfamiliar with techniques that make the most of handpainted yarns, Laura teaches. In her classes, Laura recommends the use of pattern stitches to either break up or emphasize the long color stretches in her yarns and advises knitters to pay attention to the special properties of hand-dyed yarns in

art," she explains. "Although many hands touch this yarn, color is put on by me and me alone," insists Laura. "I have an insouciant attitude about mixing colors. You don't get 'wow' by doing the expected."

Laura dyes natural fibers (cotton, wool, mohair, cashmere, and angora) and lots of nylon, which she likes because it is soft and malleable and can be readily milled for texture. She produces small dye lots of no more than five pounds to encourage both lively production and continued experimentation. Color cards are available, but some of her yarns, such as Wild Stuff, defy classification.

Laura's signature is novelty yarn. She mixes hand-dyed yarns with custom-milled novelties to create unique effects, exemplified in Mo/Bird, a hand-dyed mohair and eyelash yarn, packaged in big sweater balls. Other novelty blends feature Laura's hand-dyed fibers with confetti, metallics, and other fancy binders.

She calls her best-known custom yarns her "Family of Stuff." Combining up to 30 textures in a color group, Laura hand-ties the yarns end-to-end after they are dyed. The original member of this family is Wild Stuff,

Clockwise from above: Dazzling balls of custom-dyed novelty yarns defy definition; the personal time Laura makes for artwork each week almost always includes some weaving; mini-hanks, used for accent, provide a wild bouquet of texture and color.

Right: A palm laden with an exotic mix of color and texture. Bottom: Prism's novelty yarns are color-coordinated to mix and match solids and handpaints.

general. Not surprisingly, many of her classes focus on knitting with custom yarns that have both novelty and handpainted components.

Proving that custom yarns and fabric can be united to create distinctive garments, Laura's Cantina Kimono, from her wearables collection, incorporates knit triangles of Cool Stuff and reversed-appliqued velvet. Cantina is a "progressions colorway" in which the colors are arranged in shades through a progression (in this case, the rainbow). Laura dyed the rich rayon/silk blend velvet and trimmed the garment with Quicksilver, a knit rayon ribbon. The resulting piece is a wonderful mixed-media presentation of wearable art.

Future watch Although Laura has witnessed continuous growth in the popularity of hand-dyed and custom yarns, she does not want her business to expand beyond its present size. She recognizes Prism Yarns' advantage over larger commercial yarn manufacturers. "With hand-dyed yarns, you can quickly respond to the market. It's not hard to take a risk when you produce small dye lots."

Small dye lots also give Laura and her customers an opportunity that mainstream yarn companies cannot so easily afford: experimentation, both for the yarn design-

er and adventurous knitters who eagerly seek new and extraordinary creative experiences. Laura plans to continue dedicating time to educating knitters, though her duties as president of The National Needlework Association have limited her teaching schedule.

Laura's enthusiasm for color and texture continues to fuel her business. Prism Yarns will introduce two or three new yarns and a handful of new colorways each season, along with fresh designs and innovative ways to use its custom yarns.

"There is always room in the world for more beauty," Laura declares, advising the knitting public not to worry about stash size. "Some of us just love yarn."

Cantina kimono designed by Laura Bryant

A pair of progressions—graduated triangles based on a multiple of 15 stitches and a shaded colorway—give creative structure to the adventurous knitter.

MATERIALS

Yarn Prism *Cool Stuff A* 6 skeins Cantina (6–8oz/ 170–228g, 300yds/274m, cotton, rayon, nylon, polyester, silk, linen); *Quicksilver B* 2 skeins Cantina (2oz/56g, 160yds/146m, 100% rayon).

Needles One pair size 8 (5mm) needles, *or size to obtain gauge.*

Extras 3 frogs. Crochet hook size F/5 (3.75mm), 3½ yds 45" wide velvet in blue, fusible interfacing.

NOTES

1 See *Techniques* p. 228 for ssk, sl 1-k2tog-psso, single crochet (sc), and reverse single crochet (rev sc). *2* Cool Stuff consists of various yarns tied together in random lengths to give a variety of colors and textures in the same yarn. When you reach a knot, place it on the wrong side. *3* The body is worked in a "freeform" style, beginning with the largest triangle and working each triangle onto the previous one. The triangles can be joined on the side as they are worked, eliminating seaming, or worked individually and sewn together. *4* To make the coat, refer to diagram for triangle placement and the number of stitches used to begin each triangle. *5* Work all triangles in A and crochet edging in B.

COAT

For ease in working, make a copy of the diagram and mark off each triangle as it is completed. Since the triangles are equilateral, the direction of each individual triangle isn't important. The shaded triangles are left open and filled with velvet fabric after knitting is completed. Following the diagram, make shapes by joining triangles to form hexagons, partial hexagons and strips. You can also pick up sts along the outside edge of a tri-

angle in a shape to begin a new triangle. Work triangles and shapes as follows:

TRIANGLES

Standard Triangle

With A, cast on an odd number of sts. *Row 1* (WS) Purl. *Row 2* K1, ssk, work to last 3 sts, k2tog, k1. Rep rows 1–2 until 5 sts remain, ending with a WS row. *Next row* (RS) K1, sl 1-k2tog-psso, k1. *Next row* Purl. *Next row* K3tog. Fasten off last st.

Triangle joining 1 side

With RS facing and A, pick up and knit an odd number of sts along a straight edge of one or more triangles, picking up 1 full stitch or row in from edge. Work as for standard triangle.

Triangle joining 2 sides

With RS facing and A, pick up and knit an odd number of sts along a straight edge of one or more triangles, picking up inside 1 full stitch or row. *Row 1* (WS) Purl. *Row 2* K1, ssk, work to last 3 sts, k2tog, sl last st, pick up and k1 st in the adjoining triangle 1 st or row up (you have already worked 1 row). Pass the slipped st over the picked up st. Rep rows 1–2, picking up sts in first triangle every other st or row, until 5 sts remain, ending with a WS row. *Next row* (RS) K1, sl 1-k2tog-psso, sl 1, pick up and k1 st from adjoining triangle, psso. *Next row* Purl. *Next row* K3tog, pick up and k1 st from adjoining triangle, pass first st over 2nd st. Fasten off last st.

HEXAGON

(*Note* 6 equilateral triangles will fit together to form a hexagon.)

Make a standard triangle, then make 4 triangles the same size, each one joining the side of the previous triangle. Complete hexagon by making 6th triangle, joining 2 sides, or leave open for a velvet triangle.

FINISHING

When all knitting is completed, with RS facing and B, work 1 rnd sc then 1 rnd rev sc around

Adventurous

Size
One Size.

Finished measurements
Underarm 58"
Length approx 43"

Gauge
18 sts and 24 rows to 4"/10cm
over St st on average of yarns
using size 8 (5mm) needles.
A triangle beg with
15 sts = approx 3" each side.

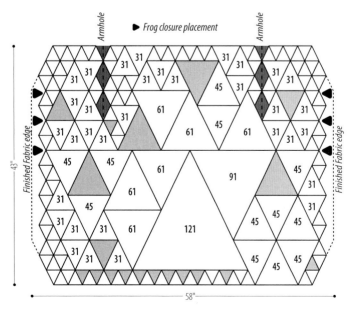

▶ Frog closure placement

Armhole Armhole

Finished Fabric edge Finished Fabric edge

43"

58"

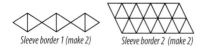

Sleeve border 1 (make 2)   *Sleeve border 2 (make 2)*

Diagram Notes
1 The number in each triangle indicates the number of sts to cast on for that triangle.
2 For small white triangles without numbers, cast on 15 sts.
3 The shaded triangles are left open, and filled with velvet fabric after knitting is completed.

Cantina kimono

each opening left for fabric. Do not crochet around outside edge of piece. Rep edging around sleeve borders 1 and 2.

Inserting velvet
Lay the velvet out on a flat surface, RS up. Lay the knitting on top of fabric, carefully stretching and tugging to make the triangles even. Pin, then baste the knitting to the fabric, through the "ditch" made between the sc and rev sc rnd. Cut the fabric away on the back side, leaving approx ½" outside of basting. Carefully topstitch over basting with a sewing machine.

Lining
Lay coat down, WS up. Lay fabric the long way (selvage at top and bottom) with RS up, on top of coat. Do not cut the length, as the coat will drop and full length is needed. Pin a large box pleat (approx 4") at center back and a smaller pleat (approx 2") at each front, at both top and bottom edges. Keeping grainlines straight, extend fabric for approx 1½" beyond the points of front triangles. Fold fabric back along this line, then cut, leaving approx 3" beyond the fold. This will become the front edge and self facing. Mark and cut an opening in velvet for the sleeves (*see diagram*). Without moving the fabric, at center front opening, mark an angle on the fabric points at top and bottom that extends the angle of the knitting. Remove fabric. Cut fusible interfacing for both front facing sections, and fuse along fold line. Machine stitch the angles marked at top and bottom for facing; trim and turn. Hand stitch the box pleats at shoulder areas and bottom for approx 2". Sew shoulder seams on both coat and lining. Reinforce the bottom of the armhole slash with tiny machine stitches, close to the slash.

Outside edging
With RS facing and B, work 1 rnd sc around entire outside edge of coat, including back neck, then work 1 rnd rev sc. Fasten off. Rep edging around both armholes.

Sleeves
From remaining fabric, cut 2 pieces 21" long. Fold in half (the foldline becomes the bottom edge of sleeve before 2nd border is added). Pin Sleeve border 1 to folded edge, leaving ½" from points to fold. Cut sleeve at an angle from border to armhole, leaving a seam allowance plus 1" for ease of stitching. Remove border, stitch continuous seam for sleeve and self lining, clip, trim, turn and press. Replace border, baste, and stitch. Treating both layers of sleeve as one, sew to lining armhole opening. Press seam allowances toward body.

Pin lining into coat, laying finished front and armhole edges of coat over the raw edges of lining. It is easiest to do this by placing coat and lining on a dressmaker's dummy or on a borrowed friend. The coat will lengthen due to the weight of the yarn; pinning in the lining while vertical will equalize the fabric and knitting. Pin, baste and machine topstitch in the ditch along these edges. Turn bottom of lining up along bottom edge. Hand stitch in place. The knitting can be stabilized by hand tacking the lining to points of various triangles throughout the body. Stitch the frog closures to the fronts, placed in the spaces between the top three points (*see diagram*). Topstitch Sleeve border 2 along bottom edge of sleeve. (Sleeve border 2 is not lined.)

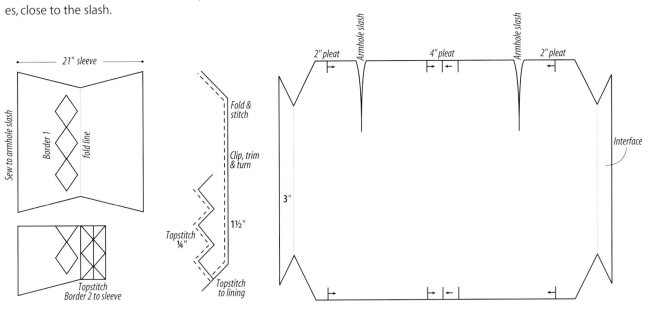

PRISM YARNS LAURA BRYANT

Mosaic maze designed by Laura Bryant

The variation in two hand-dyed yarns, one fancy, one smooth, gives a subtle interest to this mosaic yet tones down its large-scale pattern.

MATERIALS

Yarn Prism *Bon Bon A* 5 (6,7,8) skeins Autumn (2oz/57g, 94yds/85m, 100% rayon); *Super Dazzle B* 4 (5,6,7) skeins Brass (1oz/28g, 90yds/82m, 100% nylon).

Needles One pair size 8 (5mm) needles, *or size to obtain gauge.*

Extras Size G/6 (4mm) crochet hook, stitch markers.

NOTES

1 See *Techniques,* p. 228 for single crochet (sc) and reverse single crochet (rev sc).

BACK

With A, cast on 72 (86, 100, 114) sts. Work chart until piece measures 22 (23, 24, 25)" from beg, end with a WS row. Bind off firmly with A.

FRONT

Work as for back until piece measures 19 (20, 21, 22)" from beg, end with a WS row.

Shape neck

(RS) Work 28 (35, 41, 48) sts in chart pat, join a second ball of A and bind off 16 (16, 18, 18) sts for front neck, work to end in pat. Working both sides at the same time, bind off at each neck edge 3 sts once, 2 sts once, then dec 1 st every other row 0 (1, 1, 2) times—23 (29, 35, 41) sts remaining each shoulder. Work even in pat until piece measures same length as back. Bind off firmly with A. Sew shoulder seams. Place markers 7 (7, 9, 9)" down from shoulders on front and back for armholes.

Sleeves

With RS facing and A, pick up and k58 (58, 72, 72) sts between armhole markers. **Next row** P15, place marker (pm), p to last 15 sts, pm, p to end (**Note** Markers are to

aid in keeping pat during shaping. They mark the beg and end of a rep.) Work in chart and AT SAME TIME, dec 1 st each side every 4th row 8 times—42 (42, 56, 56) sts. Work even until sleeve measures 4 (4½, 5, 6)", end with a WS row. Bind off with A.

FINISHING

Sew side and sleeve seams. With RS facing, A and crochet hook, work 1 rnd sc, then 1 rnd rev sc around neck, sleeve and bottom edges.

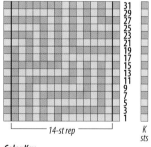

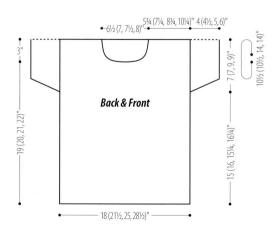

Back & Front

5¾ (7¼, 8¾, 10¼)"   4 (4½, 5, 6)"
6½ (7, 7½, 8)"
3"
19 (20, 21, 22)"
7 (7, 9, 9)"
10½ (10½, 14, 14)"
15 (16, 15¾, 16¾)"
18 (21½, 25, 28½)"

31 29 27 25 23 21 19 17 15 13 11 9 7 5 3 1

|— 14-st rep —| K sts

Color Key
- Autumn (A)
- Brass (B)

Chart Notes
1 Each chart row consists of k sts and sl sts. On each row, sts to be knit on the RS and purled on the WS are indicated at the right of the chart. All other sts in that row are slipped purlwise with yarn in back.
2 Work each chart row twice, reading the chart from right to left for RS rows, and then left to right for WS rows. On the WS, purl the same sts that

Intermediate

Sizes
S (M, L, XL)
Shown in size M.
Directions are for smallest size with larger sizes in parentheses.
If there is only 1 set of numbers, it applies to all sizes.

Finished measurements
Underarm 36 (43,50,57)"
Length 22 (23, 24, 25)"

Gauge
16 sts and 32 rows to 4"/10cm over chart using size 8 (5mm) needles.

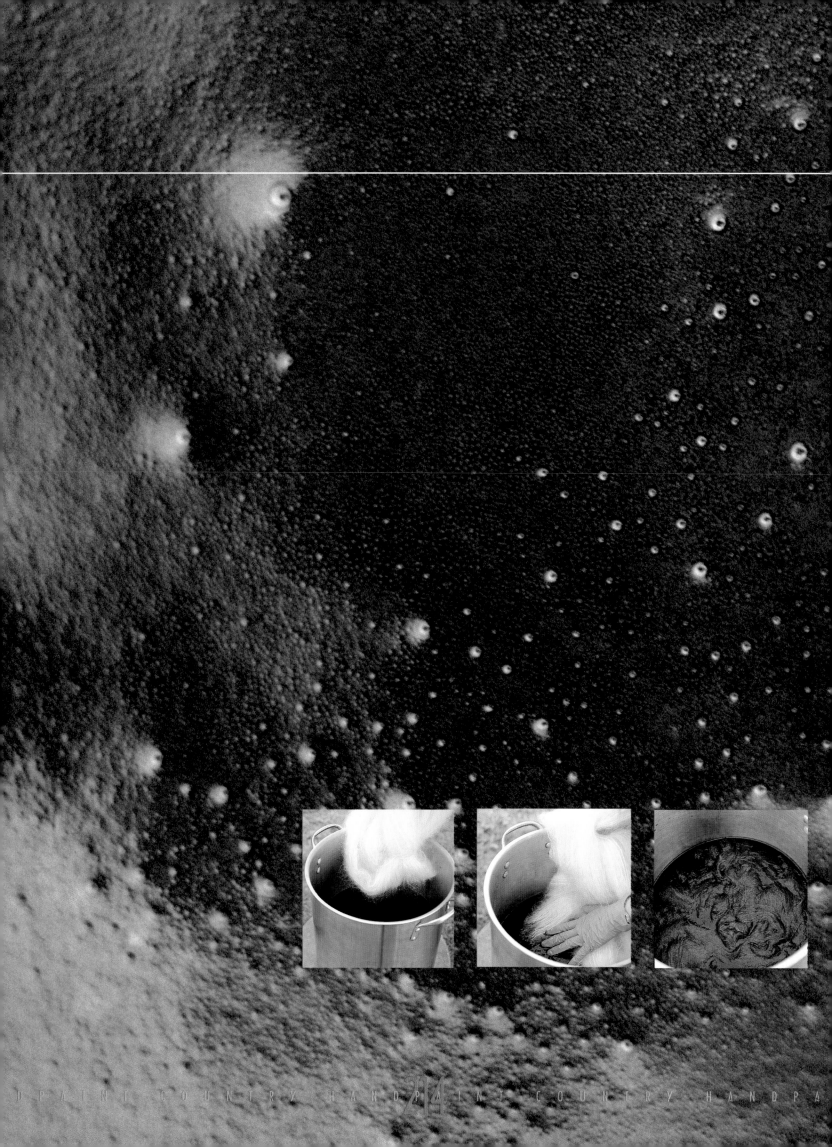

Knitter's guide

What designers tell us

Garment: Mosaic Maze, page 213

For this simple tee, I used a mosaic stitch. I selected two different yarns—a highly textured novelty called Super Dazzle and a smooth ribbon called Bon Bon—in contrasting but coordinating colorways. I wanted enough commonality for the colors to blend in a pleasing way, yet enough contrast to show the pattern.

A nice feature of mosaic stitch is something I try to achieve in weaving as well: from a distance the pattern offers one overall effect, but as you draw nearer, the details begin to be revealed. When you get too close to mosaic stitch, as when you are knitting, the pattern often is not clear. You need to retreat about six to ten feet to allow the pattern to resolve optically.

I often urge students to swatch unexpected combinations. The tee-top grew out of one such swatch. The maze mosaic stitch is relatively easy to knit, but looks incredibly complicated. I found that it took careful color selection and subsequent swatching to ensure that there was enough contrast in the colors to show the pattern, but not so much as to make your eye crazy. Because there was so much texture and color happening in the pattern at once, the garment had to be very simple in shape. I chose drop shoulders, and to keep the

Designer: Laura Bryant
Yarns: Prism Yarns

sleeves from "flying out" at the bottom, I used a lot of decrease as I knit away from the armhole edge. The final knitted fabric did not have much roll, so a simple crochet and reverse crochet were all that were needed to finish the edges.

Garment: Cantina Kimono, page 210

For the coat, I chose Cool Stuff in a Progressions colorway. Stuff yarns are combinations of many different yarns that are gauge and color-coordinated, then tied together in changing lengths. This creates a palette of color and texture that automatically shifts as you knit. The development of my yarns, colorways, and designs are also tied together. A style of knitting I am doing might inspire a type of colorway, as is the case with Progressions colorways. They grew out of my experiments with modular knitting, where I decided it would be great to have shaded colorways to help define the shapes. My designing style is suited to hand-dyed yarns: basic shapes, unusual details, proper fit, and simple but interesting pattern stitches.

The kimono design came from my desire to combine hand-dyed velvet with knitting. I wanted to integrate fabric into the surface as well as the lining. I decided to use triangles as modules, leaving some open for fabric insertions. I used the

Garment: Painted Plaid, page 69

I chose the Wool Crepe because it is fine enough to be doubled. For the gingham pattern, I needed a "dark" and a "light" colorway with enough contrast so that they could be combined to produce a "medium" range that would show well in a color block. Moose Creek and Wild Mushroom worked best, and I used garter stitch to blend the colors.

Garment: Moguls, page 68

I selected the Moguls yarn because of the fun of working with high texture and the richness of its color. Pairing it with worsted weight yarn lowers the expense of the finished garment, helps the garment hold its shape, and highlights the Moguls better than using that yarn alone. The stitch pattern is very easy but produces a complicated effect. Because Moguls appeals to beginner knitters, I wanted to design a garment that is easy to knit, offering maximum effect with minimum effort.

Handpaint Hints

Just try ABSS, which stands for Anything But Stockinette Stitch! It's pretty simple, and offers a world of possibilities.

Designer: Sally Melville
Yarns: Mountain Colors

Moguls is gorgeous in every colorway. To choose a color for the vest, I just could have closed my eyes and pointed.

Cantina colorway in a somewhat random way, allowing stripes to go in different directions and the triangles to alternate between strongly outlining and melting into one another. One triangle dominates the back; then triangles grow ever smaller as you work to the front and bottom border. Each triangle is a multiple of 15 stitches, the smallest having 15 and the largest, 121 stitches. The fabric is further integrated into the design by becoming the front border and the sleeves. Knitted borders for the sleeve tie it all together.

Handpaint Hints

With hand-dyed yarns, the tendency is to let the yarn and colors do the work and just knit, but stockinette is often disappointing. What is beautiful in the skein, where strands are long and thin, can become mottled, blotched, or striped when knit in stockinette, where that thin line has been made wider and shorter. Turn a piece of stockinette over and observe how much more attractive the purl side is!

My best advice is to swatch, swatch, swatch—and don't settle for something until you know it is wonderful! Get a good stitch dictionary and try a variety of stitches until you feel confident that you have something worthy of your time. The extra minutes you spend swatching will help guarantee a great product!

I have found that any stitch that uses knits and purls on the surface such as seed, checkerboard, and zigzag patterning works well with handpaints. For more advanced knitters, try slip stitches, mosaics, and simple Fair Isles. Smaller intarsia areas, which concentrate colors in shorter stripes, are also attractive. Consider adding a second yarn, either in a solid or contrasting colorway. Simple quilted stitches using a variegated and a solid can be effective as well.

The interest in hand-dyed yarns is in the color and often the texture as well. Simple shapes with one great detail, such as an asymmetrical closure or great buttons are often all that is needed to make a distinctive garment. Or, as in the case of the mosaic maze, a terrific pattern stitch that showcases the color and texture can be chosen. Highly intricate lace, cables, and other technical tours de force are probably best left to monochromes.

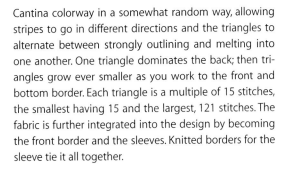

These swatches show alternative colorways worked in a checkerboard pattern, using only a light and middle color, without the dark color used in the Painted Plaid pullover (right, Moose Creek with Red Tail Hawk; left, Midnight Sapphire with Grass Valley). The upper swatches are worked in doubled Wool Crepe as in the Painted Plaid instructions, the lower swatches are worked in a single strand of 4/8's wool. This alternative makes the garment less expensive. Knitting note: For the checkerboard pattern, there is only a DC and an MC but no LC. Work as for Gingham st pattern, using DC wherever it calls for DC or LC.

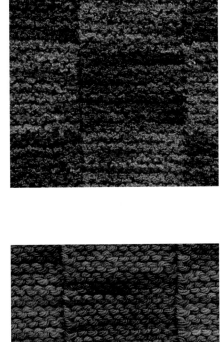

What designers tell us

Garments: Stacked and Diagonal Stoles, page 190

My friend and fellow designer, Rick Mondragon, inspired me to "exploit" the exact color sequence in a dip-dyed yarn for an ikat effect. He advised me to discover the repeat, which you can do by measuring how far the color sequence runs before repeating itself. This dictated the dimensions of both of the stoles, and also required that they be worked circularly, then cut afterwards.

Because both color and texture are in play, I chose to contrast them in the stoles, using fuzzy mohair with a smooth silk/merino blend in a solid color. One of the stoles "stacked" the same colors on top of each other; the other stole staggered the colors diagonally. I knit the solid yarn with smooth texture every other row to make the fabric look woven and also to achieve a reversible, yet somewhat different look on each side, which is very important in a stole.

Garment: Pi in the Sky, page 192

The biggest complaint I hear about handpainted yarn is the unwanted striping effect. I decided to use the striping to best advantage by creating an unusual jacket made up of a radiating circle. Stripes underscore this dynamic pattern and inter-

Designer: Lily Chin
Yarns: Tess' Designer Yarns

Garment: Mixed Miters, page 148

Choosing yarns was difficult because Great Adirondack offers so many colors and intriguing fibers. I finally settled on bright colors and fairly smooth, simple yarns for the mitered vest. The vest was inspired by my love of geometric motifs, something frequently seen in my designs. It uses a combination of bright hand-dyed yarn with a darker solid that controls and contains the colorway.

The garter ridge pattern highlights the beautiful colors and gives some simple surface texture. This technique sets off the wonderful color repeats and often shows them off better than if the garment were knit entirely of hand-dyed yarn.

Garment: Cropped Kimono, page 150

Great Adirondack offers so many yarns in each colorway that it was easy to combine a variety of fibers in this jacket while maintaining a unified feel. The jacket is knit primarily of darker reds and cranberries, with colorways close in value--a technique that tends to blend the many fibers and textures together in the effect of an overall color field.

The jacket is constructed in strips, which are emphasized by vertical ridges of a darker yarn, and accented by a solid shawl collar. It reflects my interest in non-traditional construction techniques. Yarns used in this design form small patches as they progress up each strip, creating interest in an otherwise simple garment shape. The many yarns used in this project have a wonderful variety of textures—

Designer: Ginger Luters
Yarns: Great Adirondack Yarn Company

Garments: Billy The Kidd and Circular Chevrons, pages 88, 90

I chose a jacket and bag because I wanted pieces that were unisex. The mixed fibers and textures in the same colorway enticed my spirit. When working with hand-dyed yarn, I usually exploit a repeat, which was impossible in these yarns. Because I found them challenging, I decided to let the yarns speak for themselves and outlined the painted blocks of colorway with a yellow/green for a pieced look.

For the jacket back, I was thinking "fringed yoke," but abandoned that idea when fringe became distracting to the mitered yoke and shaped sleeves. The miter is the technical interest, which runs down the front, back, and sleeves. The acid yellow/green solids frame variegated areas that are all intarsia or "intarsections" accomplished a block at time.

Designer: Rick Mondragon
Yarns: Chasing Rainbows Dyeworks

esting directional design. The texture dictated garter stitch, which was necessary for the reversible collar.

In the jacket, the use of two very different yarns held together lends both body and surface interest. Alone, a jacket in Spritzer, the pigtail, would not hold up, while the alpaca/silk blend by itself is too straightforward and lacks the punch that a dramatic garment needs. Mixing yarns like this is very inspiring—you should see how many swatches and other ideas came from this project!

Handpaint Hints

Even if you use the most basic of stitches as I have, you will notice that the coloration imparts significant interest. Avoid fancy stitches, as they can often get lost with so much color happening. Just be aware of the patterning that may come out of the color spacing unexpectedly or randomly. I have often heard the argument that handpainted garments should be kept simple, since the yarn garners so much attention. This is not always so, as you can see in the circular jacket. If anything, working with yarn that "speaks for itself" can help you concentrate on garment shaping and construction, rather than worry about color placement.

Beware, knitting with hand-dyed yarns can be very addictive. Just take it one swatch at a time and see what happens and where it leads. You may be surprised at the destination.

boucles, ribbons, and smooth cottons—which all work wonderfully together.

Designing with handpainted yarns is my absolute favorite way to work! I love the deep, rich colors, the excitement of frequent color changes, and the challenge of enhancing and showcasing delicious yarns.

Handpaint Hints

These beautiful yarns are a delight to knit. Don't be afraid to use them—give in to the temptation when they "call" to you! Think carefully about how you will knit with them. Traditional designs in plain stitches are often not the best choices for these very special yarns.

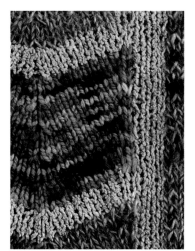

Although I like to exploit the repeat of multicolored yarns, that method did not work with the Chasing Rainbows yarn. Hand-dyed yarns have properties unique to both dyer and process. I try to find ways to create something special with each.

Handpaint Hints

Know your yarns, swatch your yarns, wash your yarns. Different yarns may behave differently. Blending too many colors in a piece can make it busy and muddy. Know when enough is enough, which for me meant no fringe. Keep it simple when it comes to stitch fabrication, shape, and motifs. I used stockinette stitch, a cardigan shape, and blocks and stripes for a motif. Since I had two

color choices, solid and variegated, I added the miter and bobbles for that special "designer look" for the jacket. The matching bag just followed its lead.

what knitters need to know

Immersion-dyed yarns

1) Dye, skein, pot

2) Immersing skein

3) Skein simmering

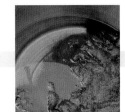

4) Exhausting dye

5) Yarn coming out of pot, note color variation

6) The exhaust water is clear

Dip-dyed yarns

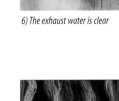
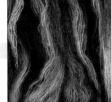

1) One skein in 3 different dyebaths

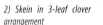

2) Skein in 3-leaf clover arrangement

3) Color wicking up yarn

4) Skein presented as dyed

5) Skein in circular arrangement

6) Notice long color stretches

Demystifying hand-dyed yarns

Space-dyed yarns

1) Applying a short stretch of the first color

2) Continuing to apply colors in sequence

3) Middle color in sunset colorway

4) Sequence is complete

5) Colors merge so that no white remains

6) Space-dyed colorways can be reduced

Handpainted yarns

1) Skein in tray with a variety of dyes

2) Applying colors randomly

3) Mixing dyes on the skein

4) Colors are not evenly distributed

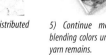

5) Continue merging and blending colors until no white yarn remains.

6) Painted skein ready for steaming

7) Yarn lofts as it is rewound into larger skein

7) Yarn rewound into larger skein

7) Right, space-dyed skein; left, same yarn rewound

7) Rewound so colors cross pleasingly.

· Immersion-dyed yarns

Features   Nearly solid,
Monochromatic

Considerations
    Knit this as you would a solid.

    Especially suited to detailed stitch pattern.

· Dip-dyed yarns

Features   Multi-colored repeats
Long color stretches
Color merges with neighboring colors along length of strand

Considerations
    Exploit striping with multi-directional knitting: diagonal knitting, entrelac, miters, side-to-side.

    Break up striping with slip stitches and short rows.

· Space-dyed yarns

Features   Multi-colored repeats
Short color stretches
Color merges with neighboring colors along length of strand
Colorways often available in a variety of yarns
Colorways are reproducible

Considerations
    Multi-directional knitting, slip stitches, and short rows work well with space-dyed yarns

    Especially suited to garter stitch and small knit-purl combinations (seed, moss).

    If a color begins to stack or ghost (follow itself across a fabric), change the width of the knitting or the needle size, work paired rows alternately with two skeins from the same dye lot, or try a stitch pattern with a changing stitch count from row to row.

· Handpainted yarns

Features   Colors applied randomly along length and depth of hank
Colorways are not reproducible
Colorway contains more colors than other methods: color merges with its neighbors on strands above and below as well as along length of strand
Colors may not be distributed evenly through the hank; a color may appear only in the first third of a skein.

Considerations
    Pick a strong design: mitered squares and multi- directional knitting, intarsia, and fairisle work well with the rich spread of color.

    Pick an asymmetrical silhouette to work with the ever-changing colorway. Work from two balls to insure a consistent spread of color.

A glossary of dye terms used in Handpaint Country

Colorfast:
When dye is considered to be permanent, meaning that it has bonded with the fiber and is set.

Colorway:
The way color is sequenced along fiber, usually associated with the space-dye technique. Colorways are both repeatable, meaning that they can occur several times on a circular hank, and reproducible, hank by hank, usually in many fibers.

Dip-dye:
To dip different sections of a dye skein in the dye bath. This can be done all at once using several baths, or sequentially.

Dye bath:
The prepared liquid solution of dyestuffs, mordants, and any other auxilliaries used to color set fiber.

Dye skein:
A circular hank wound and prepared for dyeing.

Exhaust:
The liquid leftover when the dyeing is finished. This can be clear or a colored residue.

Gradation-dye:
To dye yarns in several shades or "grades" of the same color, often associated with the immersion dye technique.

Hand-dye:
To dye fiber by hand, can be associated with all dye methods.

Handpaint:
To paint fiber by hand, usually with the aid of brushes or squirt bottles, in a multi-colored arrangement with no repeat. Recently, as dyers have drawn from various dye techniques to customize the ever-evolving look of hand-dyed yarns, "handpaint" has come to mean hand-processed fiber with a painted look.

Hank:
The circular arrangement of a dye skein, usually wound on a large diameter wheel or swift. Some yarns are left in the hank, others are rewound into smaller skeins or balls.

The Dye Factor-solids

Not all dye skeins begin white.

The Dye Factor-solids

Cashmere (from left to right): natural, scoured, and over-dyed cashmere.

Scoured cashmere: impediments are washed out with detergent and yarn lofts as it dries.

Over-dyed cashmere: the natural tweedy tan is over-dyed a soft gray—note the original color is not overpowered.

The Dye Factor-solids

   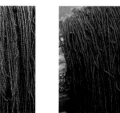

Over-dyeing adds richness because layering one color over another adds depth.

Cashmere over-dyed with black.

Cashmere over-dyed with amethyst. Over-dying with solids is done with the immersion dye technique.

Cashmere over-dyed with teal green. Note the results of color on color.

Cashmere over-dyed with purple.

Over-Dyeing - when once is not enough

Over-dyeing involves two variables, the dye factor and the fiber factor. The dye factor is the way in which newly applied dye saturates an already-dyed yarn. The fiber factor is the effect fiber content and yarn structure have on the way the yarn takes color.

The Dye Factor-colorways

Commercially dyed chenille and same yarn space-dyed.

Chenille begins khaki colored and is then space-dyed in a colorway.

Space-dyed colorway over white chenille (right) and khaki chenille (left). While both are dyed in colorways, the over-dyed hank has deeper, richer tones.

The Dye Factor-over-dyeing already hand-dyed yarns

Over-dyeing burgundy raw silk.

Working black dye into the burgundy hank.

The original burgundy silk, the burgundy over-dyed black silk, a hank of black silk. Notice that the over-dyed hank takes on color from both dye processes to create a new color we might call plum.

The Fiber Factor - solids

  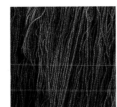 

The fiber content and the yarn's structure affect the way it takes color when dyed, Here three different fibers: raw silk, cashmere, and pima cotton have been immersed in the same dye.

Raw silk

Cashmere

Pima cotton

The Fiber Factor - solids

Four different fibers immersion-dyed. Most hand-dyed solids are intentionally not completely monochrome.

Micro-fiber ribbon dyed mint green. The flat mesh ribbon traps the dye and the shine makes this novelty yarn look lighter than it actually is.

Brushed mohair dyed blue. The deep color is softened by the fuzziness of the mohair

Glitter merino dyed purple. The gold glitter creates an optical illusion by reflecting the colors around it.

Techno-hair, otherwise know as fake fur, dyed chocolate brown. The hairs make it appear more heathered than it actually is.

The Fiber Factor - colorways

Five different fibers dyed in the same repeatable colorway, shown top to bottom in alpaca boucle, techno-hair, glitter merino, raw silk and micro-fiber ribbon. Notice that neither the ribbon nor the techno-hair are rewound, but presented the way in which they were dyed.

Immersion-dye:
To submerge fiber in a dye bath; usually associated with mono-chromatic dyeing.

Mordant:
The bonding agent used to set dyes, which can vary depending upon the fiber content and the preference of the dyer.

Over-dye:
To dye fiber that has been previously dyed.

Resist dye:
To dye fiber so that color cannot penetrate in places; usually accomplished by overcrowding a dyepot, which can prevent color from circulating evenly.

Scour:
To wash fiber to remove substances that might hamper the dye process.

Self-exhausting:
Dyes that leave only clear liquid residue because all of the color is exhausted onto the dye skein.

Sequential-dye:
To dye the same fiber in several stages. This can be accomplished by dip dyeing, in which sections of a hank are dyed in order, or by overdyeing in which the same hank is dyed in a base color and then dyed in another color for a richer look.

Snap:
To straighten a hank of yarn without rewinding it; usually associated with a dyeskein.

Space-dye:
To dye fiber in a certain sequence, which is usually repeatable.

Variegated:
Multi-colored fiber or yarn in any color range, sequenced or random.

DESIGNER BIOS

Beth Brown-Reinsel, page 125

"Working with handpainted yarn is a challenge for me as a textural designer. Ganseys and Arans are my primary focus, and sometimes knit/purl patterns can be lost in the colors. So I added intarsia cables, which are fun to knit and work well on the space-dyed background. In the yoke, I placed conventional Gansey textural patterns and increased their visibility by using solid colors. The mohair content of this yarn lends a soft glow to the garment, but could cause tangling in the intarsia areas. For this reason, I encourage the use of bobbins for the cables."

Beth Brown-Reinsel loves teaching knitting and works out of her Victorian home in Delta, PA, writing, designing, and publishing her own line of knitwear patterns.

Lily Chin, pages 188–189

I'm a New York City native who's been involved in some aspect of the fashion industry since age 13. My mom's sewing skills got me summer jobs in the garment industry. Since I grew up in the "rag trade," I've always been fascinated with garment construction. Knitting and crochet are my medium for garment design. By going straight from yarn to fabric to garment, I have control.

Lily lives in New York City where she's a very active designer with many Seventh Avenue credits. She is currently at work on a collection of knits by young urban knitters.

Bev Galeskas, page 105

I learned to knit in the late '70s at a Saturday workshop offered by a local yarn store. I stayed up all night knitting and the next day went to the book store and was lucky enough to purchase Elizabeth Zimmermann's *Knitting Without Tears* and *Mary Thomas's Knitting Book*. Reading these, I learned that not only did I know how to knit, I could make anything I wanted. So I knit, and knit, and knit, and never stopped.

In the early '90s I started experimenting with felted knitting, enjoying the challenge of discovering how to knit the shape needed to achieve the desired results after felting. When swatching with a new wool, I just cannot resist the urge to throw a swatch in the washer to see how it felts.

Bev Galeskas launched Fiber Trends in 1994 with a mere five patterns. It has grown to include numerous designers and patterns for all types of knitting, but felting patterns remain a strong focus.

Melissa Lumley, page 181

Melissa Lumley's fascination with textiles began as a child when her mother taught her to knit, crochet, and sew. Her 7th grade math teacher encouraged her to begin designing her own sweaters. At 14 she learned to weave at The Putney School, where she now teaches Fiber Arts. In addition to teaching, she does custom dyeing and weaving, and designs sweaters for several small companies. Her sense of color and pattern is strongly influenced by the textiles of Turkey, where she spent her childhood, and by the hills and gardens of Vermont, where she now lives with her husband and two children.

Ginger Luters, pages 146–147

Most of my life has been spent in California, though I love to travel. My husband, Arnie, and I live in the Sierra Mountains of northern California.

I've worked in various art forms nearly all my life, and have always been drawn to fibers. My MA in Fine Art was earned after my sons were grown and away at college themselves. I taught knitting, weaving, and design at Saddleback College in southern California for 12 years and then began to teach creative knitting and computer design workshops nationally. My work focuses on the exciting use of color, unusual construction approaches, and simple, elegant garment shapes. I'm currently working on a creative knitting book.

Sally Melville, pages 66–67

I began knitting as a Brownie at the age of 9 and I immediately felt that I had been born to do it! It's interesting how often in life we can look back at what we loved as children and see how it played itself out in our lives. My natural gauge was very, very loose. There was no one to tell me to just use smaller needles, so I thought, 'I guess me and commercial patterns don't mix, better design my own!' By 16 I was designing sweaters.

Sally is still designing sweaters, teaching, and writing from her home in Waterloo, Ontario, Canada. She is hard at work on a series of learn-to-knit books aimed at new knitters who want good technique and great projects.

Susan Meredith, page 35

I live and work in Edgewood, New Mexico, where I teach lace knitting, design lace shawls and garments, and work as a production weaver. I find inspiration in the quiet and solitude of a life alone in the high plains desert landscape.

I love the way the colors work in La Boheme, the sheen of the rayon and the softness of the mohair complement each other. It seemed the perfect yarn

for a simple undulating lace repeat, which gave the colors an extra bit of movement and interest.

Rick Mondragon, page 89

I've always liked clothes and seldom liked the fit, so I began to make them for myself. At an early age I learned how to crochet, sew, and knit (in that order) and have done so for most of my life. I sewed my way through college; that is how I made my living. I worked for a woman who made custom clothing, and she taught me a lot about garment design. Of course it was mainly for women's wear so I read and studied how to fit for men, myself specifically.

I've worked in many different fields, owned different businesses. Along the way, I had a stint in a weaving and yarn shop as a salesperson, teacher, and finally designer. I drafted and created designs for handwovens as well as knits.

Rick Mondragon lives in Sioux Falls, South Dakota where he is the editor of Knitter's Magazine.

Kathleen Power Johnson, page 77

I'm usually energized to push the knitting envelope, taking a technique where it hasn't gone before. I find that rule-breaking is the most creative thing you can do in knitting. One of my first published designs broke the rules about combining complex pattern stitches with handpainted yarn. It worked well, and I learned to trust my intuition.

Entrelac was—and continues to be—the technique that has most fascinated me. What an envelope that was to push! In my handpaint designs, I've used the natural tendency of the colors to stripe to cooperate with the geometry of entrelac rather than to fight it. In choosing yarns, we decided to use gradations of color intensity within the entrelac matrix—an effect you'll see to some extent on each garment. At the same time, I enjoyed developing shaping that works with the entrelac. Since a little entrelac goes a long way, the simple stockinette A-line skirt is designed to set off the entrelac rather than compete with it.

Teacher/designer Kathleen Power Johnson lives in Florida where she is working on a book on entrelac.

Linda Romens, page 18

I enjoy designing with La Lana's wool because the colors Luisa achieves with the plant dyes are vibrant without being harsh.

In the Anasazi vest I was trying to design a work that appears very complicated, similar to a Fair Isle pattern, but would be simpler to make than either Fair

Isle or intarsia color patterns. I accomplished this by using mosaics, which only require carrying one strand of yarn in a row. Typically I design patterns I would wear myself, so I though a man's vest would be a nice change!

Linda Romens lives and designs in New Mexico.

Kara Spitler, pages 48–49

My mom taught me to knit when I was 7. I was 10 or 11 before I knit a sweater than I could wear. I first discovered multicolored yarns at a knitting retreat in 1995. Judy Ditmore was there with her yarn. I love her colors and have been knitting with her yarns ever since. Handpainted yarns can be a challenge, but it is one that I continue to enjoy.

Knitting is an avocation for Kara Spitler whose days are spent as a court reporter in federal court in Denver, Colorado.

Barbara Venishnick, pages 159, 163

Barbara has loved knitting since her mother taught her at the age of 5. After earning a Fine Arts degree, Barbara and husband Joe moved to New York City where she designed woven fabrics for a large textile house. After a move to Connecticut, she became the full-time mother of two girls, Olivia and Anna. However, she always managed to squeeze in knitting time. When her daughters went off to school, she began working in a yarn shop, altering patterns and designing garment for clients. Now she designs for knitting publications and yarn companies.

Anna Zilboorg, page 201

When I left New York, which is all shades of gray, I was starving for color. All I could imagine was my house festooned in skeins of yarn dyed all shades of all colors. So I set about dyeing. Soon I had large baskets of samples, all with recipes, and was ready to knit everything. Not quite everything. Recently, under Merike's tutelage, I've begun playing with rainbow dyeing—a much more chancy thing than single-color dyes with predictable recipes. Also I've been spinning, so rainbow-dyed roving is another new world to explore. Multicolored yarns beg for textures, so I've left the flat world of stranded knitting at present and am wallowing in stitch patterns.

Anna Zilboorg lives and knits at her home in the country in Virginia.

Other designs in the book are by the dyers: Cindy Brooks, Laura Bryant, Traci Bunkers, Valentina Devine, Maie Landra, Cheryl Oberle, and Rosalie Truong.

Celeste Pinheiro, where are you?

Photography
Alexis Xenakis
Photos were shot on location throughout the journey, and include the closeup and scenic shots.

Typography
Titles: ITC Kendo
Headers: Arquitectura
Headlines, Subheads: Futura T Med
Body copy, Endpages: Myriad MM 330.580
Technical column: Myriad MM Italic 400.300
Technical charts: Myriad MM Italic 700.300

Paper
Text: Westvaco 80# Sterling Ultra Satin
Endpapers: Westvaco 100# Sterling Ultra Satin
Dust jacket: 80# Sterling w/film laminate

Printing
Sheetfed - Sioux Printing. Sioux Falls, SD

XRX, Inc. Prepress department: Dennis Pearson, Manager; David Xenakis, Publishing Services; Natalie Sorenson, Book Project Coordinator

Digital color photos: Everett Baker; Howtek Scanmaster 4500 drum scanner

Prepress color correction and management: Jason Bittner, David Xenakis
All fabric and model photography enhanced and color corrected from the actual garments and yarns.

Composing: QuarkXPress 4.04
XRX Prepress Dept.

Color separations: Adobe Photoshop 6.0
XRX Prepress Dept.

Illustrations: Adobe Illustrator 8.0, Jay Reeve, Natalie Sorenson, XRX Prepress Dept.

Color proofing: Epson Stylus 5000
Epson-Dupont CMYK simulation

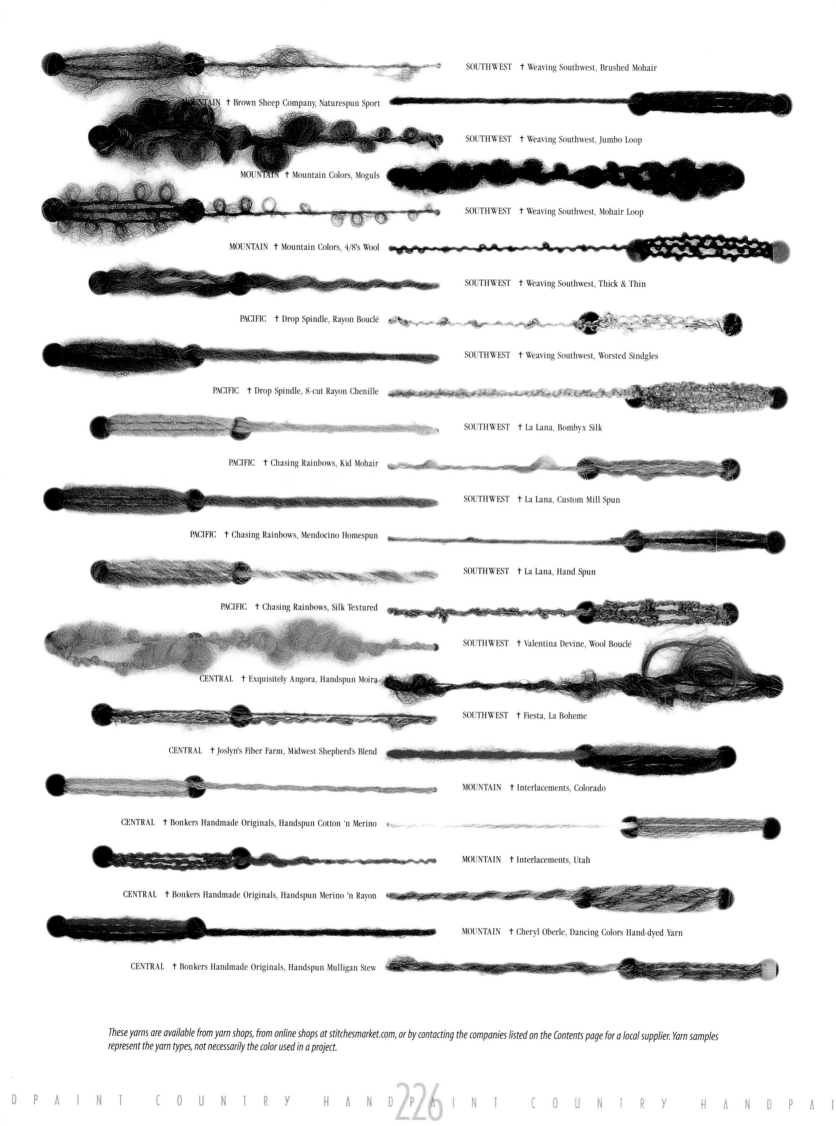

SOUTHWEST † Weaving Southwest, Brushed Mohair

MOUNTAIN † Brown Sheep Company, Naturespun Sport

SOUTHWEST † Weaving Southwest, Jumbo Loop

MOUNTAIN † Mountain Colors, Moguls

SOUTHWEST † Weaving Southwest, Mohair Loop

MOUNTAIN † Mountain Colors, 4/8's Wool

SOUTHWEST † Weaving Southwest, Thick & Thin

PACIFIC † Drop Spindle, Rayon Bouclé

SOUTHWEST † Weaving Southwest, Worsted Sindgles

PACIFIC † Drop Spindle, 8-cut Rayon Chenille

SOUTHWEST † La Lana, Bombyx Silk

PACIFIC † Chasing Rainbows, Kid Mohair

SOUTHWEST † La Lana, Custom Mill Spun

PACIFIC † Chasing Rainbows, Mendocino Homespun

SOUTHWEST † La Lana, Hand Spun

PACIFIC † Chasing Rainbows, Silk Textured

SOUTHWEST † Valentina Devine, Wool Bouclé

CENTRAL † Exquisitely Angora, Handspun Moira

SOUTHWEST † Fiesta, La Boheme

CENTRAL † Joslyn's Fiber Farm, Midwest Shepherd's Blend

MOUNTAIN † Interlacements, Colorado

CENTRAL † Bonkers Handmade Originals, Handspun Cotton 'n Merino

MOUNTAIN † Interlacements, Utah

CENTRAL † Bonkers Handmade Originals, Handspun Merino 'n Rayon

MOUNTAIN † Cheryl Oberle, Dancing Colors Hand-dyed Yarn

CENTRAL † Bonkers Handmade Originals, Handspun Mulligan Stew

These yarns are available from yarn shops, from online shops at stitchesmarket.com, or by contacting the companies listed on the Contents page for a local supplier. Yarn samples represent the yarn types, not necessarily the color used in a project.

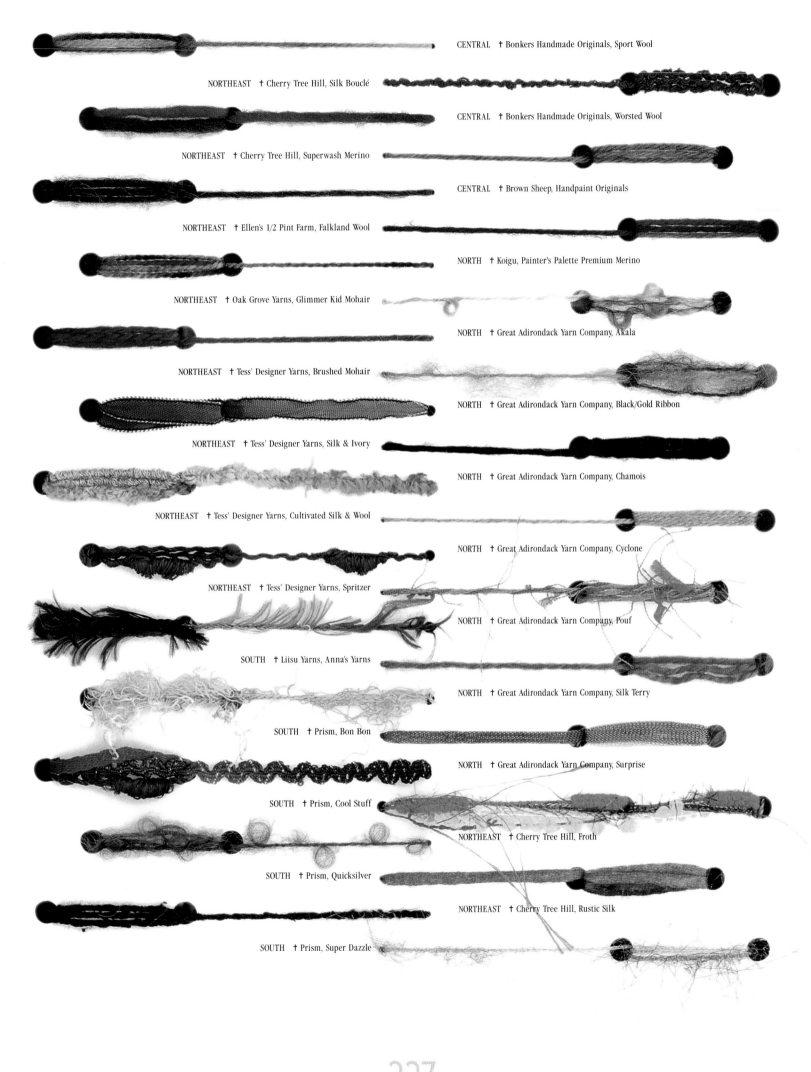

CENTRAL   † Bonkers Handmade Originals, Sport Wool

NORTHEAST   † Cherry Tree Hill, Silk Bouclé

CENTRAL   † Bonkers Handmade Originals, Worsted Wool

NORTHEAST   † Cherry Tree Hill, Superwash Merino

CENTRAL   † Brown Sheep, Handpaint Originals

NORTHEAST   † Ellen's 1/2 Pint Farm, Falkland Wool

NORTH   † Koigu, Painter's Palette Premium Merino

NORTHEAST   † Oak Grove Yarns, Glimmer Kid Mohair

NORTH   † Great Adirondack Yarn Company, Akala

NORTHEAST   † Tess' Designer Yarns, Brushed Mohair

NORTH   † Great Adirondack Yarn Company, Black/Gold Ribbon

NORTHEAST   † Tess' Designer Yarns, Silk & Ivory

NORTH   † Great Adirondack Yarn Company, Chamois

NORTHEAST   † Tess' Designer Yarns, Cultivated Silk & Wool

NORTH   † Great Adirondack Yarn Company, Cyclone

NORTHEAST   † Tess' Designer Yarns, Spritzer

NORTH   † Great Adirondack Yarn Company, Pouf

SOUTH   † Liisu Yarns, Anna's Yarns

NORTH   † Great Adirondack Yarn Company, Silk Terry

SOUTH   † Prism, Bon Bon

NORTH   † Great Adirondack Yarn Company, Surprise

SOUTH   † Prism, Cool Stuff

NORTHEAST   † Cherry Tree Hill, Froth

SOUTH   † Prism, Quicksilver

NORTHEAST   † Cherry Tree Hill, Rustic Silk

SOUTH   † Prism, Super Dazzle

HANDPAINT COUNTRY TECHNIQUES

CABLE CAST-ON

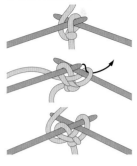

CHAIN CAST-ON

INVISIBLE CAST-ON

LONG-TAILED CAST-ON

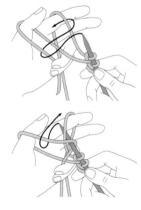

MAKE 1 (M1) KNIT

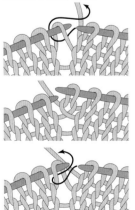

CAST-ONS
CABLE CAST-ON
Uses A cast-on that is useful when adding stitches within the work or at beginning of a row.
1 Make a slipknot on left needle.
2 Working into this knot's loop, knit a stitch and place it on left needle.
3 Insert right needle between the last 2 stitches. From this position, knit a stitch and place it on left needle. Repeat step 3 for each additional stitch.

CHAIN CAST-ON
With crochet hook, chain the number of cast-on stitches required, plus a few extra. With needle and main yarn, beginning at end of chain where stitches were just completed, pick up and knit the exact number of cast-on stitches, picking up stitches in loops at back of chain. Work the piece, usually beginning with a right-side row.

INVISIBLE CAST-ON
1 Knot working yarn to contrasting waste yarn. With needle in right hand, hold knot in right hand. Tension both strands in left hand; separate the strands with fingers of the left hand. Yarn over with working yarn in front of waste strand.
2 Holding waste strand taut, pivot yarns and yarn over with working yarn in back of waste strand.
3 Each yarn over forms a stitch. Alternate yarn over in front and in back of waste strand for required number of stitches. For an even number, twist working yarn around waste strand before knitting the first row. Later, untie knot, remove waste strand, and arrange bottom loops on needle.

LONG-TAILED CAST-ON
Make a slipknot for the initial stitch, at a distance from the end of the yarn (about 1½" for each stitch to be cast on).
1 Arrange both ends of yarn in left hand as shown. Bring needle under front strand of thumb loop, up over front strand of index loop, catching it …
2 … and bringing it under the front of the thumb loop. Slip thumb out of loop, and use it to adjust tension on the new stitch. One stitch cast on.

INCREASES
MAKE 1 (M1) KNIT
If instructions don't specify, use either the left- or right-slanting increase.
Uses A single increase.
1 For a *left-slanting increase* (M1L), with right needle from back of work, pick up strand between last st knitted and next st. Place on left needle and knit, twisting the strand by working into the loop at the back of the needle.
2 This is the completed increase.
3 Or, for a *right-slanting increase* (M1R), with left needle from back of work, pick up strand between last stitch knitted and next stitch. Knit,

twisting the strand by working into the loop at the front of the needle.

MAKE 1 (M1) PURL
Left-slanting: Work as for Make 1 Knit, Step 1, except purl, twisting the strand by working into the back loop.
Right-slanting: Work as for M1 Knit, Step 3, except purl.

DECREASES
SSK
Uses SSK is a left-slanting single decrease.
1 Slip 2 sts separately to right needle as if to knit.
2 Knit these 2 sts together by slipping left needle into them from left to right. 2 sts become one.

SSP
Uses A left-slanting single decrease.
1 Slip 2 stitches separately to right needle as if to knit.
2 Slip these 2 stitches back onto left needle. Insert right needle through their 'back loops,' into the second stitch and then the first.
3 Purl them together.

SL1-K1-PSSO
Uses A left-slanting single decrease.
1 Slip one stitch knitwise.
2 Knit next stitch.
3 Pass the slipped stitch over the knit stitch.

SL1-K2TOG-PSSO
Uses A left-slanting double decrease.
1 Slip one stitch knitwise.
2 Knit next two stitches together.
3 Pass the slipped stitch over the k2tog.

SL2-K1-P2SSO
Uses A centered double decrease.
1 Slip 2 sts together to right needle as if to knit.
2 Knit next stitch.
3 Pass 2 slipped sts over knit st and off right needle.
4 Completed: 3 sts become 1; the center st is on top.

SL2-P1-P2SSO
1 Work as for SL2-k1-p2sso, Step 1.
2 Purl next st.
3 Pass 2 slipped sts over purl st and off right needle.

BIND-OFFS
3-NEEDLE BIND-OFF
Uses Instead of binding off shoulder stitches and sewing them together.
Place right sides together, back stitches on one needle and front stitches on another. *K2tog (1 from front needle and 1 from back needle). Rep from* once. Pass first stitch over 2nd stitch. Continue to k2tog (1 front stitch and 1 back stitch) and bind off across.
For a ridge effect on the right side of the work, work as above but with wrong sides together.

SSK

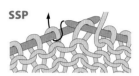

SSP

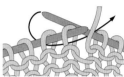

SL2-K1-P2SSO

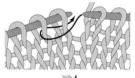

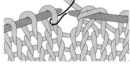

3-NEEDLE BIND-OFF

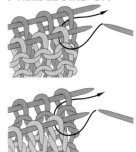

ABBREVIATIONS

approx approximately	***dec(s)('d)*** decrease(e)(ed) (es)(ing)	**'** foot (feet)	***mm*** millimeter(s)
beg beginning		***inc(s)('d)*** increase(e)(ed) (es)(ing)	***MC*** main color
CC contrasting color	***dpn(s)*** double-pointed needle(s)	***k*** knit(ting)(s)(ted)	***oz*** ounce(s)
ch chain		***LH*** left hand	***p*** purl(ed)(ing)(s)
cn cable needle	***g*** gram	***M1*** make one stitch	***pat(s)*** pattern(s)
cm centimeter(s)	***hdc*** half double crochet	***m*** meter(s)	***pm*** place marker
dc double crochet	***"*** inch(es)		

INTARSIA KNITTING

GRAFTING

I-CORD

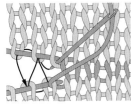

ATTACHED I-CORD

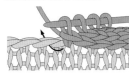

SHORT-ROW WRAPS
Knit side

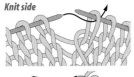

Purl side

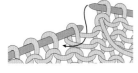

CUTTING A STEEK

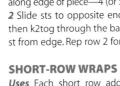

machine stitch

cutting line

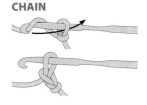

HANDPAINT COUNTRY TECHNIQUES

OTHER TECHNIQUES
INTARSIA KNITTING
When changing from one color to the next when working intarsia, it is necessary to twist the yarns to prevent holes. Pick up the new color from under the old color, as shown, and continue working.

GRAFTING
Uses An invisible method of joining knitting horizontally, row to row. Useful at shoulders, underarms, and tips of mittens, socks, and hats.
Stockinette graft:
1 Arrange stitches on two needles.
2 Thread a blunt needle with matching yarn (approximately 1" per stitch).
3 Working from right to left, with right sides facing you, begin with Steps 3a and 3b:
3a Front needle: yarn through 1st stitch as if to purl, leave stitch on needle.
3b Back needle: yarn through 1st stitch as if to knit, leave on needle.
4 Work 4a and 4b across:
4a Front needle: through 1st stitch as if to knit, slip off needle; through next st as if to purl, leave on needle.
4b Back needle: through 1st stitch as if to purl, slip off needle; through next st as if to knit, leave on needle.
5 Adjust tension to match rest of knitting.

I-CORD
I-cord is a tiny tube of stockinette stitch, made with 2 double-pointed needles.
1 Cast on 3 or 4 sts.
2 Knit. Do not turn work. Slide stitches to opposite end of needle. Repeat Step 2 until cord is the desired length.

ATTACHED I-CORD
1 With dpn, cast on 3 (or 4) sts, then pick up and k 1 st along edge of piece—4 (or 5) sts.
2 Slide sts to opposite end of dpn and k2 (or k3), then k2tog through the back loops, pick up and k 1 st from edge. Rep row 2 for I-cord.

SHORT-ROW WRAPS
Uses Each short row adds two rows of knitting across a section of the work. Since the work is turned before completing a row, stitches must be wrapped at the turn to prevent holes. Work a wrap as follows:
Knit side
1 With yarn in back, slip next stitch as if to purl. Bring yarn to front of work and slip stitch back to left needle as shown. Turn work.
2 When you come to the wrap on the following knit row, make it less visible by knitting the wrap together with the stitch it wraps.
Purl side
1 With yarn in front, slip next stitch as if to purl. Bring yarn to back of work and slip stitch back to left needle as shown. Turn work.
2 When you come to the wrap on the following purl

row, make it less visible by inserting right needle under wrap as shown, placing the wrap on the left needle, and purling it together with the stitch it wraps.

CUTTING A STEEK
1 Baste with a contrasting color yarn exactly where you want to cut. Keep most of the basting on top so it shows.
2 Machine stitch using the smallest straight stitch you can. Stitch down the ridge formed by the sts closest to the basting on one side and back up the ridge next to it. Repeat on the other side of the basting.
3 Check to see that the stitching is in the right place.
4 Cut on the basting yarn.

CROCHET
Note To join yarn to piece, work a slip stitch.
CHAIN (CH)
Make slipknot to begin.
1 Yarn over hook, draw yarn through loop on hook.
2 First chain made. Repeat Step 1.

SINGLE CROCHET
(SC; U. K. DOUBLE CROCHET)
1 Insert hook into next stitch.
2 Yarn over and through stitch; 2 loops on hook.
3 Yarn over and through both loops on hook; single crochet completed. Repeat Steps 1–3.

REVERSE SINGLE CROCHET (REV SC; U. K. REVERSE DOUBLE CROCHET)
Reverse direction of work; work from left to right.
1 Insert hook into next stitch to right.
2 Yarn over, bring yarn through stitch only. As soon as hook clears the stitch, flip your wrist (and the hook).
2b There are now two loops on the hook, and the just made loop is to the front of the hook (left of the old loop).
3 Yarn over and through both loops on hook; one backward single crochet completed.
4 Continue working to right, repeating Steps 1–3.

DOUBLE CROCHET (DC; U. K. TREBLE CROCHET)
1 Chain 3 (counts as first double crochet).
2 Yarn over, insert hook into next stitch. Yarn over and through stitch only. There are now 3 loops on hook.
3 Yarn over and through 2 loops on hook.
4 Yarn over and through remaining 2 loops on hook. Repeat Steps 1–3.

HALF-DOUBLE CROCHET (HDC; U. K. HALF-TREBLE CROCHET)
1 Chain 2 (counts as first half-double crochet).
2 Yarn over, insert hook into next stitch. Yarn over and through stitch only. There are now 3 loops on hook.
3 Yarn over and through all 3 loops on hook: one half double crochet completed. Repeat Steps 1–2.

CHAIN

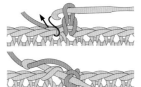

SINGLE CROCHET (SC)

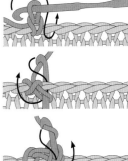

REVERSE SINGLE CROCHET (REV SC)

DOUBLE CROCHET (DC)

HALF-DOUBLE CROCHET (HDC)

ABBREVIATIONS

psso pass slipped stitch(es) over
rep repeat(s)
rev reverse
RH right hand
RS right side(s)

rnd(s) round(s)
sc single crochet
sl slip(ped)(ping)
ssk slip, slip, knit these 2 stitches together
st(s) stitch(es)

St st stockinette stitch
tbl through back loop
tog together
W&T wrap and turn
WS wrong side(s)
wyib with yarn in back

wyif with yarn in front
yd(s) yard(s)
yo yarn over

COLOPHON HANDPAINT COUNTRY REVISITED

Clockwise from top: Taos Pueblo; Rio Grande Gorge; Vermont covered bridge; sunset on the road; Traci Bunkers in a sunflower field; a quiet moment at Valentina Devine's plateau; Rachel Brown and Cheryl Oberle; Judy Dercum and horno;—"The air was soft with the incredible Southwestern light on the patio of the Mable Dodge Luhan House," Judy says, "and in a moment of spontaneous fun Alexis stuck my swatches on the adobe oven…"

"Mud is a beautiful thing to photograph against. Why would you go anywhere else?" Luisa Gelenter is laughing and talking about New Mexico's adobe landscape, the background canvas for the polychrome designs of *Handpaint Country*. It seems like yesterday when Luisa, author Cheryl Potter, and I were trekking down the canyon of the Rio Grande. "You wanted old, sun-bleached tree trunks, but we don't have any," Luisa remembers, "So I asked, 'Will boulders do?' That's when we headed to the Gorge—almost dinosaur land, with gigantic black lava boulders. Three golden eagles were circling above, and I thought it very propitious…"

Our first morning in the Land of Enchantment did not augur well for things to come. We had camped in Albuquerque, planning to shoot in its picturesque Old Town. A sudden snow storm—yes, feet of snow—forced us north, to Luisa country. She became our location scout, restaurant guide, and photoshoot gofer: you wanted a charred tree to hang yarns on? You got it. Your college-age assistants suddenly walked off the set to attend a class? Luisa found able Taos artist, photographer Lenny Foster. You wanted kids, a country setting? Luisa had them assemble at Christina's lovely adobe home in Taos' outskirts. You wanted an evocative model? She lent us La Lana's signature model Sarah Maultsbe. The only thing Luisa wasn't able to do, it seems, was keep the sun shining just a tad longer.

"I knew you wanted to use the wonderful daylight," Valentina Devine says, "that's why you took my house apart. Things were flying off the walls and out of my studio!" And into Valentina's back yard, which is actually a hill of volcanic tufa. "It's very porous, soft rock," explains Valentina. "You can easily carve steps into it." Thirty-nine of them, to be exact, which lead up to a plateau that Valentina calls her 'deck.' "When we sit there in the hot tub under the stars, we can see the lights of Santa Fe thirty miles away. But you didn't look like you'd enjoy a soak when you showed up—you looked sort of green and purple. My Russian-born mother cured all kinds of ailments with very simple remedies. So I fixed you some hot tea with honey and a shot of vodka. Do you remember? After a while you started to look better."

Valentina's tea, two cups to be exact, and that soft, violet dusk above Los Alamos—I could almost see night's veil sweep across my 'set,'—is all I *do* seem to remember.

The rest is a colorful blur. Couldn't Cheryl hang yarn on the branches, or run up those steps with that tree trunk any faster? Alas, like the Greek mythological hero who lost a race with the moon, I lost mine with the sun.

It seemed I was also losing the battle with the flu. I was still napping in the car the next day as we approached Luisa's studio on the outskirts of Taos. When I stepped outside I found myself in a different place: there was something about the sage brush, the adobe house behind the high latilla fence, and the mountains in the distance that evoked a hillside a world away. Seeing all those dye pots steaming outside reminded me of my mother and sisters stirring their own huge copper *kazani* (cauldron) under the mulberry tree.

As Luisa and her assistant wheeled racks of dyed wool outside, I knew my mother would feel at home here. And even get some free advice, as it turned out. "You wanted photos of fleece drying in the New Mexico sun," Luisa says, "but we dry indoors. We don't want the sun to make the fiber harsh!" If only my mother and sisters,

ther away… A 240-year-old farmhouse on the coast of Maine is where Melinda Bickford works. "I can't believe you drove all the way from Montpelier," Melinda says, "and you had just driven up from Valley Forge!" It took us all day to get there from Vermont, across the winding roads of New Hampshire. Melinda's home and studio look out to the sea, but it was getting late, and the sky was overcast. "It was quick, quick, quick," Melinda says, "all those cameras, yarns, my two dogs…" As Melinda helped us haul everything to the rocks on the shore, her daughter Tess fired up a pot of hot water.

Clockwise from top: Judy Ditmore climbing at The Garden of the Gods; Vermont pumpkins; lobster and Fruit Loops at Tess' Designer Yarns; D'Elin Lohr heads a convoy at Shell Beach; Cheryl Potter in the dyebath; our Taos crew that included Photo Assistant Lenny Foster, Photographer Alexis Xenakis, Location Scout Luisa Gelenter, Fashion Director Nancy Thomas, XRX Book Editor Elaine Rowley, and Photo Stylist Rick Mondragon.

who sang as their yarns dried on the rocks, had known this—before knitting my first Aran sweater.

We left Luisa's studio behind to meet Rachel Brown, considered by many to be hand-dyeing's grande dame. She welcomed us to her Weaving Southwest gallery, and gave us carte blanche to—you guessed it—start hauling stuff outdoors. "I figured you were in a creative frenzy," Rachel says of the whirlwind of activity that accompanied our arrival. Soon we were carting rugs, bleached aspen-pole ladders, and yarn baskets outside, making Rachel's storefront look like a Sunday bazaar.

Long ago, Rachel saw a friend dip a cone of yarn in a dye pot, and although the result left much to be desired, she was intrigued. "With a resist method," she says, "I would dye yarns one primary color, then a second, then a third. Of course, they came out looking like all the colors of the rainbow: red, orange, yellow, green, blue, violet, all in one skein! But then I washed them with an overall dye…" It made all the difference, and Rachel went on to dye "tons, and I mean tons, of yarn." Some of that yarn, knit into a shawl and adorned with beads, was now draped on our model, Sarah. She touched an archway wall in downtown Taos and we had a cover.

We then followed Cheryl Oberle, the designer of the cover shawl, to the St. Geronimo Lodge in a quiet part of Taos that used to be an orchard. We wanted her framed by her work, and she was amazed to see her sweaters cling to the adobe walls like so much spaghetti. In this special spot, the site of Cheryl's Knitaway, she "feels the magic that is New Mexico."

Not all the *Handpaint Country* garments had come from just up the street. Some began their journey a bit fur-

"I love that photo of the yarn that looks just like seaweed," Melinda says, "and that basket with the lobster was just too much." I kept thinking of those poor little creatures—ten pounds' worth—that Melinda had bought for supper from the lobster pen up the road, and of that hissing pot. A mad dash to the house brought back a 'model' that posed for us just so. The fee? Freedom—there were nine lobsters for dinner that night. And Melinda wants to know, "Are you going to tell everybody that you had Fruit Loops?"

Shooting in Vermont in fall during what the locals call 'leafing' season must come close to being in photographer's heaven. The landscape was breathtakingly beautiful, and we had the good fortune to find a covered bridge. Did you know that some had gates? This no-longer-used span was sliced by the light that shone through its weathered timbers. A few skeins hung, a short lens installed, a wide-angle view that captured the high, beamed ceiling soaring like a cathedral. Heaven doesn't get much better than that.

And there were the pumpkins: "We descended upon this farm stand and asked if we could take some pictures," says Cheryl Potter. "All those wonderful vegetable displays, all that squash, all those pumpkins! We took over the place for almost three hours, but no one seemed to mind. And the texture of the yarns against those gourds…You should have seen the puzzled faces of the shoppers."

Or of Ned the Llama, and his friends Chili, the Alpaca and the flock of sheep at Ellen's 1/2 Pint Farm the next day. "Ned kept an eye on everything, always," says Ellen Minard. "He wanted to know exactly what was happening." And there was a lot to see, what with roving mas-

querading as boa constrictors, hanging from every tree branch. But unlike my Maine model, Ned was definitely not interested in posing—and he let us know when Ellen and husband Keith attempted to drape a yarn wreath around his long wooly neck.

Then there was that other coast—and another set of steps, lots and lots of them—a continent away at Shell Beach near Pismo. "It was totally surreal," says D'Elin Lohr, laughing. "I had spent days and days cleaning my house, and what did you do? You flew in, dashed all around, took yarns off shelves, filled baskets, stuffed it all in your van—including my tapestry loom—and headed for the ocean! I'd love to see a photo of all of us carrying bundles up and down all those steep, steep steps to the beach. All the while it kept threatening to rain."

The threat became a reality at Nancy Finn's in Willits, California. It rained, and rained, and rained. What was there for our crew to do but go on a wine-tasting tour of Sonoma and Napa vineyards? But the rain wasn't about to stop, and we decided we'd better come back another time. "I thought if we had to wait a year it wasn't going to happen," says Nancy." But come back we did, and by then Nancy had moved to her new studio that adjoins a ravine of Douglas fir, maples, wildflowers, a seasonal creek, and tree trunks draped in lichens and moss. What else could a photographer ask for? No poison oak, perhaps. But that now is a distant memory. What I do remember is the image painted by Nancy's words: "When I stand where I work and look out the window, I see the coastal range and the fog spill over the hills. It's always changing, moving. It mesmerizes me; I can watch it forever."

We could have lingered in Northern California, but Montana, and Mountain Colors, beckoned. By now Cheryl and I knew the drill, and Diana McKay and Leslie Taylor good-humoredly went along: "We absolutely love any excuse to go to the river in the middle of a work day," Diana says. "Besides, we're surrounded by vivid, vibrant color—why not try to capture it in the book? And I figured, if things got wet, we'd just have to put new tags on them. And sure enough, a couple of skeins did start floating down the Bitterroot River and we had to go after them."

The Mountain Colors folks weren't the only ones who got wet. Our next escapade took us through an ocean of green, the middle of the country, to Wisconsin, home of Joslyn Seefeldt. A silver canoe lay near the edge of Clear Lake, and with Joslyn's blessing, we lined its floor with plastic and began dumping bags of yarns in it. Have you

ever photographed a canoe? You'd think, in this placid lake, the thing would sit still. "I was holding the canoe line," Joslyn says, "and you kept saying, 'Please relax it a little…' That's because as soon as you started shooting it began to drift, stretching its tether." That simply wouldn't do, photographically. The picture called for a languid shot, with a *relaxed* rope. So I kept shooting and saying, "Beautiful, beautiful, please relax the rope a little." But Joslyn held fast. "You kept telling me, 'Let go a little, let go a little more, please let go…' and I started to say, 'but…but…' "

When I finally took my eye off the view finder, the canoe was ten yards away. Against her better judgement, Joslyn had granted my request—and let go of the tether! Now what? I called out to a young man who was fishing nearby, "We'll give you twenty bucks if you snag that canoe!" "I was dumbfounded," Joslyn says. "There was the canoe, with all that yarn, out in the lake, and I watched this kid try to hook it with his fishing line! The longer he tried, the further the boat drifted. That's when I decided it was going to involve swimming. I have never dived into a lake with my clothes on, but somebody had to get that yarn."

It never occurred to me that the somebody should have been me. Have I ever, in my shooting career, felt any less gentlemanly than I did watching Joslyn dive in while I, instinctively, grabbed for my sharp shooter and started clicking? But I *am* too much of a gentleman to show you pictures of a very soggy Joslyn triumphantly towing to shore the canoe and its precious cargo. I was delighted when art director Bob Natz chose that shot of the canoe—minus Joslyn—for our *Handpaint Country* poster.

Near another body of water, we shot under the swaying palms at Laura Bryant's waterfront home in St. Petersburg, Florida. "I'm always trying to look at things

from a different perspective," Laura says, "but skeins sticking out of palm trees? That was fun." While shooting on her boat, moored under a cool grove of trees out back, we wondered: Could Key West be far? Several days' sail, we learned.

It took Judy Ditmore just three days to make it all the way from Hemingway's Key West hangout to her home and studio in Colorado Springs—on her Harley! "There's something wonderful about being on a bike," Judy says. "Out there with the elements, all your senses are heightened. For me it's a very creative time, and my head takes off. I get inspired to create new things." For our shoot at the indescribably beautiful Garden of the Gods, Judy climbed off her bike and onto the rocks.

From Colorado's heights, our *Handpaint Country* journey took us to the sunflower fields of Kansas. Traci Bunkers had set up a display in a corner of her new studio—only to see it dismantled and transported to the fields. "The rain was coming down while you were taking my picture, " Traci says, "and I felt a little like a sunflower myself." But soon the sun came out, and we resumed our shoot amid silvery cornstalks. "Watching you wrap my spinning batts around the cornstalks was surreal," Traci says. "The setting, your music, we seemed in our own little private world."

That's what those brave pioneers must have felt, in their 'prairie schooners,' the covered wagons that took them across the country over the Oregon Trail. Its tracks can still be seen near the home of yarn pioneer Harlan Brown, and I couldn't believe our luck when we saw a wagon in a nearby park. Within sight of Scotts Bluff, a landmark to those traveling the Oregon Trail, we draped that wagon with all the Brown Sheep Company yarn it could hold.

The wagon trail jump-off point was St. Louis, Missouri, the Gateway to the West. Its silvery Arch celebrates its history— and frames Rosalie Truong's small community garden. Amidst blooming flowers, leafy vegetables, and hanging from a lovely pergola, Rosalie's yarns shimmered under the noon sun.

A journey that logged over 30,000 miles had begun twenty-five miles outside of Saratoga, New York, at The Great Adirondack Yarn Company. But Patti Subik was too busy with a horse show to clean house. "You were having too much fun with my clutter and all my stuff for me to worry about whether my house was neat," she says. "It was fun to be there at the beginning, watching you start from scratch. And I love the fact that the book will give the person who buys the yarn a chance to see where it was created."

Well, not always. That isn't really Koigu's pond on page 135, but a bend of the Big Sioux River outside Sioux Falls. Not that we wouldn't have loved going back to Canada to visit our friends Maie and Taiu. "We have put on an addition since you were here," says Taiu Landra. "No more dyeing on the kitchen stove. And I like your pond. Ours is still being used as a runway: we have geese, and they teach their little goslings how to fly on the hill behind the barn. Their first attempts are very funny, because they just come plopping down in the water."

From the Big Sioux we traveled to the Schuylkill River that runs through Valley Forge National Park, where we caught up with Linda MacMillan and Marike Saarniit. Our journey ended in Corales, New Mexico, home of Fiesta Yarns. "At the time of your visit Molly Cavin and I were totally immersed in Fiesta," Cindy Brooks says. "Now it's in our past. But *Handpaint Country* will be a way to hold on to it—forever."

We couldn't have said it better ourselves: What a wonderful way to hold on to this journey and 21 memorable stops.

—*Alexis Xenakis*
Sioux Falls, South Dakota

Next page: Prairie Schooner at Scott's Bluff, Nebraska.